SEA SLANG
of the
TWENTIETH CENTURY

ROYAL NAVY: MERCHANT NAVY
YACHTSMEN
FISHERMEN: BARGEMEN: CANALMEN
MISCELLANEOUS

by

WILFRED GRANVILLE

Introduction and Etymologies
by
ERIC PARTRIDGE

THE PHILOSOPHICAL LIBRARY
NEW YORK

Published, 1950, *by the Philosophical Library, Inc.*
15 *East* 40*th Street, New York* 16, *N.Y.*

Printed in Great Britain

To

CAPTAIN ANTHONY F. PUGSLEY, C.B., D.S.O.
ROYAL NAVY

FOREWORD

THE slang of the seafarer must ever be the despair of a glossographer, for new words and phrases are being coined almost daily by quick-witted seamen in the ships of the Royal and Merchant Navies, by yachtsmen, fishermen, the men of the lightships, and the crews of the barges and 'narrow boats' that work our inland waterways.

No glossary of nautical unconventional speech can claim to be complete any more than can a dictionary of Standard English, for language, like history, is constantly in the making. However, I have tried to present as full and authentic an account of twentieth-century sea slang as my association with all types of seafarers and a long study of the subject have enabled me.

The late Admiral W. H. Smyth in his excellent *Sailor's Word Book*—which, however, contained many technicalities—recorded the slang of the nineteenth century, and Frank C. Bowen in *Sea Slang*, a 'Dictionary of Old Timers' Expressions and Epithets' (1929), preserved many last-century terms and phrases as well as a good crop of modern sea slang; and, as recently as 1946, Commander John Irving published a small book of *Royal Navalese*, a glossary of ' Forecastle and Quarterdeck Words and Phrases ', which contained Old Navy expressions and many present-day terms but which was not confined to slang.

The period covered by the present work is from 1900 to 1949. I have recorded, rather fully, the slang of the Royal Navy in the wars of 1914–18 and 1939–45, and have included as ' slang ' a number of terms that stand just outside its boundary. These, however, can be said to have become ' naturalized ' by usage. Many phrases which seem to be peculiar to the R.A.F. are proved to be of naval birth and to have passed into the sister service when the Royal Naval Air Service amalgamated with the Royal Flying Corps to form the Royal Air Force in April 1918.

I have also included, as borderline examples, a few slangily used initial-formed words such as *asdic*, *buco*, and *masby*. I have purposely omitted cockney rhyming slang which characterizes the speech of the lower deck of His Majesty's ships: for this type of slang is not sea-born but went afloat with its users.

Over a number of words—especially lower-deck ' pejoratives ' —I have had to risk seeming emasculate in order to be immaculate; but where decorum has obliged me to euphemize, the knowledgeable will, I have no doubt, supply their own interpretations.

It is inevitable in a book of this kind that the compiler should cover much of the ground explored by others, who, themselves, must necessarily have worked in the fields of those that preceded them; and I have made acknowledgements in the text of any apparent borrowings, it being impossible to approach the numerous authorities I have had to consult in the compilation of this glossary.

In the works of the following authors I have found terms with which I have checked my researches: John Masefield (*passim*); William McFee; Eric Partridge (whose monumental *Dictionary of Slang and Unconventional English* has been invaluable); Edward FitzGerald; George Goldsmith Carter; Frank C. Bowen; Peter F. Anson; Thomas Woodrooffe; Allen Baddeley; Charles Morgan (*The Gunroom*); Lionel Dawson; Gilbert Hackforth Jones; Robert Harling; Martyn Sherwood; L. C. T. Rolt (*Narrow Boat*); John Moore; and the pseudonymous writers ' Bartimeus ', ' Taffrail ', ' Tackline ', ' Sea Wrack ', ' Giraldus ' and ' Etienne '.

To my friend Eric Partridge I owe much for encouragement and assistance in the planning of the book; for writing the Introduction and supplying etymologies.

I have to thank the novelists Winston Graham and Jaspar Power for special terms.

Of the officers and men of the Royal Navy—my ' old ships ' —who have helped in the making of the book, I am particularly grateful to Petty Officer V. W. Ellis, D.S.M., R.N., and Ldg Stoker W. H. Bindon, R.N., a submariner, for a valuable list of current lower-deck slang. To my friends in the Merchant Navy, in the East Coast trawlers and drifters, and all who ' mess about in boats ', my thanks for their co-operation.

WILFRED GRANVILLE

INTRODUCTION

The most advanced nations are always those who navigate
the most.—EMERSON.

IT IS with pleasure that I accept an invitation to write the introduction to a book so badly needed and so competently and
comprehensively written as *Sea Slang of the Twentieth Century*
by Wilfred Granville.

There used to be a popular song about every nice girl loving
a sailor (' for you know what sailors are ') and there still is a
popular libel about Jack having a wife in every port. He hasn't
even a girl in every port. But, like the Greeks, the sailor ' has
a word for it '; his verbal resources, copious and apposite,
seem to be almost as remarkable as his manual adroitness and
his ability to cope with even the most untoward circumstances.
Resourceful in action, resourceful in speech; cheekily cheerful
in all circumstances, impudently invincible in his verbal response
thereto; gifted with wit as well as with humour: that is your
sailor, whether Royal Navy or Merchant Navy, yachtsman or
bargeman, fisherman or canalman.

Clearly, the need to set courage and patience and humour
against the caprice, the danger, the hardship of life at sea, has
affected the nature of the sailor's speech: has imprinted upon it
an unmistakable yet almost indefinable character. A character
original, independent, sturdy, virile, courageous, whimsical,
pawky, realistic, picturesque.

One very striking characteristic of nautical speech has been
indicated by Jean Richepin (1849–1926), that French poet who,
in *La Chanson des Gueux* (1876), *Les Blasphèmes* (1884) and *La
Mer* (1886), sang the common man, the beggar, the ordinary
seaman, the underdog; that dramatist, both in verse and in prose
of the last quarter of the nineteenth century; and that novelist,

psychological yet realistic, of the half-century ending with his death: by Jean Richepin, who, in the van of ethical and sociological thinking in French literary and cultured circles for at least forty years, is now almost forgotten except by historians of literature: by Jean Richepin, who, in *La Mer*, included a poem called ' Parler Mathurin '—Sailors' Speech, *mathurin* being a popular French deviation from *matelot*[1], a sailor. There, said Richepin

> *Les mathurins ont une langue*
> *Où le verbe n'est point prison.*
> *L'image y foisonne à foison,*
> *Or vierge dans sa rude gangue.*

A rough paraphrase: Sailors have a language in which the words do not constitute a prison; images of speech flourish, like virgin gold in its crude, harsh ore.

The ore vastly exceeds the gold; the pedestrian prose the poetry. But much ore is useful; much prose, although pedestrian, is amusing or instructive. Of the sailor's speech in general, not of his slang in particular, the late lamented Anglo-American, Logan Pearsall Smith[2] once remarked that ' if we take the words in common use among English sailors, the terms, special or general, connected with the sea and ships, we find a vigorous and extensive vocabulary, very characteristic of the hardy and practical people who employ it '; yet equally applicable to the sailor's slang terms, his colloquialisms, his catch-phrases.

But the language of sailors has not attracted very much attention. The Royal Navy has been called ' the Silent Service '. Although its officers can be exceedingly expressive, the lower-deck even voluble, neither officers nor men have tended to be particularly expressive in print; the same holds good, to a lesser degree, of the Merchant Navy; but, to a perhaps even greater degree, of fishermen.

Of the unconventional speech of English sailors, the following are the chief records: Admiral Smyth, *The Sailor's Word Book*, 1867; W. Clark Russell (popular novelist of the sea), *Sailors'*

---

[1] See the glossary.
[2] See too the essay in his delightful *Words and Idioms*.

Language, 1883; ' Taffrail ' in an article published in 1917; Fraser & Gibbons, *Soldier and Sailor Words and Phrases,* 1925; Frank C. Bowen, *Sea Slang,* 1929; and now, far more comprehensive than those others, Wilfred Granville's book, restricted though it is to speech current in the twentieth century—speech that inevitably preserves many older terms.

Nautical slang, like every other slang, is at once original and traditional; independent and allied to other slangs and to popular speech. For instance, it shows affinities[1] to the slang of the Army and the Air Force and occasionally borrows from them, as the ensuing pages will prove. It enlists a few terms from rhyming slang, a predominantly Cockney form of linguistic activity—but then, the Cockney element is very noticeable in nautical slang; it has at least one rhyming-slang term of its own, the now slightly obsolescent *old Jamaica,* the sun, via *old Jamaica rum.*

In the nautical slang of the Royal and the Merchant Navy, we notice that the unconventional speech of the officers and that of the men is now, in the main, identical; this wasn't true of the Royal Navy and of the Merchant Service in 1914, still less in 1900, and less again in (say) the 1860's. The slang of the two Navies has become increasingly democratic. Yet there are still many terms used mainly by the officers; many others, mainly by the men. For the Royal Navy, Wilfred Granville has differentiated these by the designations ' wardroom ' and ' lower-deck '. The vocabulary of Royal and Merchant Navy officers tends to be more educated, more cultured, more witty and more allusive than that of the men; that of the men, more earthy, more humorous, more Rabelaisian than that of the officers. The officers tend to regard seamanship more as a form of technics; the men, rather as a craft. Whereas the men's speech tends to be reminiscent of the Elementary, the officers' recalls the Public School.

But *tends* is, in the current cliché, ' the operative word '. The language of the officers and the language of the men have far more in common than in distinction. And that distinction hardly

[1] See my introduction to *A Dictionary of Forces' Slang: 1939–1945,* wherein I have collaborated with Wilfred Granville and Frank Roberts.

operates at all in the slang and colloquialisms of fishermen and bargemen and canalmen, although it does characterize those of yachtsmen.

But my burblings are of little account: mere excrescences upon the jovial, self-reliant face—mere motes in the steady, twinkling eye—of the sailor's speech. A sherry before a good dinner.

' Dig in, lads! Fill your boots.'

ERIC PARTRIDGE

A

A.B. An Able-Bodied Seaman—one who has passed through his training as an Ordinary Seaman (cf. O.D.), and can steer a ship and carry out the 'marline-spike work' of his rating. See MARLINE-SPIKE SEAMANSHIP.

A.B.C. Admiral Sir *A*ndrew *B. C*unningham (later, Admiral of the Fleet Lord Cunningham). Cf. OLD CLOSE-THE-RANGE.

A.B.G.s, the. *All Big Guns*—the 'Dreadnought' type of battle-ships of the pre-1914 era.

abaft the screen. On the quarter-deck: behind the thwartships steel curtain which divides the upper deck from the quarter-deck.

Aberdeen cutlet. A cured (dried) haddock. Aberdeen is a centre of the Scottish fisheries; the term is comparable with (say) *Welsh rabbit*.

above board. Honest and straightforward; with nothing concealed. Cf. CHARLEY MORE. One of the many nautical words and phrases that, as befits a great maritime nation, have got into the very texture of the English language.

acid. Sarcasm; withering criticism. See BOTTLE.

acid drop. One who is always complaining. (Lower-deck.) A DRIPPER or captious critic who is not able to suggest a remedy for what he scorns.

act green. To be gratuitously stupid. (Lower-deck.) Cf. GREEN COAT, WEAR THE.

acting Dicky. One appointed temporarily to a ship; a naval officer 'lent' to a ship or Shore Establishment for special duty, or to relieve someone who is 'sick on shore'. He is 'lent' because he is still borne for payment in the ship in which he holds a permanent appointment and to which he will return when his period of duty is over.

15

acting dish. One substituted for that promised on the mess menu. Any dish resembling it. Used ironically, e.g. *acting rabbit pie*, a corned beef one. In the austerity days immediately after the 1939–45 War ' Viennese steak ' has been a typical *acting dish*.

addlings. Pay accumulated during a voyage. Probably derives from the Yorkshire dialect *addle*, to earn (money).

admiral. A shell of the Conus species, a rather handsome specimen.

Admiral, tap the. See BLEED THE MONKEY.

Admiral, Vice Admiral, and **Rear Admiral.** Respectively the first, second, and third boat to arrive on the Newfoundland fishing banks.

Admiral's mate. A ' mess-deck menace '; one who always knows the ship's movements; when leave will be granted; who is to be promoted or disrated, etc. A boastful know-all. Ironic; cf. SEA LAWYER.

Admiralty ham. Potted or canned meat. Ironic.

Admiralty pattern=SEALED PATTERN.

Admiralty weather. Bad weather which might have been arranged by the Admiralty, for it always happens when a man is going on leave.

adrift. Missing; (of persons) ' absent over leave ' or from one's place of duty.

advice boat, the. Any dispatch vessel used by the Admiralty for conveying important messages to the Fleet.

aerial sausages. Small dirigibles used for reconnaissance by the Royal Naval Air Service in the 1914–18 War. The name comes from the fact that these airships had a three-in-one sausage appearance, thus differing from the BLIMP which had a blunt nose and tapered stern. Cf. also GAS BAGS.

aft, be taken. To be placed IN THE RATTLE. A defaulter is usually taken aft to the officer of the watch when ' run in ' by a Petty Officer, and he is then ordered to appear before the Commander at the defaulter's table on the following forenoon.

aft, get. To become a naval officer.

16

aft through the hawsehole. Applied to a man who has risen from the lower-deck to officer rank. Cf. DARTS.

afterguard, the. In the Royal and Merchant Navies, the officers whose quarters are in the after part of the ship. Technical rather than unconventional. Cf. BRASS and GOLD LACE.

afters. The sweet course at dinner on the lower-deck. A colloquialism adopted from civilian life; common in the Army and the Air Force as well as in the Navy.

Ag and Fish. The Ministry of *Ag*riculture *and Fish*eries.

Aggie on horseback. Nickname of H.M.S. *Weston-super-Mare*. A clever pun, suggested by:

Aggie's. One of the late Dame *Agnes* E. Weston's ' Sailors' Rest Hostels ', which are found in the principal naval ports. These hostels are run on club-like lines and there is sleeping accommodation for a large number of men; many of the ' cabins ' are dedicated to the memory of naval officers killed in action. A slightly religious atmosphere prevails. The hostels are usually full and are very popular. See MOTHER OF THE NAVY.

agony. Anything causing undue strain or difficulty. A term indigenous to the training ship *Conway*.

aground on her empties (i.e. sitting on her empty bottles). Said of a Depot Ship that stays alongside a jetty or lies at a buoy. (Wardroom.)

air disturbers. Telegraphists. Cf. SPARKER.

air goat. The snipe, a marsh bird that resembles that animal in some of its characteristics.

airyard matey. A mechanician in a Fleet Air Arm Station. Cf. DOCKYARD MATEY.

Alec. A. V. *Alex*ander, the First Lord of the Admiralty during nearly all of the 1939–45 War.

Alex. Alexandria, the one-time naval port in Egypt. Cf. :

Algy. Algiers, the North African naval port.

All Aloney. The Cunard White Star liner *Alaunia*.

all my eye and Betty Martin (usually shortened to [*that's*] *all my eye*). A British naval rating attended the wrong church and sat through a Latin service. The only words he could understand—he afterwards told a pal—were the apparently senseless ' all my eye and Betty Martin '. What he actually heard was ' Ah mihi Beate Martine ' (' Oh, help me, Blessed Martin! '). So the naval version of the story goes. But the Catholic service does not contain the phrase, and the explanation is obviously apocryphal.

all night in. A night on which a man has no watch to keep and throughout which he can therefore sleep in his hammock.

All parts bearing an even strain ? A catch-phrase question meaning, ' Is everything running smoothly ? '

All proved, ten bob out ? The stock question in Naval Accountant circles at the end of the ' putting-up ' of the Ship's Company's pay on the eve of the actual payment. This ' putting-up ' ensures that there is no money ' over ' when all the hands have been paid. Each man has his own pay envelope which has his name, rating and Ship's Book Number on the outside, together with the exact amount of pay due to him. All the envelopes are placed in partitions in a large pay box and the job of paying out is simple: all the paying officer has to do is to pour the money from the envelope on to the recipient's cap which is placed on the pay table. Sometimes at the ' putting-up ' a ten shilling or a pound note will be left over and it is clear that someone will have that amount less in his envelope; which means that all the envelopes have to be checked and the error discovered—hence the irony in the question. If there is no cash over the payment is ' all proved '.

all shipshape and Bristol fashion. Said of a ship that is 'in all respects ready for sea ' and is about to ask ' permission to proceed '. From the fact that Bristol was once a very great seaport. The phrase has become part of the language.

all standing, brought up. (Figuratively) taken by surprise; unable to supply an answer to a question or to cope with something. A sailing ship was brought up ' all standing ' when she had all sail set and came up into the wind.

all standing, turn in. To go to one's bunk (cf. CART) fully dressed, as when anticipating air attack or a sudden call on deck during the night, i.e. to turn in just as one stands.

all-boat. One in which no space is wasted. (Yachtsmen's.)

18

all-hands ship. One in which all hands are made to work on deck, none excused.

along of. Alongside of; because of. A lower-deck vernacular usage as in, e.g., ' It was all along of Nobby Clark being adrift that we got our " leaf " jammed '; ' I served along of 'im when he was a Torpedo Lootenant in the old Tiger in '14.'

alow and aloft. Above and below decks. ' Alow and aloft she was a picture '—said in admiration of a trim vessel.

alphabet destroyers. Those named after letters of the alphabet and not belonging to a particular class such as the Tribal, Hunt, and Battle classes.

Alphabetical. Nickname for anyone possessing more than two initials, e.g. A. B. C. Jones is inevitably called *Alphabetical* Jones.

Altmark, the. Any ship or Shore Establishment run on severe disciplinary lines. From the German prison ship of that name which was captured by the British destroyer *Cossack* in 1940.

'Am and Tripe. H.M.S. *Amphitrite*. (Lower-deck.) (By the well-known linguistic process of ' Hobson-Jobson ', whereby a difficult ' foreign ' word is simplified to the needs of the uncultured. The process is not confined to English.)

ambi. Short for *ambitious*. A term of contempt for one whose conduct is so irreproachable that he must be out to catch the eye of Authority and so get promotion. A term indigenous to the training ship *Conway*.

A.M.C. Armed Merchant Cruiser, one of those passenger liners which are converted for duty as convoy escorts in time of war. Commanded by retired Admirals with the rank of Commodore, Royal Naval Reserve, and manned by officers and men of the Reserves, they did splendid work in both the 1914–18 and the 1939–45 Wars. The A.M.C.s *Rawalpindi* and *Jervis Bay* fought gallant actions with German ' pocket battleships ' to save their convoys from destruction. Both these ships were sunk, but their example of courage and loyalty forms a glorious page in the history of the Royal Navy. In the first World War there was a stand-up fight between the British Armed Merchant Cruiser *Campania* and a German one, the *Cap Trafalgar*, in which the latter was sunk. See MUCKLE FLUGGA HUSSARS.

ammo. Short for *ammunition*. Cf. BRICKS.

anchor, swallow the. See SWALLOW THE ANCHOR.

anchor the arse. To sit down on the deck.

anchor to windward. To play for safety. To keep on the right side of Authority. Cf. WINDWARD OF, GET TO.

anchored in Sot's Bay. Incapably drunk and unable to ' manœuvre '.

ancient mariner. A seagull, believed to possess the soul of a departed mariner. See CHIEF STOKER.

Andrew Mack. H.M.S. *Andromache*. (Lower-deck.) By ' Hobson-Jobson '.

Andrew, the. The Royal Navy, after one Andrew Miller, a Press Gang ' tough ' who shanghaied so many victims into the Navy that they thought it was owned by him. Also *Merry Andrew*.

Andrew Miller. See preceding.

'Andy Dromedary, the. H.M.S. *Andromeda*.

Angel's Whisper. Defaulter Call, or Reveille. Cf. CHARLEY.

Angry Cat, the. A 1914–18 War name for the French battleship *Henri IV*, which became famous for her exploits at Gallipoli. By a pun on *Henri Quatre*.

ankle bone. A crayfish.

Annie. H.M.S. *Anson*. Cf. R.A.F. *Annie*, an Anson aircraft.

ante-up. To settle one's debts, to pay up. (A poker term.)

Any Bloody How. H.M.S. *Howe*. (Lower-deck.)

any ears ? This question is asked of a lower-deck GANNET who searches the almost empty stew-pot for bits of meat.

A.P. (1) Admiralty pattern. The orthodox method of doing a thing, the correct ' form '. (Originated at Royal Naval College, Dartmouth.) Cf. JONNICK. (2) An Assistant Paymaster (Paymaster Sub-Lieutenant or Lieutenant) R.N. 1914–18 War nickname. More usually he was referred to as PAY.

aplets. Drift nets. (Herring fishery term.) Perhaps a corruption of *epaulettes*; a particularly luxuriant epaulette does vaguely resemble a drift net spread out on golden sands to dry.

'Appy Day. A miserable, pessimistic type, a grouser of the worst kind; mostly as a nickname. Ironic. ·Cf. DRIP PAN.

Arch Tiffy. The Warrant Engineer of the engine room of one of H.M. Ships. Literally, a chief ar*tifi*cer.

Archdeacon, the. Nickname for H.M.S. *Venerable.*

Arctic smoke. A sea-fog off Iceland.

Are you happy in the Service ? Asked of a shipmate when he is given a particularly unpleasant job to do.

arisings. A term used in Naval Accountant circles for the ' leftovers ' of food, a return of which must be rendered to the Director of Navy Accounts.

Ark, the. The famous aircraft carrier *Ark Royal* which was so often ' sunk ' by Nazi propaganda in the 1939–45 War. She had many narrow escapes and, as was inevitable for such a trouble-seeking ship, she was finally sunk—although quite late in the war.

arles. A retaining fee paid to Scottish fisher ' lassies ' employed in the herring industry as gutters, ' kipperers ', packers, etc. They follow the herring round the coast from the Moray Firth for the great autumn season at Great Yarmouth and Lowestoft; some even go as far as Newlyn in Cornwall for the winter fishery. The usual Scottish spelling is *airles*. *Arles* derives ultimately from Latin *arrha*, an earnest—money paid to cement a bargain. (This technicality has been admitted here solely *à titre de curiosité*.)

arm the lead. To prepare the lead for sounding by filling the cavity with tallow which picks up a sample of the bottom. (Now a technicality.)

armies. *Arm*ament ratings generically.

Armstrong's patent. Any hand-operated gear: boat's falls, hand winches, etc. Cf. JOHNNY ARMSTRONG. Obviously a pun on the *strong arm* needed.

Arries, the. Boys of the training ship *Arethusa* on the Thames.

arse of the ship. The stern; this phrase, like the ' arse of a block (pulley) ' is used almost as a technicality in the Royal Navy.

arse-perisher. See BUM-FREEZER.

21

Arso. *Ar*mament *S*upply *O*fficer. (Wardroom.)

artificial eye. A small eye worked in the end of a rope, not quite as elaborate as an eye-splice.

as handy as a cow in a spit-kid. Said of an awkward person—a man with ' two left feet '. A spit-kid is a mess-deck spittoon.

as long as the maintop bowline. Very long indeed. The maintop bowline is the longest rope in the ship; used to haul out the weather leach of the sail when sailing close-hauled. When a man is listening intently his ears are said to be ' hauled out to the bowline '.

ash-can. A depth charge, which looks like one.

ash-cat. A fireman in the Merchant Navy. Cf. BLACK WATCH, BUNKER-CAT, CLINKER-KNOCKER, and DUSTMAN.

astern of station. Behindhand in work or not abreast of affairs. (Wardroom.)

at eighty feet, be. To be fast asleep. A submariner's term; when a submarine is at that depth she is said to be asleep.

at the rate of knots. See RATE OF KNOTS.

at the run. Only in the Army and R.A.F. are things done *at the double*; in the Royal Navy they are carried out *at the run*. (Technical.)

Atlantic greyhounds. The liners which ply between England and America. Cf. OCEAN GREYHOUNDS. (Journalistic.)

Atlantic rangers. Herrings. Cf. SEA ROVERS.

atmospheric. An old term for a telegraphist rating.

away all lefts. Deprived of good conduct badges, which are worn on the left arm. (Lower-deck.)

axed. ' Sacked ' as redundant when the Royal Navy is cut down. The term dates from the time when Sir Auckland Geddes used his ' economy axe ' to cut down the strength of the Navy after the 1914–18 War. Cf. BLUE TICKET.

B

babbing. A hookless and rodless method of eel-fishing by a baited line peculiar to the Fen district and the East Anglian coast. Excellent results are obtained. This mode of fishing is known as ' bobbing ' on some parts of the coast; *babbing* is simply a dialectal form of *bobbing*—the bait bobs about.

Baby. A Sopwith-built aeroplane used in the 1914–18 War by the Royal Naval Air Service.

baby killers. A 1914–18 term (mainly journalistic) for the German battleships which bombarded the open towns of Scarborough, Whitby and Hartlepool on the morning of December 16, 1914. There were numerous children among the dead. The same term was applied to the Zeppelin raiders that attacked London and the coastal towns.

baby's head. A meat pudding. (Lower-deck.) It is round and bald.

baccy firm. A lower-deck ' firm ' that specializes in the marling of ship's tobacco. The charge used to be threepence a pound. Leaf tobacco is marled and rolled in spunyarn. See DHOBEY FIRM and GOFFER FIRM.

back-breakers. The pumps in the old sailing ships.

backing and filling. Acting in a state of indecision; ' dithering '. The sails of a ship back and fill when she is ' in irons ' and unable to make any headway.

back-slack. Smart, cheeky back-answers; ' handing out the slack ', giving such answers. (Merchant Navy.)

back-strapped. (Of a ship) held by the tide in such a position as to be unable to manœuvre.

back-water. (Figuratively) to retract a rash statement.

bacon ducks. Fried bread. (Lower-deck.)

bad service. Any naval appointment which seems to offer little chance of promotion or of being noticed. Before the 1914–18 War it was considered *bad service* to be in destroyers.

badge-cap. A Merchant Navy officer's uniform cap bearing the company's badge. Such officers invariably refer to their caps as badge-caps. They seem very reluctant to wear uniform except on formal occasions or when paying visits to owners who insist on uniform being worn.

badgeman. The possessor of good conduct ' badges ' or stripes, which are awarded for several years' exemplary behaviour— or undetected crime as their owners would put it. The first badge is given after three years' service; the second after five years, and the third on completion of thirteen years' service. Each badge earns its owner the sum of threepence a day. Cf. STRIPEY. (Technical rather than unconventional.)

Badger Bag, the. Father Neptune and his Court at the ' crossing the line ' ceremony.

bag, 'ammick and bird cage. The sailor's ' all '. ' It's the Navy all over, chum; as soon as you gets 'appy and comfortable in a ship, it's up bag, 'ammick and bird cage and you're off to another hookpot.' (Lower-deck.)

bag meal. A meal of sandwiches, pies, etc., given to a rating working away from the ship or proceeding on draft.

bag shanty. A brothel. (Lower-deck.) A *bag* is an old prostitute.

baggies. Bluejackets. An old Army term, dating from when the crews of troopships wore baggier bell-bottoms than they do today.

bagging on the bowline. Sailing wide of a course.

baggy. A bluejacket. (A soldier's term coined during the ' trooping ' days.) From the seaman's baggy trousers.

bags of mystery. See BANGERS.

bake. A disappointment, a ' sell '; any untoward circumstances when happy ones were anticipated. Sometimes the lower-deck gets a *bake* instead of a *roast* for dinner.

bald-headed ship. A topmastless schooner or a square-rigger without skysails,

24

ballast, to carry. To show one's ability to carry one's liquor.

balloonatics. (Royal Naval Air Service, 1914–18 War.) Officers and men working with kite balloons. For its 1939–45 Air Force sense, consult *A Dictionary of Forces' Slang, 1939–1945*.

banana balancer. A ship's steward or a wardroom waiter. See FLUNKEY.

banana boats. Flat-bottomed invasion barges that, with raised ramps forward, have the appearance of a banana.

bandage roller. A naval sick-berth attendant. Cf. SICK-BAY TIFFY and POULTICE-WALLOPER.

bandies. Bandsmen of the Royal Marines. *Bandy* is the Band-master.

bandmaster. A pig's head. (Lower-deck.)

bandstand. (1) The circular gun-platform in a small escort vessel. (2) A cruet.

Bandy. See BANDIES.

banger. A knock-kneed messmate who 'bangs' his knees together.

bangers. The tinned variety of naval sausages. Cf. BAGS OF MYSTERY, LINKS OF LOVE, and MYSTERY TORPEDOES.

banjo bill. A spoonbill. (Longshore and wildfowlers' term.) From the shape of its bill.

Bank, the. Dogger Bank.

bannock-fluke. A turbot. A Firth of Forth fishermen's term, adopted from dialect. (Derivation obscure; perhaps in reference to the Scottish oatmeal, or barley-meal delicacy called a bannock.)

banyan party. A picnic ashore in the shade of the banyan trees on the East Indies Station.

banzai party. A shore party. Such a party was a great occasion when the Royal and the Japanese Navies were on very friendly terms. From the Japanese *banzai*, a general felicitation, meaning '10,000 years; for ever': 'May you live for ever'.

bar, one's. The bar on which one's hammock is slung. 'A chap on my bar told me that we shall probably be drafted this week-end.'

barber's cat. A talkative messmate.

barber's clerk. One who thinks more of his personal appearance than of his work; a skulker who always wants to be ' watch ashore '.

barberizer. A gadget used for ' shaving ' (planing) a ship's decks.

Bardia Bill. A six-inch gun well known to those who were in Tobruk in 1941. The enemy used it, several times a day, to express his hate.

bare Navy. The bare rations allowed to the ship's company.

barf. A dialect corruption of *barth*, a shelter or anchorage (*berth*). The general meaning in East Anglia seems to be a shed, e.g. ' Barf House ' is an old Yarmouth term for a herring-curing house. The term may be related to the Welsh *barth*, a ground floor, which could be a one-storey shed; in English dialect, a *barth* is predominantly a shelter for cattle.

bargain. A catch of fish. (East Anglian fishery term.)

barge roads. Mooring in a river or estuary set aside for barges.

bargee. ' There ain't no sich animal.' If you respect yourself, never use *bargee*, in reference to a member of the crew of a barge. It is a purely journalistic term for a *bargeman*.

bargemen. Maggots in ship's biscuits.

bark. The tanning used for the sails of fishing craft and barges.

barmaid's blush. Another term for MOUNTBATTEN PINK.

barnacle. An officer of some seniority who clings to a soft job to the envy of his juniors. A wardroom version of the lower-deck term, DEPOT STANCHION.

Barnacle Bill the Sailor. The hero of a bawdy song popular on the lower-deck and also outside the Royal Navy. His real name is somewhat grosser.

baron. One of the politer names for a C.W. CANDIDATE. Cf. W.C.s and SEA-GOING WREN.

baron, on the. Free; as a treat. ' We had a smashin' party and everything on the baron.' (Lower-deck.) Cf. HARRY FREEMAN'S.

barrack mould. Depression felt by officers spending a few days in naval barracks where they know few people and have not enough time to cultivate society.

barrack ranger. One who seems to have a permanent job in naval barracks. Cf. DEPOT STANCHION.

barrack routine. The routine through which a naval rating has to go every time he reports to the barracks of his Port Division pending draft to a new ship. He has to see the Surgeon, Dental Officer and other functionaries and be passed fit in every respect for drafting to ' a ship of war at sea '. (A technicality admitted here for its general interest.)

Barrier blight. Depression felt by the officers and men during the South Pole Expeditions.

bash. Short for DOBASH.

Basil. The R.N.A.S. nickname (1914–18) for a kite balloon.

basket. Euphemistic for *bastard*.

bat boat. A naval seaplane of the 1914–18 period.

Bataviers. Liners of the Muller Line which ply between London and Holland. With a reference to *Batavia*, the old name for Holland, from *Batavi*, the Latin name for the tribe inhabiting that region.

batchy. (1) One who in the North of England would be termed ' gawmless '. A variant of *bats*, which is short for *bats in the belfry*. (2) A nickname for anyone surnamed Payne or Paine.

Bath Brick. Malta, from the colour of the stone buildings. (Royal Navy.)

bathing beauty. Blancmange. (Lower-deck.) It shivers and has lovely curves.

batta-money. Naval prize money. (An Eastern term.) After the 1914–18 War considerable sums of prize money were paid out to officers and men; after the 1939–45 War these sums were considerably lower.

battle-bags. Small airships used by the Royal Naval Air Service in the 1914–18 War. Cf. BLIMP.

battle-boats. Warships of the 1914–18 War. Cf. BATTLE-WAGONS.

battle-bowler. A steel shrapnel helmet. Cf. TIN TITFER.

battle-wagon. (1) Any battleship of the Vanguard, Anson, Howe, or Duke of York type. (2) Any capital ship.

battler. A battle-wagon. See WAGONS.

Battles, the. Battle Class Destroyers built at the end of the 1939–45 War and named after famous battles—Jutland, Narvik, etc.

Battling Ls, the. The ' L ' Class of Torpedo Boat Destroyers of the 1914–18 War; *Lance, Lively*, etc.

Battling Third, the. The Third Destroyer Flotilla of the Harwich Striking Force in the 1914–18 War.

batman. A junior cadet in H.M.S. *Worcester*, who acts as servant to seniors.

Bats or **Batty.** Deck-landing officer. (Wardroom.) From the bats he uses to indicate to the pilot when to land.

Bay. Short for Robin Hood's Bay, that ancient and picturesque fishing village on the Yorkshire coast which for centuries has provided the Royal and Merchant Navies with fine seamen. At one time a very flourishing port, its fishing activity has declined since the end of the nineteenth century, although its menfolk still choose the sea as a career, many being owners or part-owners of coasting steamers. ' Bay ' can be described as the cradle of Master Mariners.

Bay, the. The Bay of Biscay.

Beach, the. The world on shore; civil life generally. (Royal Navy.)

beach-cadger. An ex-seaman tramp who haunts the foreshore at a seaside resort.

beach, hit the. To go on shore leave.

beach-loafer. An occasional variant of SHORE-LOAFER. (Royal Navy.)

beach-rangers. Longshoremen who hang around harbours and ports doing odd jobs, and occasionally work as stevedores. They are usually ex-seamen whose characters are so bad as to preclude their employment in merchant ships.

Beach Sigs. The Beach Signal parties in Combined Operations. They landed with the first wave of the invasion forces and set up communications ashore.

beach-tramper. A coastguard. Cf. SHINGLE-TRAMPER.

beached. Discharged from the Royal Navy.

beacher. A short spell ashore; just time enough for a couple of pints at the local. (Lower-deck.) Cf. DICKY FLURRY and DICKY RUN.

beagle balls. Rissoles at the Royal Naval College, Dartmouth. The modern explanation of the origin is that all the College beagles were killed off at the beginning of the 1939–45 War, and immediately afterwards a new type of rissole appeared on the College menu—beagle balls; but the term has been in use many years, Frank C. Bowen recording it in his entertaining *Sea Slang*, 1929; obviously it was prompted by *dogs* (sausages), current since about 1860.

Beal, the. A Dorset pronunciation of Portland *Bill*.

beating up. Becoming very efficient and conscientious in the execution of one's duties about the time of the half-yearly promotions. This is also known as 'lashing up'. 'Old So-and-So is getting very " Pusser " these days, isn't he?' —' Oh, he's all right. I expect he's beating up for his brass hat.' A sailing craft ' beats up ' when she is heading for harbour.

beckets. Technically, handles of a bucket. Hence, slangily, pockets. ' Take your hands out of your beckets when you speak to me, you young swab.'

bedroom areas. Fishery grounds where the fish sleep and are therefore easy to catch in the trawl-net.

beef chit. The wardroom menu card. Cf. TOMBSTONE.

beef screen. The place where the ship's meat is kept. (Royal Navy.)

beef trip, the. The routine trip to bring the meat ration from shore. Also a convoy escort of meat-carrying vessels in wartime.

beer gang. Stewards in liners. They collect the empty beer bottles from the saloons and cabins.

beetles. Shallow-draught motor lighters used for carrying troops at the Gallipoli landing in 1915. Cf. X-SHIP.

beetster. A net-mender. The verb *beet* means to mend (nets). Perhaps directly from the Dutch *beteren*, to repair, to make better; but probably an adoption of English dialect *beet*, ' to mend '—itself deriving from Old English *betan*. The term is in general use in Great Yarmouth during the herring season; ' beeting ' goes on all the year round, most of the work being done by the fishermen's wives.

before the mast, sell. See SELL BEFORE THE MAST.

before the stick. Before the mast in a WINDJAMMER.

Behemoths, the. Ships of the King Edward the Seventh Class which comprised the Third Battle Squadron in the 1914–18 War. Unwieldy and unsteady, they were also known as the ' Wobblies ': cf. WOBBLY EIGHTS. In the Bible (Job. xl, 15–24), Behemoth is a strong, very large animal, supposed to be the hippopotamus. A Hebrew word: *behemoth* literally means ' the great beast '.

behind the chests. In the dark corners of the chest space on the orlop deck of the training ship *Conway*. Excellent places in which to lose oneself. Cf. *sanc* ('BRITANNIA' SLANG).

belay. Technically, to make a rope fast; hence, slangily, to cancel an order.

belaying-pin soup. The rough treatment meted out to merchant seamen by ' bucko ' officers in a sailing ship. The seamen were chased with belaying-pins.

bell, little one. One light stroke on the ship's bell at the end of the Last Dog Watch. See DOGS.

bell, warm the. To arrive for duty early. To put the clock on.

bells. Bell-bottomed trousers.

belly. The swell of a sail in the wind.

belly muster. Medical inspection at the Royal Naval College, Dartmouth, to detect incipient measles or chicken-pox.

bend. To damage. 'You bend 'em; we mend 'em.' (Repair party motto.)

bender. A really good lie which even the celebrated TOM PEPPER would have respected.

bends and 'itches. The art of knotting and splicing, which figure so largely in a New Entry's training. Cf. MARLINE-SPIKE SEAMANSHIP.

30

Benjamin. The youngest member of a ship's company who, in the Royal Navy, is privileged to sound sixteen bells at midnight on New Year's Eve.

Benjy. A gunroom shortening of LITTLE BENJAMIN, OUR RULER.

Bessy Lork. A North of England name for a gudgeon. (Why so named, I have been unable to discover. Like many nicknames of this nature, its origin is lost in the mists of time.)

best Welsh. The best bunker coal from the Welsh pits. (A colloquialism.)

better than a slap in the belly with a wet fish. A gunroom phrase meaning that things aren't as bad as they might have been. There is a select group of synonymous phrases: see Eric Partridge's *A Dictionary of Slang and Unconventional English*.

Beware of your latter end. A naval warning to ' watch one's step '. It is often at the latter end of a man's service that he is apt to do something careless and thus blight his whole career.

Bible. A Service manual on any subject whatever.

bible-puncher. A parson. (Lower-deck.)

Biff. A nickname for Smith. Cf. SMUDGE. Rhyming with *Smith* mispronounced *Smiff*. (Lower-deck.)

biffer. A signal exercise in Morse (lamp or flags) or semaphore. (Naval signalese.)

Big eats—fill your boots! The lower-deck invitation to any meal. Cf. LUVERLY GRUB; DIG IN, FILL YOUR BOOTS!

Big Lizzie. H.M.S. *Queen Elizabeth*. (Lower-deck.)

big-ship men. Officers and men who serve in battleships, as distinct from destroyer and small-craft men.

big-ship time. Commissions spent in battleships.

big stink. A large motor boat. (A term indigenous to the training ship *Conway*.)

big stuff. Battleships or Cruisers. (General naval slang.)

Bight, the. Heligoland Bight, the scene of a naval engagement in 1915.

bilboes. Irons in which obstreperous seamen were placed. Cf. GARTERS. Ultimately from *bilbo*, a sword noted for the excellence of its temper and manufactured originally at *Bilbao* in Spain. Cf. Standard English *toledo*.

bilge cod. The fish course at meals in the training ship *Conway*.

billyboy. A schooner-rigged vessel rather like a barge. The type is obsolescent, although there were several plying between the Humber and the Tyne as late as 1930.

Billy Ruffian. H.M.S. *Bellerophon*. (Lower-deck.) By ' Hobson-Jobson '.

bimster. A stonachy (three-tailed cat whip; see STONNICKY) used in H.M.S. *Worcester* for mild chastisement; cf. TOGIE (Royal Naval College, Dartmouth), TEASER (H.M.S. *Conway*). From *bim*, a thinned form of *bum*.

bin. A space forming a mess on the lower-deck. It is usually curtained off. Cf. the civilian sense 'loony bin'.

binder. A last drink before leaving a ship; ' one for the gangway '.

'Bine. Short for a *Woodbine* (cigarette). Naval lower-deck.

binge the cask. See BULL THE CASK, which is more usual.

binnacle lights. Apprentices in the Merchant Navy. At one time they attended to the riding lights.

bird. A naval trouble-maker. See KING'S HARD BARGAIN and cf. CROW, FOWL, PELICAN.

Bird Sanctuary, the. The W.R.N.S. Headquarters in Sanctuary Buildings, London. *Wren* = bird.

Birdie. Lieutenant Bowers, R.N.R., who lost his life with Captain Scott in the South Pole tragedy. An ' Old Worcester ', Bowers was a fine and popular officer, and an indefatigable worker; Scott spoke very highly of him in his Journal. The nickname derived from his prominent nose.

birdmen. Aviators, friendly or otherwise. A naval colloquialism adopted from the ' intrepid birdmen ' of the popular Press.

bird's nest. A smaller look-out barrel placed higher up the mast than a crow's nest; used in whaling ships. The higher position enables the look-out to spot whales at a greater distance.

birds. Vessels belonging to the Steam Navigation Company. They have ' bird ' names.

biscuit. A small mattress used in a hammock. For its Army and Air Force senses, see *A Dictionary of Forces' Slang: 1939–1945*. Partly from its hardness and partly from its colour.

biscuit-eating stiffs. Old-timer seamen of the Merchant Service who learnt their job the hard way—subsisting on ' salt-horse ' and weevil biscuits.

biscuit-tin. One of the early Torpedo Boats. According to those who served in them, this is the material from which they were made.

Bish. The ship's Padre.

Bish, to act. To officiate in the absence of the Padre at Divisions, or at a burial service at sea. (Wardroom.)

Bishop! A derisive exclamation peculiar to the training ship *Conway*. It greets any stale information and matches the shore-going catch-phrase, ' Queen Anne's dead! ' (John Masefield, *The Conway*.)

bit o' wood. A London River bargeman's affectionate term for his craft: ' She isn't a bad bit o' wood, sound as she was fifty year ago and the fastest bit o' timber on the River.'

bitter weed. An acidulous, grumbling type; a ' messdeck horror '. He wears the expression of one who has tasted something bitter and invariably has a ' weed ' on. (Lower-deck.)

bi-wing boys. The pilots of biplanes, e.g. Gloster Gladiators or Swordfish aircraft, of the Fleet Air Arm in the 1939–45 War. Cf. FLYING HORSE and STRINGBAGS.

black book. The mythical book kept at the Admiralty to record the 'blacks' put up by malefactors in the Royal Navy.

black cutter. A training cutter used at the Royal Naval College, Dartmouth.

black fishing. Salmon poaching at night.

black flat. A type of vessel peculiar to the River Mersey. It is of shallow draught and its function is the regulating of barge traffic on the Mersey and the neighbouring canals. It is painted black and lies low in the water.

black gang. The stokers in coal-burning ships. Cf. OIL SPOILERS.

Black Indies, the. Newcastle-upon-Tyne, North and South Shields and Sunderland—all coal ports.

Black is the white of my eye. A sailor's protestation of innocence. A very old Navy expression.

Black Jack. The chequered buoy off Calshot Point at the entrance to Southampton Water.

black-list men. Naval rating defaulters undergoing punishment; or those merely ' in the report '. These, to use an Air Force expression, have put up *blacks*.

black lugs. The ' laps ' of a cod which, being discoloured, detract from its quality in the fish market. This discoloration is caused by the fish being insufficiently ' bled ' at sea. The first process in the curing of a cod is the bleeding of the fish, and if this is not done soon after it is landed in the trawler and the cod remains too long on the ice, the blood congeals; hence the term.

black meat. Bacon. (East Anglian.)

black Navy, the. Destroyers. A term born in the early days of the destroyer flotillas when these ships were painted black.

black pan. A pan containing the remains of the cabin food in a liner which is the 'perks' (perquisites) of the *black* gang or stokehold men who come off watch at eight bells in the evening. (Merchant Navy.)

black varnish. Bottled stout sold in the naval canteen.

black watch. Stoker ratings in the old coal-burning ships.

blackbird song, the. This seems to be known only to the men of the Devonport Division, and the first verse goes something like:

> *Where be thic blackbird tu?*
> *Us know where he be,*
> *He be in thic wurzle tree*
> *and us be after 'e.*

It is sung to the tune of the marching song of the Devon Regiment and is immensely popular with the ratings in GUZ.

blackguard's pay-off. The lowest scale of long-service pension, paid to a man whose character is so bad that he has never been awarded a good conduct badge.

blackheads. Black-headed gulls. (Wildfowlers'.)

blackies. The generic term for blacksmiths in the Royal Navy.

black-out. (1) A temporary loss of consciousness experienced by aviators or by men undergoing severe mental strain. From the sensation of blackness as one faints. (2) The darkening of a port as a precaution against air attack—a sense that in the 1939–45 War rapidly became part of Standard English.

black-outs. The official undergarments of the ' bloomer ' type issued to members of the Women's Royal Naval Service (' Wrens ') in the 1939–45 War. Cf. PASSION KILLERS.

blad. A rain squall. An East Coast term used among fishermen. Perhaps from Scottish and Irish dialectal *blad*, ' to slap heavily '.

Blanco. A variant of CHALKY as a nickname for White.

blanker. A Naval Service Certificate with a CLIPPED CORNER.

blanket. A whale's blubber. (Whalers' term.) It blankets the vital organs.

Blanket Bay. One's hammock or bunk; the abode of sleep. ' Me for Blanket Bay after this lot.' Cf. the archaic *go to Bedfordshire*.

blanket, to. To steal another boat's wind by coming up to windward of her. Fishermen's and yachtsmen's term.

blare. A mixture of tar and pitch used on the East Anglian fishing craft. (George Goldsmith Carter, *Looming Lights*, 1945.) Adopted from Northumbrian and East Anglian dialect.

blasphemy and voicepipe. The ship version of the Whale Island term GATE AND GAITERS.

blast. Much the same as a BOTTLE: a very severe reprimand. Also known in the Fleet Air Arm as a *rocket*.

blast bags. Those canvas shields strapped on gun-casings which served as anti-flash screens in the 1914–18 War. After the Battle of Jutland in 1916 a more efficient form of protection was devised.

bleat. A grouse or ' whine '; cf. MOAN and DRIP. From the querulous bleating of sheep.

bleed the buoy. To let the water out of the buoy.

bleed the monkey. To steal grog from the cask; cf. TAP THE ADMIRAL, by which it was suggested.

blimp. A small coastal patrol airship used by the Royal Naval Air Service in the 1914–18 War. The term was coined by Horace Short, who may have intended it as a blend of '*bloody limp*'.

blind guard. A coastguard look-out post that is hidden from the view of the main coastguard station.

blind rocks. Those just under the surface of the water and not visible at any state of the tide. (A colloquialism that has become a technicality.)

blind roller. An unlooked-for heavy sea on a calm day.

blind sail. A low-cut sail that blots out the helmsman's view.

Blip, oh! An ironical cheer when a boat collides with another. (H.M.S. *Worcester* cadets.)

blister. A bulge built in the side of a battleship to take the shock of torpedoes and to reduce damage to the hull.

bloater. (1) The early type of aircraft used by the Royal Naval Air Service during the first year of its existence, *circa* 1912. (2) (**B—**) A resident of Great Yarmouth, Norfolk, the home of the famous 'Yarmouth' bloater.

blob. (Usually in the plural.) A mine-net float.

blockards. Herring fry. An East Anglian term.

blocker. One of the block-ships used at Zeebrugge on St George's Day, April 23, 1918. These were obsolete vessels filled with cement and sunk in the entrance to the harbour.

Bloke, the. In the Royal Navy, the Commander—the Senior Executive Officer in the ship. In the Merchant Navy, the First Mate.

blood. The red maximum-mark on the steam pressure gauge in a ship's stokehold.

Blood and Guts, the. The Red Ensign of the Mercantile Marine, now known as the Merchant Navy.

blood boat, the. That which is used for the BEEF TRIP.

blood for breakfast. The threatened consequences of lubberliness; 'If the Captain sees any of you men with your caps flat-a-back, there'll be blood for breakfast'; cf. GUTS FOR A NECKTIE.

36

blood money. A Service gratuity or prize money.

blood wagon. A Naval (or Army or R.A.F.) motor ambulance.

bloody flag, the. The red flag which is run up as a signal to 'engage the enemy more closely'.

bloody-minded. A rebellious state of mind caused by annoying circumstances which have placed a man in such a position that he has to CARRY THE CAN for another's misdeeds.

blow. A gale of wind, or any wind above Force Six in the Beaufort Scale.

blow fish. Whales, which 'blow' spouts of water.

blow the grampus. To pour water over a sleeping sailor. (An old Merchant Navy term.)

blower, the. The ship's internal telephone system. In the old days one blew down the voice-pipe to attract attention and gave the message when there was a response; now the telephone is in every part of the ship, and it too is known as *the blower*.

blubber hunter. A whaling ship. Cf. SPOUTER.

blue boats. Skiffs or gigs used on the Dart by cadets of the Royal Naval College, Dartmouth.

blue ensign club. A yacht club that is privileged to wear the blue ensign in its suit of flags. This ensign is primarily that of the Royal Naval Reserve; members of the Reserves (R.N.R. and R.N.V.R.) may apply to the Admiralty for warrants to wear the ensign, undefaced, in their yachts. Royal Yacht Clubs and certain privileged sailing clubs are entitled to the ensign but it must be defaced by the club's device in the fly and they must have a warrant from the Admiralty to do so. The wearing of the 'blue' has a number of privileges as well as a certain standard of etiquette which is demanded of its wearers. Cf. RED ENSIGN CLUB.

blue fever. Venereal disease. (Naval lower-deck.) (Blue = unmentionable.)

blue fish. The shark, from its dark-blue appearance.

Blue Funneler. A 'Blue Funnel' (Alfred Holt) liner. Cf. WELSH NAVY.

Blue God, the. Father Neptune, god of the blue sea.

Blue Island. The Isle of Skye.

blue jobs. Naval officers or men. An Army and Air Force term. Cf. BROWN JOBS. A 1939–45 coinage.

Blue Marines. The Royal Marine Artillery, which was a separate unit until amalgamated with the Royal Marine Light Infantry about the time of the 1914–18 War. Cf. RED MARINES and KHAKI MARINES.

Blue Nose certificate. A ' diploma ' presented to those who have crossed north of the Arctic Circle. It is a document rather resembling an illuminated manuscript and worded: ' We, Neptunus, Monarch of all Seas, do hereby declare that our Loyal Subject . . . . on this day hath passed north of the Arctic Circle into the Realms of the Midnight Sun. Having thus penetrated the rigours of the Frozen North it is our Royal Pleasure to bestow upon him the Ancient and Universally Honoured *Diploma of the Blue Nose*. Given under Sovereign Hand on this day . . . month . . . year . . . on board His Britannic Majesty's Ship . . . .'

Blue Peter. The Navy's Long Service and Good Conduct Medal, awarded for fifteen years' exemplary behaviour.

blue pictures, the. Salacious programmes in the cinemas at Eastern ports; a cinema-cum-brothel.

blue shirt. The blue International Code flag hoisted when a ship needs assistance.

blue slipper. Treacherous blue sand peculiar to the shores of the Isle of Wight. One slips on it.

Blue Squadron, the. The Royal London Yacht Club—from the predominating colour of its ensign and burgee. A privileged club, its members are permitted to wear a Blue Ensign, defaced with the arms of London in the fly; the burgee is royal blue and bears the London arms. Cf. BLUE ENSIGN CLUB.

blue ticket, get the. To fall under the Geddes economy ' axe ' (in 1922). Officers thus picked out were asked to retire on pension, or they would be forcibly retired as redundant. The ' blue ticket ' informed them of their misfortune.

blue-eyed boy. One who is in favour with the Captain or Commander and can do no wrong. ' Oh, *he's* the Captain's blue-eyed boy.'

blues. (1) British bluejackets, a Victorian term which survived a few years of the present century but is now obsolete, MATELOTS being the current term. (2) Blue uniforms worn in Home Waters. (3) A Royal Marine officer's best uniform.

blue-water sailor. One who sails ' deep sea '; as opposed to a coastal-waters man. A colloquialism that has been admitted to the best linguistic circles.

blue-water school, the. The people who believed in the supremacy of British sea power as the best defence of Britain in pre-1914 days. Cf. preceding.

blunt end. A landlubber's name for a ship's stern. Cf. SHARP END.

board in the smoke. To take someone by surprise. From the literal sense, ' to attack under a smoke screen '.

boardsmen. Those members of a fishing boat's crew who bait and shoot the lines. (East Anglian.)

boatmen. Men who work the ' narrow boats ' on the inland waterways.

boat's shoved off, the. A phrase meaning that a man has ' had it '; he is too late for tea, the liberty boat, payment, or what have you. The opposite of catching the boat.

Boats. (1) The Boats Officer who runs the ship's boats, trains crews, etc. (Wardroom.) (2) Submarines; or the early Torpedo Boats of the 1914–18 War.

bob. A bob-fly, which is a barge's burgee fitted on a swivel that allows it to run free.

bob-a-day gunner. An officer who undertakes gunnery duties in the absence of the appointed Gunnery Lieutenant. He used to receive a shilling a day extra pay.

bobber. One of the workers at fish wharves who help to unload trawlers.

bobbing. (1) (Of a ship) flashing a Morse code message. (Flag-deck language.) (2) = BABBING.

bob-tailed. Cruiser-sterned.

bodkin. An old term for a Midshipman's dirk. Cf. DO-LITTLE SWORD.

body-and-soul lashing. A length of spunyarn tied belt-wise round a seaman's oilskin to prevent its being blown over his head and taking him overboard. The rope could always be grabbed by a nearby messmate if the wearer should slip on deck and be in danger of going over the side. Cf. *to keep body and soul together*.

body-snatcher. A Regulating Petty Officer (cf. CRUSHERS). He snatches the bodies of the unruly and takes them on to the quarter-deck before the officer of the watch.

boffins. In the Navy, officers over the age of thirty-five. (In the R.A.F., ' backroom boys ' or scientists.) The name is partly echoic; cf. the dialectal *boffle* for *baffle*.

bogeyman. A fishery-protection craft, usually a naval sloop under a Lieut.-Commander, R.N., whose job is to prevent fishing vessels from poaching inside the three-mile limit.

boiler-cleaning leave. Leave granted to members of the ship's company when their ship is undergoing the periodical cleaning of boilers. Often shortened to *boiler leave*.

boileritis. Anything that may be wrong with a ship's boiler tubes; cf. CONDENSERITIS. Humorously satirical of *-itis*, a suffix indicative of disease.

bomb alley. Any particularly vulnerable area afloat or ashore: e.g. the Thames Estuary during the London blitz 1940–41 or during the flying bomb period 1944–45; Malta; the strip of enemy-occupied coast between Tobruk and the British lines in Egypt.

Bombay duck. A bloater. (Lower-deck.)

Bombay oyster. A glass of milk and castor oil served in training ships.

Bond. The duty-free supply of liquor to H.M. Ships each month. ' Be careful with the gin: it's the last bottle till our Bond comes.' (Wardroom.)

bonkers. Light in the head; slightly drunk. (*Bonk* is echoic for ' to hit '; therefore cf. the civilian *crackers*.)

bonxie. A Scottish name for the Great Skua.

boom off. To keep someone at a distance, e.g. an inquisitive or unwelcome caller. ' If the Press people come for details, boom them off as politely as you can, Number One; this show isn't to be released'; i.e. *shoot* them off.

boomey. A sailing barge fitted with a *boom* and rigged yachtwise. Boomeys are almost, if not wholly, extinct. Cf. SPRITTY and STUMPY.

boot-necks. Royal Marines who, at one time, had a leathern flap on the neck of their tunics. Hence also, LEATHER-NECKS.

bor. A Norfolk term of address heard among herring fishermen. Either sex may be addressed thus: ' I don't think much of the weather, bor; fares' (it seems) ' to me we'll see some dirty weather.' If more than one person is addressed the form would be, ' together ': ' Well, together, how's things?' This ' bor ' and ' together ' idiom is peculiar to East Anglia. (See the novels of Michael Home, *passim*.) *Bor* is perhaps short for *neighbour*, but cf. Middle High German *bur*.

Bose. Short for Bo'sun. (Lower-deck.)

boss. A boatswain in the Merchant Navy.

Boss Serang. A native Leading Hand in charge of a working party. Used on the East Indies Station.

bo'sun. A boatswain, the oldest rank in the Royal Navy, dating from the time when His Majesty's Ships were commanded by Army Officers. The *bo'sun* was responsible for seamanship and the crew's efficiency.

bo'sun bird. A tropical bird, whose pipe resembles that of the SPITHEAD NIGHTINGALE.

bo'sun's call. The colloquial form of *boatswain's call*, the twittering pipe used by the Bo'sun or Quartermaster to precede routine ' calls ', e.g. ' Hands to breakfast and clean ', ' Clear lower-deck '; it is also used for piping a senior officer on board. Cf. SPITHEAD NIGHTINGALE.

Bo'sun's key. A marline-spike. (Lower-deck.) Cf. PUSSER'S KEY.

bo'sun's nightmare, the. A particularly exasperating and intractable wire used in the early type of magnetic-minesweeping gear.

bo'sun's stool. A kind of chair which is used for hoisting men aloft, e.g. to paint the masts or funnel. The Standard English term is *boatswain's chair*.

bottle. A good ' ticking off '. Short for *bottle of acid,* now obsolescent. An Old Navy expression.

bottle, collect a. To go ashore to receive a reprimand from the Commander-in-Chief.

bottle bumper. A bittern. From its ' booming '. (Wildfowlers'.)

bottlenose. (1) A nickname for a puffin. (Wildfowlers'.) (2) A porpoise. Both from the bulbous ' nose '.

Bottle the Whisky. The famous Polish destroyer *Blyskawika* whose exploits in the 1939–45 War will make thrilling reading if ever they are told. Residents of Cowes, Isle of Wight, will remember her with gratitude for her spirited defence of the town when it was heavily raided by enemy aircraft in May, 1942. (By ' Hobson-Jobson '.)

bottle the tot. To carry out the illegal practice of saving one's daily rum ration and bottling it against leave or a ' birthday '.

bottoms. Lighters lying abreast and aground in the mud are referred to collectively as *bottoms* and numbered as in ' ranks '; *first bottom, second bottom,* etc.

bottom's out of the glass, the. An observation made when weather is particularly ' dirty ' and causes the mercury in the barometer to disappear.

bow wave. A cap that has been shaped to achieve this effect. (Royal Naval College, Dartmouth.)

bowler hat, get a. To be invalided or discharged from the Navy. Cf. TAKE FELT.

bowls. The barrel-shaped floats used for the warp of a herring net. (East Anglian.)

bows under. The naval version of the shore-going term *snowed under*—with work.

Bowse down! ' Be quiet! ' Literally, to tighten a bobstay by haul-on the fall.

box wallah. A commercial traveller passenger in a liner. (Merchant Navy.) From *box wallah,* which, in Indian, used to mean a merchant, a man engaged in commerce.

brag rags. Medal ribbons. (Royal Navy.)

brains of the Navy, the. The self-description of the Communications Branch, which includes the 'tels', coders, radar ratings. Cf. EYES OF THE FLEET.

branch kagg. Specialist talk; 'shop'. See KAGG.

brass. A collective term for the officers. (Lower-deck.)

brass hat. A cap with oak leaves round its peak worn by Naval Officers with, and above, the rank of Commander, R.N., R.N.R., or R.N.V.R. Whence:

brass hattery. The junior naval officers' collective term for Commanders, Captains and above. Cf. preceding.

brass-bounder. A Merchant Navy apprentice. From his brass-bound uniform.

brassed off. The Navy's version of the Army's 'browned off' and the Air Force's 'cheesed off'. Probably arose from the excessive polishing of BRIGHTWORK that goes on in the Navy.

braves. Men, 'warriors', the ship's company. Cf. THE TROOPS.

Brazilian Navy. The Special Branch of the R.N.V.R. Cf. GREEN STRIPERS.

Breadcrumbs! When this cry goes forth from the Sub-Lieutenant or Senior Midshipmen, the Junior Midshipmen place their fingers in their ears. It is a signal that the 'Sub' wishes to say something that is not intended for the ears of the 'CRABS'. In the old days large breadcrumbs were put in the ears.

break ship or **break out of ship.** To leave a ship or shore establishment without permission; to take French leave. 'Knocker White was RUN IN for breaking ship.' (Lower-deck.)

break surface. To wake up from sleep. (Submariners' term.) Usually shortened to *surface*, e.g. 'Has the Old Man surfaced yet?'

break the hatch. To open a submarine's hatch when it has surfaced. (Now technical.)

brenner. A sudden gust of wind at sea. Cf. ROGER. An East Anglian term, either a variant or a cognate of *burner*: cf. the slang senses of *scorcher*.

bricks. Projectiles of whatever calibre. (Royal Navy.)

Bridge of Sighs. A narrow gangway across the broadside torpedo tubes in a submarine.

bridle. A wire rope.

brig, the. The cells. (Naval colloquialism.) Cf. OVER THE WALL.

bright-lights leave. Leave in Greenock given to the ships of the Home Fleet based on Scapa Flow. (1939–45.)

brightwork. Any part of a ship that requires to be polished daily with ' brass-rags '.

brightwork juice. Metal polish. (A term indigenous to the training ship *Conway.*)

brigs, the. The sailing squadron of brig-rigged vessels used for training naval cadets or boys at the beginning of the twentieth century, the last being used about 1903.

briny, the. The ocean. *A whiff of, a trip on, the briny.* (Journalistic.)

' Britannia ' slang. On my desk lies a small ash tray inscribed: ' Made from old copper taken from H.M.S. *Britannia,* cadet training ship at Dartmouth, 1869–1905 '; it was in 1905 that the last cadets left the old ship. Little of the slang used by them has survived her passing; but, since 1905 is in the twentieth century, I am listing the following terms which have been recorded in the writings of ' Bartimeus ', ' Taffrail ', ' Sea Wrack ', Captain Lionel Dawson and other naval officers who were themselves in the *Britannia*: *News, threes, sixers* and *niners* were, respectively, First, second, third and last termers. A *chief captain* was the Cadet Captain in the *Hindustani,* that tender to the *Britannia* which housed the first and second term cadets. *Ruxing* meant teasing, (ragging) or creating any kind of disturbance, riotous behaviour generally; a *till-rux* was an inspection of (or as modern cadets would term it, a ' blitz ' on) a *private till* for suspected hoarding of food, sweets or cigarettes; *stodge* was food of any kind (the *stodger* is Dartmouth's equivalent of the Public School's ' tuck-shop '; to *stodge anyone* is to stand him treat at the stodger). *Ship's prices* were those charged by cadets for stodge smuggled on board by the ship's ' black market '. A *Garry-biscuit* was a very popular delicacy composed of chocolate cream between two Garibaldi biscuits and was also known as a ' Garry sandwich'. (Garibaldis are still known as 'squashed flies' at Dartmouth.) A *ship's bun* was provided gratis in the forenoon to stave off hunger till lunch, a *bun-flag* being hoisted at *bun-time*. *Nerving* meant impudence or 'sideness', and offenders were usually chastened by a whack from a Cadet Captain's *togie*, a short length of hemp with a knot at the end. *Guff*, meaning 'cheek', has survived the *Britannia*, for guff rules are still observed at the Royal Naval College, Dartmouth. *Sancs*, short for *sanctuaries*, were places where senior cadets foregathered for illicit smoking; and 'niners' had their own hideout, which was known as *niners' sanc*. A *gam* is an exclusively *Britannia* term for a hammock and gives no clue to its origin. The *mumpery* was that isolation 'ward' in the *Hindustani* which was used during a mumps epidemic. *Mods* were moderate punishments entailing extra drill. *Loot* was an abbreviation for 'Lieutenant' and is still in use. *Beagle bitch* was the whip to the *Britannia* pack. Other *Britannia* terms will be found throughout this work.

Brittlesea. A local and yachtsmen's pronunciation of Brightlingsea, Essex.

broach cargo. To steal from the ship's freight.

Broad Fourteens, the. A sea area off Ymuiden on the Dutch coast.

Brock's benefit. Any spectacular display of gunfire. The firm of Brock is famous for its fireworks. A son of one of the firm's owners was killed at Zeebrugge in 1918 as a Commander in the R.N. Air Service.

brockey. Nickname for anyone prone to acne. (Lower-deck.) Probably from English and Scottish dialectal *brocked*, mottled with black and white: cf. *brock-faced*, having—like a badger—a white streak on the face.

broke. (Of an officer) dismissed his ship and the Navy. Cf. DÉGOMMÉ.

brot tow. A man who collects old tow ropes. Perhaps cf. the obsolete adjective, *brotel*, 'brittle'.

brow, the. A ship's gangway.

brown food. Malt liquor, an essential part of the matelot's sustenance.

45

brown George. A ship's biscuit; ship's biscuits generically. (Merchant Navy.)

brown jobs. The Navy's collective term for the Army. Cf. BLUE JOBS.

browned off for (a job). A lower-deck colloquialism borrowed from the Army. ' I can't go ashore tonight, I'm browned off for guard duty.'

browning shot. A first shot at the enemy, no particular ship being selected as target. From the sporting phrases *browning a covey —firing into the brown.*

brute force and bloody ignorance. A lower-deck opinion of gunnery instructors' methods.

Brylcreem Boys, the. The Navy's term for the Air Force. From the hair-cream advertisement depicting an airman user of Brylcreem.

bubbly. Navy rum. Also WINE. (Lower-deck.) A humorous sense-perversion of the usual slang meaning, ' champagne '.

Buccaneers, the Blackfriars. The London Division of the Royal Naval Volunteer Reserve, whose Headquarters are in the old Flower Class sloop, moored off the Thames Embankment near Blackfriars Bridge.

Buck. The naval nickname for all surnamed Taylor. Probably from the name of a once-famous rough-rider.

bucker. A porpoise, because of its bucking propensities.

buckie. A whelk. A Scottish-coast term. Perhaps from the whelks found in the neighbourhood of Buckie in the Moray Firth.

bucko. A Merchant Navy bully, now not so common as in the days of sail, when *Bucko Mates* struck terror into the hands and ship's apprentices.

> *Her skipper was mate of a bucko ship*
> *Which always killed one man per trip.* (Kipling.)

Probably from his size and strength.

Buco. *Bu*ild-up *Co*ntrol, an organization that ensured the constant supply of men and materials to the beach-heads in the invasion of Normandy, 1944.

Buffer, the. The Chief Bo'sun's Mate. He is the 'buffer' between the Commander and the upper-deck; perhaps also with an oblique reference to *old buffer*.

buffs. Leather air-inflated spherical buoys used to mark fishing-nets. (East Anglian.)

bug juice. (1) Cocoa—or kye, as it is known throughout the Navy. At one time this was issued in solid blocks, sweetened; the *kye* was cut from the block according to the desired consistency and melted in boiling water. Quite often it was eaten as 'chocolate' but a little went a very long way. Properly made, *kye* is a delicious drink and very popular during the Middle Watch (midnight to 4 a.m.). (2) Brilliantine. (Lower-deck.)

bug trap. A tramp steamer or Fleet Auxiliary.

bug whiskers. An incipient SET which has got out of control and looks 'like nothing on earth'. Cf. also SCURZE and LAVATORY BRUSHES.

bugs. (1) 'Chatty': i.e. verminous or generally inclined to 'scruffiness'. The Royal Navy fetish for cleanliness is proverbial and anyone conspicuously dirty soon becomes unpopular. It is an axiom in the Service that if you are in doubt what to do with anything you cannot go wrong if you wash it. (2) = BATCHY. (Lower-deck.)

build a chapel. To turn a ship broadside on by very bad steering.

bulgines. Old Navy for engines. From the words in an old sea shanty:
> '*Clear the track and let the bulgine run.*'

bulk. To stack large quantities of pilchards in alternate layers of salt and fish in curing houses to remain four weeks, after which time they are washed and drained of oil and sent for export. (A technical term used in the pilchard fisheries of Cornwall.)

bull the cask. To make grog by the simple—and not very successful—method of pouring water into an empty grog tub and letting it stand.

bullets. Dried peas. (Lower-deck.)

Bullock Patch, the. A gunnery range in the Portsmouth area.

Bullocks, the. The Corps of Royal Marines. (Lower-deck.) Cf. LEATHER-NECKS, JOLLIES. They are big, beefy, brawny and brave.

bumblebees. The Wildcat aircraft used by the Fleet Air Arm in 1939–45.

bumblejar. A gramophone or musical box. Cf. JUTE-BOX.

bumboatman. One who runs a bumboat—a species of floating stall that sells all manner of goods from clothing to fruit. Bumboatmen hang round ships in an anchorage crying their wares or bartering on the 'changey for changey' system.

bum-freezer. A Midshipman's round jacket cut on the Eton style. This is also known as an ARSE-PERISHER. It has no tail.

bumped, be. To hit a mine. (R.N.) From boat-racing at the English universities.

bunch o' fives. A man's fist. Adopted from civilian—especially pugilistic—slang.

bundleman. An Old Navy term for a married man. At one time sailors were allowed to take food ashore when 'proceeding' on leave, and married men seemed always to carry ashore the largest bundles. Cf. RABBITS.

bundook. A musket or rifle. (Lower-deck.)

bun flag. Navy Code flag 'B', which is flown at bun-time at the Royal Naval College, Dartmouth.

bun rush. Tea time at the Royal Naval College, Dartmouth.

bung. Short for *bung-hole*, the lower-deck term for cheese. Cf. SOAP AND FLANNEL. From its binding properties.

bung up and bilge free. Technically, the proper stowage position of a rum cask. Used slangily to describe anyone lying asleep during a MAKE AND MEND.

Bungy. Nickname for anyone surnamed Williams.

Bunje. The wardroom nickname for that member who is responsible for Physical Training duties in the ship. Cf. INDIARUBBER MAN (wardroom).

Bunker. The lower-deck nickname for anyone surnamed Brown.

bunker cat. A variant of ASH CAT.

bunny meat. Any green vegetables; food associated with rabbits. (Lower-deck.)

bunting. International code flags; flags of any sort which are made of bunting. Hence the *bunting-tosser*, a signalman.

bunts. Lower-deck abbreviation for *bunting-tosser*, a signalman. Cf. FLAG-FLAPPER and GENTLEMAN BUNTS.

buoy, go round the. To take more than one helping at a meal.

buoy, swing round the. To hang on to a good shore job with allowances, etc. (Applied to naval officers.)

Burgh, the. Edinburgh. (Wardroom.)

burgoo. Porridge. This very old term (current since about 1740) probably derives from Turkish *burghul*, ' wheat porridge '.

burgoo spoiler. A cook. (Merchant Navy.) He burns the porridge (BURGOO).

burn. A smoke or ' burn of the weed '. (Lower-deck.)

Burney gear. A paravane which was invented by Captain Burney, R.N. (A virtual technicality.)

butch. The ship's butcher, usually a Royal Marine.

butt. A flounder. (East Anglian fishermen's.)

Butt-In, the. H.M. T.B. Destroyer *Sportive* of the 1914–18 War. Her ship's badge was a goat, and she was fond of butting into the enemy.

button on. (Of a ship) to join a convoy (1939–45).

button up. To finish a job. 'Is everything buttoned up?' (Wardroom.)

button your flap. Be quiet; stop panicking! (flapping). A reference to sailors' trousers. (Lower-deck.)

buttons, get one's. To be promoted to Petty Officer (W.R.N.S.). On such promotion the black buttons of a Leading Wren are replaced by brass ones.

button-up abaft all. A naval chaplain's collar.

butty boat. A canal barge working in company with another. From the dialect word *butty*, a pal; companion. Cf. the American *buddy*.

buy it. To meet with any kind of misfortune. Of a ship, to be torpedoed or bombed. ' Old Nobby has bought a sticky number in Malta '; ' I hear the old " Ark " has bought it '. (General Navy slang.)

buy white horses. To spend money recklessly on shore leave. ' White horses ' on the crests of waves are quickly dispersed; cf. the standard English (*buy*) *a white elephant.*

buzz. A rumour. ' Is there anything in this buzz about boiler leave, Chief? '

buzz king. A messdeck oracle; one from whom all rumours emanate. A *buzz-monger* par excellence.

by guess and by God. Steaming blindly in bad weather. Trusting in God and one's sense of direction.

by-the-wind sailor. A species of jelly-fish known as *Velella*, often seen on the south coast of England. Its oblique crest acts as a sail and it often drifts a long way.

C

C.W. candidate. A Naval rating who aspires to temporary officer status through the Royal Naval Volunteer Reserve. Known sarcastically as *W.C. candidates* by their messmates. The C.W. Branch of the Admiralty is where the Commissions and Warrants are awarded. Cf. SEA-GOING WREN and WHITE PAPER CANDIDATE.

C.W. List, the. The list of naval appointments issued to H.M. Ships and Shore Establishments. (A technicality.) See preceding entry.

cab rank. A ' trot ' of destroyers, torpedo boats and small craft awaiting orders to put to sea.

cabin, doing. Undergoing cell punishment. ' Where's old Smiler —haven't seen him for days. Is he UP THE LINE? '—' No, he's doing ten days' cabin.'

cackle berries. Eggs. The hen cackles when laying them. (Lower-deck.)

Cads' Bar. The ' pub ' resorted to by junior naval officers at a shore base.

Cads' corner. The junior officers' corner of the wardroom.

cady. A hat or cap. (Lower-deck.) Adopted from (now obsolescent) civilian slang of obscure origin; perhaps cf. Romany *stadi*, a hat.

cag or cagg. See KAGG.

Callao painter, the. A Merchant Navy name for the noxious effluvia that arise from the water at the port of Callao (Peru).

Callao routine. A free and easy routine. ' I had a lovely commission in the *Squirt*—more Callao than that ' (see MORE THAN THAT). Callao, the principal seaport of Peru, is a notoriously easy station.

camel. A submarine-lifting tank.

camel night = DUFF NIGHT.

cam ship. A *C*atapult *A*rmed *M*erchant Ship, carrying fighter aircraft (1939–45).

can, carry the. See CARRY THE CAN.

Can. H.M.S. *Canopus*. (Lower-deck.)

Can do? Much use is made of ' Pidgin English ' in the Royal Navy by those officers and men who have spent commissions on the China Station. If one is not able to *do*, the answer is *No can do*. Cf. CHOP CHOP, and PIECEE ONE.

Canada. The nickname for all Canadian officers or ratings. (Wardroom.)

Canary Ward. The venereal disease ward in a naval hospital. It is painted yellow.

cane. A cap grummet.

canteen boat. The junior ship in an Escort Group. She does all the dirty work and has to CARRY THE CAN when there is trouble.

canteen medals. Stains on a man's uniform as a result of ' careless feeding '. (Also in the Army and the Air Force; probably an Army term originally.)

canteen merchant. A steward serving in the canteen of the training ship *Conway*.

Canteen open, mind yer fingers, canteen closed! The derisive shout which greets the opening of the N.A.A.F.I. canteen on board ship. It is open for such a short time and is so quickly filled that the laggards get their fingers trapped in the closing door.

canvasseens. The canvas trousers worn by seamen.

cap off, with your. A constant threat to ' awkward ' New Entries is: ' Any more flannel from you and you'll be taken aft with your cap off ', i.e. taken before the officer of the watch and told to take his cap off as a defaulter.

cap tally pint. A glass of beer served ' short ', i.e. with the depth of a cap ribbon short of a full glass. The equivalent of the shore-going term *collar-band pint*. (Lower-deck.)

Cape Doctor, the. The health-giving south-easterly wind that is so beneficial to invalids recuperating at Cape Colony.

Cape Flyaway. See DUTCHMAN'S CAPE.

Cape Horn Fever. An imaginary disease: a malingerer's complaint in rough weather off Cape Horn.

Cape Horn rain. Rum. (Merchant Navy.)

Cape Horn rig. Thick clothing and oilskins.

Cape of Birds, the. Foulness in Essex; originally called *Fowlness*.

capful of wind. A nice sailing breeze. (Verging on Standard English.)

Cap'n. A Merchant Navy shortening of *Captain*.

Captain, four-ringed. A Captain in the Royal Navy who wears the four stripes of that rank, as distinct from an officer of a junior rank who commands a ship and is known as *the captain*.

Captain Kettle set. A beard fashioned like that worn by ' the little red captain ' in Cutcliffe Hyne's famous collections of short stories, *Adventures of Captain Kettle* (1898), *Further Adventures*, etc.

Captain's cloak, the. The 39th Article of War, which is as sweeping—as comprehensive—as a cloak.

Captain's tiger. The Captain's steward in the Merchant Navy.

carfindo. A ship's carpenter. The influence of *carf*, a piece of wood, is obvious, but the second element is obscure unless it is a diminutive suffix.

Cargo Bill. Nickname for a Royal Naval Reserve officer; a term now outmoded, but occasionally used during the 1914–18 War. See SINBAD.

cargo-shifter. A variant of CARGO BILL; cf. the synonymous SINBAD.

Carney. The lower-deck name for an officer who is a ' taut hand ' on board, but sweetness itself ashore. Perhaps from a Captain Carney who led his men a hard life afloat and professed friendliness on the beach, but more probably a personification of civilian slang *carney*, ' wheedling; suave hypocrisy ', itself from *carney*, ' to coax, wheedle, flatter '.

carpet. To reprimand a subordinate, the Merchant Navy's form of BOTTLE. Literally, to have a man on the carpet.

carry round. To help a new-comer to know his duties or the general routine of the ship; to teach a novice technical details of any science. 'The P.O.s carry the officers round half the time.' (Lower-deck.)

carry the can or **carry the keg.** To accept blame for another's misdeeds or do a job that has been neglected by one who was told off to do it. ' That's all very well, Jack, but who carries the can back? ' is frequently asked when any enterprise which may bring trouble is projected. Cf. *carry the urn* (see URN).

carry three red lights. To be drunk. From the three lights shown by a ship that is not under control.

cart. A bunk in a ship. (Humorously pejorative.)

Caruso, a touch of. A turn of the ship's engines astern. ' Give 'em a touch of Caruso, Chief!' From the high-pitched sound, with reference to the famous Italian tenor.

Casey's Court. A seamen's mess in an H.M. Ship. Full of noise and liveliness, either with a reference to a once disreputable neighbourhood or to the high spirits of Irishmen (*Casey* being a common Irish surname).

cassoon. A DOCKYARD MATEY'S form of *caisson*.

caster. See CRAB, GLASS.

casual. Short for the official Accountant term *casual payment*. When an officer or rating joins a ship it is often some weeks, or even months, before his pay is properly adjusted, so that he is paid in ' casual payments ' until his pay documents arrive. This is a measure to safeguard the Paymaster and to prevent the payee getting too deeply IN RED INK.

catch fake. Such a coil in a spiral as catches up another and, instead of cheesing down cleanly, goes under the top fake and has to be recoiled. See FAKE.

catch up with him in the black-out, I'll. A wartime threat made by a defaulter who has had what he considers a hard sentence. The threat to beat up the officer under cover of darkness was never carried into effect.

catch up with the boat. To contract venereal disease. (Lower-deck.) Presumably the boat takes him ashore to Naval Hospital. Cf. CANARY WARD.

catchers, the. Torpedo Boat Destroyers. Admiral Lord Charles Beresford is believed to have given currency to this term. The destroyers ' caught ' the torpedo boats and ' destroyed ' them.

cat rig. A fore-and-aft mainsail only set on a boom and gaff and stepped well forward near the ship's stem.

Cats, the. The battleships *Lion* and *Tiger* of Jutland fame.

caulk. Sleep. When a man is asleep on deck he is said to *caulk a few seams*. Cf. ZIZZ.

caulker. A blanket or watchcoat used for sleeping on deck during ' Make and Mend '. The term, which is also spelt *corker*, dates from the early days of the Navy's history when the caulker was spread on the deck to prevent the melting pitch from soiling the sleeper's uniform.

caustic. An acoustic mine used in the 1939–45 War. This diabolical weapon detonated when the ship's engines synchronized with the beat of the mine.

Caustic, Old. A grousing, cantankerous messmate. (Lower-deck.) Cf. ACID DROP.

centre-boarder. A small yacht carrying a centre plate, which, when lowered, allows her to sail closer to the wind.

chai. Tea. A corruption of the Chinese word *tchi*: cf. the Army's corruption, *char*, and the lower-deck's PLEW.

chain-breakers. Sleeveless vests of the muscle-revealing type worn by young seamen in the Merchant Navy.

Chain Locker, the. The Registrar General of Shipping and Seamen.

chalked in, be. If a passenger in a liner inadvertently sits in the Captain's chair he may have a chalk ring drawn round him by the steward and be requested to pay for a round of drinks for the stewards—the penalty for this *faux pas*.

Chalky. A variant of BLANCO.

challenge ships. The United States ships *Orleans* and *Rochester*, which were sent into the blockaded area off the coast of Flanders in 1916 to challenge the U-boats to attack them. America at that time being a neutral country.

chamfer up. To make things tidy or shipshape; to *square-off* the messdecks for Captain's inspection. (Lower-deck.) Cf. WATER CARNIVAL.

chance one's arm. To do something against the regulations, the consequences of which—if caught out—are the loss of rank or ' rate '. The doer risks losing the badges on his arm.

Channel fever. The symptoms of homesickness felt by a ship's crew when nearing the English Channel after being a long time abroad.

Channel Gropers, the. An old Navy term for the Channel Fleet.

Channel groping. Naval exercises in the English Channel. Cf. preceding.

Channel money. A sum given to men before they land at a home port. (Merchant Navy.)

chariot. A one-man submarine. (1939–1945 War.)

Charles William. The name of the dummy used for life-saving practice at the Royal Naval College, Dartmouth.

Charley. The Navy's reveille bugle-call, which has these words:

> *Charley! Charley! get up and wash yourself.*
> *Charley! Charley! lash up and stow!*

Charley Martin's Hole. Herring fishing ground in the North Sea some distance from Yarmouth; discovered by Charley Martin.

Charley More. A one-time Maltese publican whose house sign read, ' Charley More, the square thing '. The name became a naval catch-word synonym for straight dealing. ' Here, act Charley More! ' It is seldom heard nowadays.

Charley Noble, the. The galley stove. From one Charles Noble, a sea-captain whose galley funnel—made of copper—was kept brightly burnished.

Chase-me-Charley. A radio-controlled glider bomb used by the Germans in 1941–2 for attacks upon key ships in Allied Convoys.

chassing or **chasing.** Gentle correction of junior midshipmen or laggards generally. A salutary livening-up process, good for officers and men.

chat. A young haddock. Probably from the centuries-old underworld term *chats*, a thing: young haddocks are 'little bits of things'.

Chatham rats. Lower-deck collective term for ratings of the Chatham Division. Cf. DUFFOES.

Chats. The town of Chatham, Kent, and the Royal Naval Barracks known as H.M.S. *Pembroke*. Also CHATTY CHATS.

chatty. Dirty; slovenly; generally untidy or down-at-heel. (Lower-deck.) A *chat* is slang for a louse. Cf. BUGS.

chatty and happy. A 'non-pusser' ship with a free and easy discipline; an auxiliary vessel of the HARRY TATE NAVY.

Chatty Chats. See CHATS.

cheapers. Anything cheap—but not necessarily nasty. 'Do you want to buy a wrist-watch cheapers?' (Lower-deck.)

cheerful but subdued. The aspect of a habitual naval defaulter. He obeys the instructions laid down in King's Regulations for mourners at a naval funeral: 'assume an aspect cheerful but subdued.' As the lower-deck has it: 'cheerful because he's gorn to 'is everlasting resting-place; subdued because the b . . . ain't paid his mess-bill.'

cheese-cutter. A type of cap worn by officers, petty officers and ratings of the Accountant and engine-room branches of the Royal Navy. See FORE-AND-AFT RIG.

cheese down. To coil ropes into spirals, as distinct from FLEMISH.

cheesy-eggy-hammy-topsides. An appetizing savoury popular in the wardroom.

Chef. The cook in the Royal or Merchant Navy (especially as a term of address). Cf. SLUSHY and GRUB SPOILER.

Chemist. The nickname for surgeon. (Lower-deck.) Cf. *Pills*, QUACK and SAWBONES.

Cherry Tree class. Certain ships of the Royal Navy reduced in tonnage just after the 1914–18 War to conform with the Washington Treaty. The reference was to George Washington's legendary cutting down of the cherry tree. H.M. Ships *Nelson* and *Rodney* of this 'class' were limited in displacement to

35,000 tons and their main armament was not to exceed sixteen inches in calibre.

Chest-o! A request (in the training ship *Conway*) for someone who is sitting on the owner's chest to get up and allow him to remove clothing or other articles from it.

chest stooge. A junior cadet who keeps a Cadet Captain's chest tidy for him. (Royal Naval College, Dartmouth.)

chew her oakum. (Of a ship) to be leaking and in need of re-caulking.

chew the fat. To argue a point at unnecessary length. ' When you two have finished chewing the fat, perhaps you'll get some work done? ' (Lower-deck.)

Chicago piano. A multiple pom-pom gun. Echoic of its noise. The term was common to Royal and Merchant Navies during the 1939–45 War.

chicken fruit. Eggs. (Lower-deck.) Cf. FARMYARD NUGGETS.

Chief, the. The Senior Engineer Officer in an H.M. Ship. (Wardroom.) Cf. SENIOR. In address, *Chief*.

Chief or **Chiefy.** A Chief Petty Officer. (Lower-deck.) *Chief* is frequently used as a less formal address to a Chief P.O. by an officer; *Chiefy* is the lower-deck's term of reference.

chief housemaid, the. The First Lieutenant (probably a Lieutenant-Commander) in an H.M. Ship. He is responsible for the ship's smartness and general cleanliness.

Chief Pricker, the. The Regulating Chief Petty Officer *Stoker*. Contrast:

chief stoker. A nickname for a seagull. Seagulls are said to embody the souls of dead chief stokers, partly because they occasionally ' laugh ' like one: see LAUGH LIKE A CHIEF STOKER.

china. A pal. ' What cheer, me old china? ' Cockney rhyming slang for *mate: old china-plate;* something of value, as is a good pal.

China-bird. An officer or rating who has been on the China Station and does not let any of his messmates forget the fact. His conversation is usually carried on in pidgin and he is full of China-side adventures, legends, etc. Cf. CHINKY.

China-side. The China Station. (Wardroom.) In pidgin English, *side* = place: cf. *topside*.

chin-chin joss. A church service ashore in China. (China-side slang.)

chin food. Gossip or meaningless conversation. (Lower-deck.)

Chinese National Anthem. A loud clearing of the throat, an old Chinese custom.

Chinese wedding cake. Rice pudding, a staple lower-deck ' afters ' dish—much as rice is the staple food of the Chinese.

Chink. Any Chinaman. (Very common, too, in civilian slang.)

Chinky. A rating who is always talking about his adventures on China-side. Cf. CHINA-BIRD.

Chinky toe-rot. What is known ashore as *athlete's foot*—an unpleasant complaint prevalent in the tropics.

chip one off. To salute an officer. Cf. CUT OFF A SLICE.

chippy chap. A ship's carpenter. Known also as *Chippy* or *Chips*. From the chips of wood he causes to fly about.

chips. To be given *full chips* is to be regarded as the best of fellows; to have the highest credit. ' I must say, I'll give the chef full chips for this meal.' To say of anyone that his chips are pretty high is to accuse him of being the *Captain's* BLUE-EYED BOY. (Royal Indian Navy term; *chips* being rupees.)

chit. A word borrowed from the Hindustani and meaning any written document, memorandum, note, or bill. (See *Forces' Slang*.)

chit-up. To seek anyone through the head of his department, who puts a ' chit ' on the mess notice-board. From CHIT.

chocker; chocko. See CHOKKER; CHOKKO.

chocolate gale. A strong wind from the N.W. of the Spanish Main. (Frank C. Bowen, *Sea Slang*, 1928.) *Chocolate* is a Central American native word.

chocolate, get a bar of. To receive a pat on the back from the Captain or your immediate ' boss '. A word of praise is sweet.

choke your luff! ' Be quiet! ' (Lower-deck.) Cf. PIPE DOWN!

choker. A stand-up collar worn by senior cadets at the beginning of the century. Known also as a *drain-pipe*.

chokey. Cells. Cf. COOLER. Both terms have risen from the underworld.

chokker or **chocker.** Being in a state of pessimism or BLOODY-MINDEDness; utterly ' fed up ' with life. Short for *chock-a-block* or perhaps *chock-full*. Cf. TWO BLOCKS. (Lower-deck.)

chokko or chocko. The training ship version of CHOKKER.

chooch hat. A naval officer's term for his best, ' number one ', cap worn on important occasions such as a visit to the Admiralty or the C.-in-C., *chooch* being a conflation of *Commander-in-Chief* (1939–45 coinage).

chop-backs. An ancient term for Hastings fishermen referring to the time of a hatchet skirmish with the Dutchmen.

chop chop. At once; at the run. ' Take this message to the First Lieutenant, chop chop.' Originally a ' China-side ' term, probably derived from the Cantonese dialect.

Chops of the Channel, the. The Western approach to the English Channel. There is a pun on *chops*, ' jaws ', and on the choppy seas so often experienced there.

chow. Food. Cf. SCRAN. Short for *chow-chow*, pidgin English —probably from Chinese—for ' a mixture '.

chow-line, the. The food queue in naval barracks.

christening wine. That brand of wine used for breaking across a ship's bows when she is named at the launching ceremony.

chuck-barge. The bread ' barge ', or a cask in which the ship's biscuits are kept. *Chuck* is a lower-deck name for bread.

chucks. Bo'sun, R.N. It is seldom heard in the modern navy. Origin obscure.

chuck-up. Any form of applause or encouragement. When a ship has been into action and covered herself with glory her sister ships usually give her a ' chuck-up' (cheer) as she comes into harbour.

chum. ' Chap ', ' fellow '. (Used in the training ship *Conway*.) A *new chum* is a new entry cadet in the *Conway*.

chummy ship. One with whom you exchange parties and games. Usually, but not necessarily, your neighbour in harbour.

Churchill's Armada. The Channel Convoys in the 1939–45 War.

Churchill's chicken. Corned beef. Its introduction coincided with Winston Churchill's becoming First Lord of the Admiralty.

churchwarden. A shag or cormorant. From its 'greediness'. Cf. ISLE OF WIGHT PARSON.

Cinder Track, the. A dancing 'joint' in Malta patronized by the lower-deck.

circling torpedoes. One of Hitler's 'secret weapons' which became something of a menace during the invasion build-up in 1944. The torpedoes were electrically driven and were very difficult to detect, since they left no wake. They were made to run straight until they reached an anchorage or convoy of ships and then to run in circles for about ten hours. If the 'mouldy' did no damage during its circular run it was still, at the end of it, a danger to shipping as a form of mine.

Cities, the. Ships of the City Line.

C.I.V.s. Civil Independent Volunteers, a term given to short-service officers and men who were enlisted under Lord Selborne's Scheme to provide a Naval Reserve. Synonymous with SELBORNE'S LIGHT HORSE and TICKLERS.

civvies. Plain clothes. The word 'mufti' is never used in the Royal Navy.

clagger or **clacker.** Pastry. 'Any gash clacker loafing?' means, 'Is there any more pie crust?' (See GASH.) From dialectal *clag*, to adhere, be sticky.

Clampy. The inevitable nickname for the flat-footed on the lower-deck. From *clamping* (=clumping) about the place(?).

Clans, the. Ships of the Clan Line.

clawing off. Working off a lee shore.

clean. To change clothing (not 'to wash oneself'). In the days of coal-burning ships men were piped to *clean into dirty clothing* for the evolution *Coal ship*.

clean ship. One that returns to harbour without a catch. (A whaling and fishery term.)

cleaning trick. A period of brass-polishing. A 'trick' is a spell of duty, e.g. *a trick at the wheel*.

clear lower-deck. The effervescence in a drink. If a drink is flat one occasionally hears the remark, ' Not much clear lower-deck about this stuff '.

clear one's yard-arm. To prove oneself blameless when ' reasons in writing ' are demanded. From a nautical procedure. Cf. *square yards*.

clear the decks. To remove the debris of a meal or otherwise clear a table.

Cleethorpers. Small sailing craft that fish out of Cleethorpes (Lincolnshire).

clew to ear-ring, from. Figuratively, from A to Z; thoroughly to know a subject. ' You'll never get away with that, the " Bloke " knows K.R.s from clew to ear-ring.' Technically the term refers to the condition of a square sail that has been drawn from the clew to the top of the sail (ear-ring).

clew-up. Literally, to draw the clews of a sail to the yard-arm for furling (in the days of sail). Hence, colloquially, to arrive; to finish (a job); to meet (*I clewed up with him*).

clews and lashings, hand in one's. To leave the Navy on completion of twelve or twenty-two years service. To return a hammock to stores with clews and lashings complete. ' When I 'ands in me clews and lashings there'll be no more bloody sea for me.' (Lower-deck.) See ROLL ON MY BLOODY TWELVE.

clinker-knocker. A stoker rating. Cf. ASH-CAT, BLACK WATCH, BUNKER-CAT, and DUSTMAN.

clipped corner. A man whose character in the Royal Navy has been so bad has the corner of his Service Certificate clipped to show that he is worthless. Cf. BLANKER and TICKET, BRANDED.

cloak and dagger merchant. An officer who is carrying out ' a secret mission '; also, any ' Security Officer ' who disappears from time to time.

clock. To torpedo an enemy battle or merchant ship. ' Good show, old So-and-So's clocking that Wop transport! ' (Submariners': 1939–45 War.)

closh. An East Anglian rating. (Lower-deck.)

clothing-crusher, the. That Petty Officer of the Regulating Branch who takes charge of a kit inspection on board ship. Cf. CRUSHERS.

clove hitch, in a. In an awkward position from which it is difficult to extricate oneself. The clove hitch is a very efficient knot.

club run. A routine trip with a convoy or on patrol.

Clubs. A Physical Training Instructor. (Lower-deck.)

cluck like an ash-hoist. To talk excessively; to ' natter '. ' He clucks like a ruddy ash-hoist.' Echoic. (Lower-deck.)

coached. ' Broke', financially. An East Anglian fishermen's term.

Coach Inn, the. The mess at the Royal Naval Air Station, *Cochin*. A wardroom pun.

coal fever. A state of agitation caused by the fear that a ship may not have enough coal on board to get her back to port. A Merchant Navy term born in the early part of the twentieth century.

coaling through the hose. Taking in fuel from the oiler. A term born during the change-over from coal-burning to oil-burning ships. (Stokers' term.)

Coalopolis. Newcastle-upon-Tyne. Humorous formation, on the analogy of *Cottonopolis*, Manchester.

coal-passer. A stoker in the U.S. Merchant Marine.

coast crawlers. Tramp steamers that hug the coastline; e.g., colliers from Newcastle to London. Cf. WEEKLY BOATS.

cob. A young herring. (Among East Anglian fishermen; perhaps rather dialectal than unconventional.) As a heraldic device it appears in the escutcheons of the Cobb families of East Anglia, namely the Cobbs of Sandringham and the Cobbs of Snettisham.

cob on, have a. To have a grievance or be annoyed at something: ' Don't take any notice of him, he's got a cob on.' It is a Merchant Navy stewards' term and may derive from the old nautical *cob*, meaning to strike (with the fist)—a sense in which it was used in Captain Marryat's day. Cf. the Royal Navy's WEED ON, HAVE A.

cobs. Hard roes of herring. (Fishermen's.)

cock a chest. To have a good opinion of oneself. To boast of one's prowess in work or play. A pleasing reference to self-inflation.

cock-crow. To follow the COCK-CROW ROUTE. (Bargemen's term.)

cock-crow route, the. An inshore-route kept by bargemen, so close to the land as to be within ear-shot of the cock's crow.

cock's eye. A sunny gleam in a black sky.

cocked-hat. A navigator's error in reckoning when pencilling a course on the chart. The lines, instead of meeting at the point aimed at, cross each other and form the cocked-hat.

cockle. (1) A type of two-man naval canoe in the 1939–45 War. These canoes, manned by a gallant band of Royal Marines, went up enemy-occupied rivers under cover of darkness and placed limpet mines on the hulls of enemy ships. One particularly hazardous operation was carried out in 1942 in the Gironde estuary by five ' cockles ', only one of which returned. The full story of these operations is given in Rear Admiral George P. Thompson's *Blue Pencil Admiral*, 1947. An adaptation of Standard English *cockle*, a small shallow boat, itself named after the bivalve mollusc. (2) *Cock-lolly*. A Manx shearwater.

cockroach. A pearl-fishing craft, small and, presumably, full of cockroaches.

Cocktail Islands, the. Eigg and Rum in the Hebrides.

cock-up. A mess-up, a bungled piece of work. A LASH-UP. (Lower-deck.)

cocoa bo'sun. JAM BO'SUN; a Warrant Cook.

cod's head. A vessel that, like the codfish, has the widest part of her beam well forward.

cod-banger. A cod-fisher. This term dates from the time when cod were kept in a tank on deck and were banged on the head and killed when taken out for landing. George Goldsmith Carter (in *Looming Lights*, 1945) quotes a verse of the ' Song of the Aldboro Cod-Bangers':

> *When we came to Harwich Pier*
> *The folks all flock from far and near*
> *To see us heave our cod on deck*
> *And smack 'em on the head with a bloody great stick.*

coddy moddy. A young seagull. (North of England.)

cod-hauler. A Newfoundland Banks fisherman. Cf. COD-BANGER.

cod-whanger. A man employed in the Newfoundland fish-curing industry. Cf. COD-BANGER and COD-HAULER.

coffee-pot. That pneumatic hammer in its steel cage which is placed in the bows of an acoustic-mine sweeper. When the hammer is lowered into the water and set working, its ' beat ' explodes any acoustic mines that are in the area. In appearance this gadget looks rather like a gigantic coffee-pot.

coffee-pot sailor. A man who had deserted sail for steam. (A term heard at the beginning of the twentieth century.) Steam ships were called ' kettle-bottomed coffee-pots ' by men in sailing ships.

coffee stalls. The L.C.K.s (Landing Craft Kitchen) used off the Normandy beaches to provide meals to the crews of craft which had no galleys.

cog. (1) A tin basin into which fish offal is thrown. A dialect fishery term. (2) See:

coggle. A cock-boat, a small in-shore pulling boat. Often shortened to *cog*. *Coggle* represents a ' thickening ' of *cockle*.

coil up one's ropes. To die. Cf. *go out with the ebb-tide*.

cold meat ticket. An identity disc. Cf. DEATH TALLY.

Colonel Sperry. The Sperry gyroscopic compass. (Navy.)

colour bands. The distinguishing braid worn between the gold lace of non-executive officers in the Royal Navy. They are: white (Supply and Secretariat); scarlet (Surgeons); orange (Dental Surgeons); purple (Engineering Officers); silver grey (Shipwright Officers); maroon (Wardmaster Officers in R.N. Hospitals); dark green (Electrical Officers); dark blue (Ordnance Officers); light blue (Naval Instructors and Schoolmasters); emerald green (Officers in the Special Branch of the Royal Naval Volunteer Reserve). See MARKS OF THE BEAST. A number of distinguishing braids are worn by officers in the Merchant Navy and indicate the same branches.

colour-chest. The code-flag locker on a ship's signal bridge. It has a compartment for the flag of each letter in the alphabet.

colour watches. In naval barracks and shore establishments the watches are divided into three called the red, blue, and yellow watches. This system facilitates the distribution of work and leave.

Colours. The picturesque naval ceremony instituted by ' Old Jarvie ' (Lord St Vincent) about 1790, which has been observed punctiliously ever since every day. Colours are ' made ' at sunrise and ' lowered ' at sunset. When the bugler ' sounds off ' the ' Still ', everybody faces the ensign at attention, officers saluting whilst the White ensign is hoisted. In summer, Colours are ' made ' (they are never ' hoisted ' in the Royal Navy) at 8 a.m., and in the winter at 9 a.m.

Combined ops. Combined operations. Cf. CONFUSED OPERATIONS.

come the old tinman. To bluff or FLANNEL; to be objectionably self-assured; (i.e. to play the old soldier: *tin man = toy soldier*). (Lower-deck: in fairly common use up to 1939.)

come off. Officers and men of the Royal Navy are said to ' come off ' (the shore) when they return to their ships which are lying in the stream. ' You'd better keep an eye on the libertymen tonight, I expect half of 'em will come off tight.' (Colloquial— not slang.)

Comic Cuts. The Admiralty Intelligence reports in the 1914–18 War. From the children's comic paper of that name.

comic party. A variant of the more usual FUNNY PARTY, a concert party in an H.M. Ship.

commissioned popsey. A Wren officer. (Navy.)

commissioning inspection. The routine inspection of a ship when she commissions or PAYS OFF.

common pennant. The Church Pennant, which first appeared in H.M. Ships about 1660, when it was much longer than the present one and had a ' slit fly '. The use of the pennant for Squadron Colours ceased in the 1860s, and the pennant now serves as a cable working-party flag; but when flown at half-mast it indicates that a man has fallen overboard.

comozant. St Elmo's fire. Probably a corruption of *corposant*: cf. COMPOSITE.

company-keepers. Fishing craft that sail together for the fishing grounds. (Fishermen's.)

complain. (Of a ship) to have her timbers creaking.

complete book, the. A book containing the names, ratings, birthplaces, dates of joining, etc., of the members of a ship's crew.

compo. Compensation allowance, officially known as ' Lodging and Provision '. Allowance (L. & P.A.) granted to officers and ratings who live ashore when no accommodation is provided in a ship or Shore Establishment. Cf. LODGE AND COMP.

compo number. A shore appointment that entitles an officer or rating to COMPO.

composite. Fishermen's solecistic form of *corposant* (St. Elmo's fire), the electric ball of light seen around the masts and rigging of a ship on dark, stormy nights. It is said to portend disaster. Cf. CORPSE CANDLES.

condenseritis. The leaking of condensers in old ships. For the form, cf. BOILERITIS.

Confused Operations. A sarcastic pun on *Combined Operations* when this Force was in its infancy. Cf. COSTLY FARCES.

Conkey or **Conky.** The lower-deck nickname for those possessing prominent *conks* or noses.

Consort, the. The Prince Consort buoy off Cowes, Isle of Wight, well known to yachtsmen.

contaminated area. One in which the presence of enemy mines is suspected.

conun or **conundrum.** One of the huge bobbins of pipe-line used in *Operation Pluto*. As the bobbin unwound the pipe-line was laid on the bed of the ocean. People who saw these strange things wondered what they were: hence the pun, *conun*(*drum*).

Conway pup. A cadet in the training ship *Conway*. Cf. BRASS-BOUNDER.

cookem fry. This odd expression is a survival of those lawless days when sailors had reputations so bad that they never expected to be candidates for heaven and were, therefore, reconciled to ' cookem fry ' in Hell.

cookery nook. The galley at a Royal Naval Air Station. (Wardroom.)

cookie. The ship's cook. Cf. GRUB SPOILER and SLUSHY.

cooking oppos. Two ratings told off for duty in the galley. They help to prepare the food for the mess and ' dish up ' (i.e. wash-up) afterwards. The actual cooking is done by cook ratings; *cooking oppos* are ratings of any branch and merely take their turn of duty with the rest of their mess. See OPPO.

cook of the rook. The duty cook. (Lower-deck.)

cook the log. To make false entries in, or to alter, the ship's log.

cook's chevrons. Permanent scars on the arms caused by accidental burns in the galley.

cooler, the. Detention barracks ashore, or ' cells ' in a ship, where the JACK STROPS are placed to cool off. Cf. CHOKEY.

cooper. A floating grog-shop of the kind which used to hang round the fishing fleets; usually Dutch. Perhaps so called because of the barrels carried on board.

copper punt. A raft used by the Side Party when painting or cleaning a ship's hull. Technically known as the Balza Raft, it is modelled on the rafts used by the natives on the South American coast. (Royal Navy.)

copper rattle. A stew. When it is cooking, the bones rattle in the copper pan.

Cordite Jaunty, the. That Chief Gunner's Mate who carries out Regulating Duties in any of H.M. Gunnery Schools. See JAUNTY.

Cordites, the. Any football, cricket or other sporting team from H.M.S. *Excellent*, the Navy's Gunnery School on Whale Island, Portsmouth.

corf. A floating cage for keeping alive crabs and lobsters. (East Anglian fishermen's.)

cork; uncork. To code—decode—a naval signal. Cf. UNBUTTON.

corker. See CAULKER.

corkscrew roll. The motion of a destroyer in a seaway.

Corkscrews, the. Ships of the General Steam Navigation Company, which, at the beginning of the twentieth century, had funnels painted in spiral bands.

Corncurer, the. H.M.S. *Conqueror*. (Lower-deck.)

68

Cornish duck. A pilchard. Cornwall is the home of the pilchard fishery. Cf. SPITHEAD PHEASANT and YARMOUTH CAPON.

Corpse, the. Any party of Royal Marines. Short for '*Corps* of Royal Marines', with the first element illiterately pronounced.

corpse-eaters. Great black-backed gulls. (Wildfowlers'.)

corpse candles. St Elmo's fire. See COMPOSITE.

corvette. A Wren who is a Sub(Lieutenant)-chaser. A corvette (ship) is a sub(marine)-chaser.

Costly Farces. Coastal Forces. The nickname was self-inflicted by the members of this gallant party.

cottage, the. A sailor's name for his mess or billet.

Cotug. The Tug Coastal Organization during the Normandy landings in 1944. (The word-order of *Tug Control* has been reversed, *Control* abbreviated, and the two elements amalgamated.)

coulter neb = BOTTLENOSE.

Counties, the. 'County' class cruisers.

courting the cat. 'Walking out' with a girl. (An old naval term.)

Court Martial Jack. A Union Flag hoisted at the peak of the ship in which a Court Martial is being held. At one time the signal for a Council of Captains was the firing of a gun (see ONE-GUN SALUTE) and the running-up of the Union Flag to the mizzen shrouds. A colloquialism.

covered wagon. Meat- or fruit-pie. (Used in the training ship *Conway*.)

cow. Milk. (Lower-deck.)

cow's tail. A fagged-out rope's end which needs whipping. It has the appearance of a cow's tail.

cowboy's breakfast. Bacon and baked beans; a popular dish on the ranch. (Lower-deck.)

cow gun. A naval gun of heavy calibre. 'Cow' suggests unwieldiness as in, e.g., *cow-hitch*, a clumsy knot: Cf. SEA COWS and WOBBLY EIGHTS.

cow pat. A cadet on H.M.S. *Worcester* who is told off to look after the Cadet Captain's quarters. cf. CHEST STOOGE (Royal Naval College, Dartmouth).

crab. A junior Midshipman. A pejorative term: cf. DOGSBODY, WART and WONK.

crab fat. Battleship grey paint used in Home Waters. Cf. PUSSER'S GREY.

crab, berried. A crab in spawn, a ' seed ' crab.

crab, glass. A crab that has just shed its shell. Also known as *caster*.

crack on. To increase speed. In the old sailing days it meant putting on more canvas. Cf. the modern phrase *get cracking*!

cracker-hash. Minced meat and biscuit. Also called *cracker-jack*.

crash dive. The quick submersion of a submarine to avoid detection or as a practice evolution. (The term was long ago promoted to technical status.)

crash down the swede. See SWEDE, CRASH DOWN THE.

crash it down. To sleep. (Lower-deck.) From the preceding.

crash warning. An ' independent ' Air Raid Warning in a naval dockyard, sounded only when there was immediate danger. In some districts this was known as the ' Cuckoo ' warning, from its repetitive ' cuckoo-cuckoo ' sound. Much valuable time was saved by these crash warnings.

crawly. A hermit crab. (Fishermen's, as is:)

crawly pot. A crab pot.

Crazyman's Creek. The Straits of Messina.

cream in. To come into harbour with a huge bow wave and more speed than is wise. See RATE OF KNOTS, at the.

Creek, the. The Straits of Messina. Cf. CRAZYMAN'S CREEK.

creeping and weeping. Searching for an errant torpedo by towing a dragging gear across the area in which it is supposed to have sunk. This is sometimes a very long and tedious job, with no guarantee that success will crown the work. The process of dragging outward is known as ' creeping '; the homeward trip is ' weeping ' because of the lack of success. In torpedo exercises it is a frequent evolution: often a torpedo sinks instead of remaining on the surface at the end of its run, and only the trace of oil on the surface indicates where it sank.

crespie. A grampus. A fishermen's term, adopted from Scottish dialect, to which it came through Anglo-French, from Medieval Latin *craspiscis*, either a corruption or a popular conflation of Latin *crassus piscis* (literally, ' fat fish ').

Cressies, the three. H.M. Cruisers *Cressy*, *Aboukir* and *Hogue* which were sunk in company in September 1914, the first serious naval losses of the war. Built in 1900 they displaced 12,000 tons, had a speed of 18–20 knots, and carried a complement of 700 officers and men. The *Cressy* was the first of her class to be built; the others besides the above-mentioned two, were the *Bacchante* and *Euryalus*.

Cricketers, the. A class of steam-trawlers named after famous professional cricketers. These vessels, finely built, were requisitioned by the Admiralty in the 1939–45 War and used as anti-submarine and minesweeping trawlers. The *Larwood*, *Jardine*, *Hammond*, and *Bradman* were sunk in operations off Norway in 1940.

crooner. A gurnard, which ' croons ' when caught. (Fishermen's.)

cross anyone's bows. Literally, to pass in front of the bows of a ship commanded by one senior to oneself without first asking permission to do so thus committing a breach of naval etiquette. Hence, slangily, to give offence to a senior officer, or to annoy a person, by speaking out of turn.

cross fish. A starfish. Cf. FIVE-FINGERS.

crossed killicks. Crossed anchors, the arm-symbol of a Petty Officer's rate. See KILLICK.

crow. A habitual leave-breaker, drunkard, or nuisance in a ship. Cf. KING'S HARD BARGAIN and BIRD.

crow in working rig. A seagull. Cf. GULL IN NIGHT CLOTHING.

crushers. Regulating Petty Officers, formerly known as ' Ship's Corporals ', who, being the first to leave their hammocks, crushed the cockroaches. Since the introduction of the Regulating Branch, all are ' crushers ' irrespective of rating—except the JAUNTY.

Crystal Palace Army, the. The gallant Royal Naval Division, which was trained at the Crystal Palace in 1914. Many of the force died at Gallipoli and in Flanders. The Division was formed from men who volunteered for Naval service but for whom there were not enough ships to man. Their story has been told in the official history by Douglas Jerrold.

cuddy, the. The Captain's cabin in an H.M. Ship.

cuddy leg. A Scottish fishery term for a ' full ' herring.

cuffer. Any improbable story; hence, *spinning a cuffer*. (Merchant Navy.) From *cuff*, to strike or buffet: cf. ' a *whacking* lie '.

cumshaw. A corruption of the Army Chinese word *kam sia* meaning ' thank you '. In the Navy the term is synonymous with HARRY FREEMAN'S or on the BARON—i.e., something for nothing.

Cunarders. Ships of the Cunard White Star Line.

cupboard, the. The ocean. A variant of DAVY JONES'S LOCKER.

cupola. A revolving dome-shaped gun turret used in the old battleships.

curlew carries a shilling on its back. A marshman's saying. The bird used to be sold for that price.

curlies. A Royal Naval Reserve officer's stripes of intertwined lace.

curly. The cane used for punishment in the training ship *Conway*. Cf. PENANG LAWYER.

Curly Navy. The Royal Canadian Naval Volunteer Reserve. Cf. WAVY NAVY.

Curry and Rice Navy. The Royal Indian Navy, formerly known as the Royal Indian Marine.

custard boats. The first H.M. Ships to come under the General Messing Scheme were known thus, the implication being that they had custard with their ' duff ' instead of eating it BARE NAVY.

custard bo'sun. A Warrant Cook, R.N.

cut a man down. To cut a man's hammock clews so that he falls on the deck. Cf. YARNING A HAMMOCK.

cut barge. One specially fitted for work in the ' cuts ' or canals.

cut off a slice. To give a smart salute to anything impressive in ' gold lace '. Cf. CHIP ONE OFF.

cut the painter. To depart hurriedly; to decamp; to desert a ship; to die.

72

cutch. The tan called 'catechu' which is used for preserving sails and nets. Cf. BARK. (Moray Firth term.)

cuts. (1) A beating at the Royal Naval College, Dartmouth. *Official Cuts* means a public whipping, administered only for very reprehensible conduct. (2) Short for *funny cuts*, a lower-deck term for a facetious messmate; cf. DIDO, ACT.

cutters. Fish-carrying craft which used to bring the catches from the 'fleeters' or smacks to the shore.

cutty. An abbreviation of *cutty-gun*, a short tobacco pipe.

cypher queen. An officer of the Women's Royal Naval Service who carries out cyphering duties in a Shore Establishment.

D

' D.' Short title for *Captain* ' *D* ', the commanding officer of a Destroyer Flotilla, and used in colloquial reference to him. The Commanding Officer of, say, the 18th Destroyer Flotilla is simply ' D 18 '. (A technicality.)

D.B.S. A *D*istressed *B*ritish *S*eaman, the survivor of wrecked or torpedoed ships in war-time.

D.N.A. Short for the much-maligned *D*irector of *N*avy *A*ccounts; always used in reference to matters of pay with its delays and difficulties. When an officer or man is transferred to a new ship it is often months before his pay ' catches up with him ' and, in the meantime, he has to be content with CASUAL payments from the Paymaster. No man suffers more than inconvenience through the delay because he gets every penny in the fulness of (D.N.A.'s) time.

D.N.P. A *D*ark *N*ight *P*atrol, carried out on moonless nights to prevent surface minelaying. (1914–18.)

D.S.B. The person in charge of the *D*uty *S*team *B*oat. A midshipman's term of the steam-pinnace era. ' Who is D.S.B. to-day? The O.O.W. wants him, chop chop.'

D.Y.F. *D*amned *Y*oung *F*ools. Wardroom officers under thirty years of age and presumably not responsible for their actions, at least according to the judgment of the S.O.B.S.

dab chick. A small racing yacht. From *dabchick*, the little grebe.

dab dab. See DAB TOE, of which this is a lower-deck variant.

dab toe. The stokers' name for a seaman. Cf. DUSTMAN. Perhaps with reference to *dab*, a flounder.

Dagger. Dagger ' G ', Dagger ' N ' and Dagger ' E ' refer respectively to those officers who have high specialist qualifications in Gunnery, Navigation or Engineering. A dagger device appears against their names in the Navy List.

Dago. A Spanish or Portuguese seaman. From *Diego*, a common Spanish masculine font-name.

Daily Mirror types. Officers or ships that appear in the daily papers.

Dalmatian pudding. A galley name for ' spotted dog ', boiled currant dumpling. The *Dalmatian* (dog) has a spotted coat.

Damager, the. The Manager of the N.A.A.F.I. canteen. (Lower-deck.) With a pun on *Manager* and *damages* (expenses, bill).

Damn a horse! An expression of annoyance. Short for ' Damn a horse's hind leg! '—an old expression among naval officers. It dates from the time when horses were carried in H.M. Ships during annual manœuvres with the Army. The horses' legs often damaged the ship's precious paintwork.

Dams. A word formed from the initials ' Defensively Armed Merchant Ships '; used in reference to the officers and men serving in them. This 1914–18 War term was altered to DEMS in the 1939–45 War.

damsel. A skate. (Trawlermen's.)

Dancers. The ' Dance ' Class of corvettes—named after dances: *Minuet*, *Gavotte*, *Quadrille*, etc.

Dan Leno's. The *dans* or posts that support the wings of a trawl net. After Dan Leno, a famous comedian of the 'nineties.

dandyfunk. A mess of broken ship's biscuits. Much the same as CRACKER-HASH. Probably from *dandy*, excellent, and *funk*, a smell.

danners. Dan-laying vessels used to mark dangerous sea areas. A *dan* buoy is a spar buoy with a flag.

Danskers. Danish seamen or ships. Cf. NORSKERS and SCOWEGIANS. (Merchant Navy.)

darken ship. To close scuttles at dusk in accordance with Defence Regulations in wartime. (A technicality.)

darks, the. Moonless nights at sea.

darn the water. To patrol to and fro in front of a blockaded port. The Dover Patrol did this in the 1914–18 War.

Darts. Officers trained in the Royal Naval College, Dartmouth, ' Active Service ' officers, as distinct from Reserve officers or those who have obtained their officer status from the lower-deck. Cf. AFT THROUGH THE HAWSEHOLE.

David. Admiral Sir David—later, Earl—Beatty (1871–1936) of Jutland fame.

Davy Jones's locker. The bottom of the sea. Apparently first recorded by Captain Francis Grose in 1785 as *David Jones's locker*.

Davy Jones's shocker. A depth charge or any underwater explosion. By a pun on the preceding.

dawgs. The fishermen's pronunciation of *dogs* or dogfish, the curse of the herring fishery when they attack the nets.

day boats. A canal barge which has no sleeping cabins, being used for day work only. (Colloquial.)

day on. Doing duty as Officer-of-the-Day.

> *Sing a song of ' Pompey ',*
> *Gunwharf and ' Gieve ';*
> *' Excellent ' and ' Vernon ',*
> *Day-on and leave.*
>
> > *Portsmouth*, by Norah Harley.

dayman. One who does not keep night watches at sea. Cf. IDLER.

dazzle paint. The camouflage on a ship's hull. A wartime measure to frustrate enemy submarines and to confuse enemy gunners. (Technical.)

dead head. A spar used as a mooring buoy.

dead man's fingers. Coral washed up on the beach after a gale. From the resemblance. This compound noun has at least four senses in Standard English: consult the O.E.D. or Webster's Dictionary.

dead marine. An empty bottle. One that has done good service once is prepared to do so again, as William IV said, in apology, for having referred to a *dead marine* in the presence of Royal Marine officers. What he had really meant to imply was that a dead marine, like an empty bottle, was no good to anyone. (So, at least, the Navy's version goes.)

dead men. (1) The gaskets which dangle from the yards of a badly furled sailing ship. (2) Empty beer bottles. A Merchant Navy variant of the Royal Navy's DEAD MARINE.

dead muzzler. A wind from dead ahead. It blows fair into one's *muzzle* or face. Cf. NOSE-ENDER.

dead rope. A rope that does not pass through a block (pulley).

Dead-End Kids, the. (1) Self-description of Royal Naval Volunteer Reserve Lieutenants who despair of ever becoming Lieutenant-Commanders. There were so many Lieutenants R.N.V.R. in the 1939–45 War. In allusion to ' The Dead End Kids' of the films of the 1930's. (2) Stoker ratings in submarines. A much grimmer self-naming than was (1).—For an R.A.F. sense, consult *A Dictionary of Forces' Slang, 1939–1945*.

Deadeyes square? ' Do I look all right? am I " tiddley " enough for Divisions? ' (A catch-phrase on the training ship *Conway*.)

deado. Dead drunk. Utterly incapable of speech or movement; ' dead to the world '. (Lower-deck.)

death heads = COMPOSITE.

death tally. An identity disc. (Lower-deck.) Compare the Army's *dead-meat ticket*, and see COLD MEAT TICKET.

decimal bo'sun. A naval Instructor or ' Schoolmaster ', a chaser of the decimal point and the elusive *x*.

deck ornaments. Watch-keeping officers in the Merchant Navy. Cf. EDUCATED TRIMMERS.

decky. A deck-hand in trawlers or drifters. See:—

decky learner. A ship's ' boy ' or junior hand in a steam trawler or drifter.

dee-em-tee. Baked jam roll (used in the training ship *Conway*). Perhaps = *d— m.t.*, damned empty (of jam).

deep sea beef. Haddock. (Lower-deck.)

Deep, the. The Black Deep in the Thames Estuary.

deep-water jetty. A small pier which is approachable only at high tide. At other times there is no water round it. (Now a technicality.)

deep-water sailor = BLUE-WATER SAILOR.

defaced ensign. The blue ensign defaced by a yacht club's device in the fly. See BLUE ENSIGN CLUB.

dégommé. (To be) ' unstuck '—relieved of an appointment because of failure to carry out its duties with the efficiency required. To fall from grace in some way. Literally ' ungummed ', *dégommé* was borrowed from the slang of the French Navy and Army in 1914–18.

Dems. A word formed from the initials of ' *D*efensively *E*quipped *M*erchant *S*hips '. All connected with these vessels are known as ' Dems ' personnel. Cf. DAMS.

Dems gunners. Naval gunnery ratings or soldiers of the Royal Artillery serving in armed merchant vessels. See DEMS and cf. MARITIMES.

Dennis. The nautical nickname for a pig. It dates from the time when livestock were carried in ships making long passages and were slaughtered on board ' as requisite '. All the animals possessed nicknames. Cf. BANDMASTER.

dental tiffy. A sick-berth attendant doing duty with the Dental Surgeon. See SICK-BAY TIFFY.

Depot stanchion. A man who seems to have a permanent job in a shore station, or in a naval barracks (called a *depot*).

Derby, in the. In the promotion race. Cf. ZONE.

devil. That seam on the water line which is very awkward to caulk.

Devil's smiles, the. Occasional glimpses of the sun in bad weather; cf. COCK'S EYE.

Devil's Throat, the. Cromer Bay in Norfolk, notoriously dangerous to navigation—especially to sailing vessels in bad weather.

Devil's toothbrush. A wardroom drink—brandy and gin in equal measure taken neat.

dhobey (or **dhobeying**) **firm.** A partnership of ratings who run an unofficial laundry and wash their messmates' ' pieces ' for a small fee: ' Come on! sling 'em out! Me and Ginger are running a firm '. Also spelt *dhoby*: i.e. *dhobi*, a native laundryman in India: from Hindi *dhob*, a washing.

dhobeying. Washing clothes. See DHOBEY FIRM.

dhobey- or **dhobi-wallah.** A member of a DHOBEYING FIRM.

dicky. Of short duration (in civilian slang it means ' inferior '), as in: (2) A sailor's blue jean collar.

dicky bird. Cf. SEA PIE.

Dicky Daw's rocks. A reef of rocks off Bembridge, Isle of Wight, named after one Dicky Daw, a local smuggler who, when chased by revenue men, cut inside this dangerous reef and made his escape. (I owe this lore to H. Alker Tripp, who mentions the rocks in his book *The Solent and the Southern Waters*, 1928.)

dicky flannel. A short flannel (vest), white with blue-edged, square collar worn by seamen from the 1st May to the 1st October; DICKY is a Naval diminutive. Cf. MONKEY.

dicky flurry. A variant of DICKY RUN, which is the more usual term nowadays. (Naval lower-deck.)

dicky hand. A game of cards on the mess-deck.

dicky run. A quick run ashore, just enough time for a drink. (Lower-deck.)

Dido, act. To cut capers. At one time H.M.S. *Dido* had the reputation of being a wild company ashore, and, to *act Dido* became a catch-phrase throughout the Navy. At least, that is the Navy's story: much more probably, *act Dido* is merely a variant of *cut up didoes* (to cut capers or play pranks), adopted about 1850 from the U.S.A. Nevertheless, the Royal Navy shows excellent judgment, and a nice sense of gallantry towards the ladies, by referring the origin of the expression to Virgil's Dido, Queen of Carthage (*The Æneid*, Book IV).

different ships, different cap-tallies. Other ships, other methods: *autres pays, autres mœurs*.

different ships, different long splices = preceding.

Dig in, fill your boots! The mess-deck cry when dinner is served.

dig out. To work with a will; to help oneself liberally to food. ' If you men want to win the whaler race at the regatta you'll have to jolly well dig out, you'll never do it on your present form.'

dim. Dull-witted. (Cf. SOLID.) Adopted from civilian—originally, university—slang.

Dinghy. The traditional nickname for Reed.

dink. A dinghy. ' I'll leave the dink at the jetty for you.'

dip. To drop or lose (a thing). A Leading Hand in the Royal Navy *dips his hook* when he is disrated for bad conduct or inefficiency. A yacht *dips* her burgee in salute to a warship or in

79

courtesy to a yacht belonging to a senior club, e.g. one wearing the White Ensign of the Royal Yacht Squadron.

dip chick. A naval diver. An obvious corruption of *dabchick*, a species of diving bird commonly known as the Little Grebe.

dipping needle. A needle so suspended that it shows the magnetic dip.

dipsy. A lead-line. A thinning of *deep-sea* (line).

direct operator. A wireless operator who has been employed by the company owning the ship in which he works and has not obtained the job through a shipping agency.

Dirty Duck, the. The Swan Inn at Bursledon, Hants, a haunt of yachtsmen. A term of affection rather than disparagement.

dirty money. A special rate of pay given to men doing work ' of an unpleasant nature ' in merchant ships. Cf. the Navy's DOUBLE-BOTTOMS MONEY.

discharge. A Naval Service Certificate. Cf. PARCHMENT.

dish jerkers. Merchant Navy stewards. A euphemistic form of a grosser term.

dish up. Wash up. (Lower-deck.)

ditch, the. The sea; cf. 'OGGIN. As a verb, *ditch* means to throw overboard. ' What'll I do with this old bucket, Chief? ' ' Ditch the ruddy thing, it's no further use '.

ditch crawling. Estuary sailing in small yachts; Norfolk Broad cruising. ' I haven't done any real sailing, I'm just a ditch crawler.' (Yachtsmen's.)

ditcher. One of the early torpedo boats built before the 1914–18 War. Short for *ditch-crawler*.

ditty bag. This serves the same purpose as a:

ditty box. A small wooden box that used to be given to a New Entry but has been displaced in recent years by an attaché case. Short for *commodity-box*. The ditty box contained a seaman's cherished possessions, photographs, letters, and small souvenirs picked up during his commissions abroad.

ditty box, steam. See STEAM DITTY BOX.

dizzy, get. To become ' hot and bothered '; angry with people or circumstances. ' All right, Nobby, don't get dizzy.' (Lower-deck.) Cf. STAGGERS.

dobash. A pal or girl-friend. (Lower-deck.)

Doc. The wardroom mode of address to the Surgeon.

dock, be in. Ill in the ship's Sick Bay or in hospital ashore.

dock pheasant. A bloater. Cf. SPITHEAD PHEASANT and YARMOUTH CAPON.

dock rats. Dockside loafers or part-time stevedores.

docking herself. (Of a ship) taking the bottom in harbour or settling into a mud berth.

dock-walloper. A dockside lounger who stands gazing at ships.

dockyard crawl. The rate at which the DOCKYARD MATEY is said to work.

dockyard horses. Naval ratings drawing stores. When a lorry is not available they pull the load on handcarts.

dockyard matey. A worker in a naval dockyard. Cf. AIRYARD MATEY, and YARDEE.

dockyardee. A variant of the above.

doctor, the. A Merchant Navy cook. (Fo'c'sle slang.)

dodge Pompey. To shirk work; keep out of sight and so avoid being 'lurked' for an unpleasant job. (Lower-deck.) For some reason, *Pompey* means 'Authority; those in authority; the Law'.

dodger. A canvas screen round the bridge of a small craft as protection against the weather.

do-little sword, the. A Midshipman's dirk. Capable of little damage and worn simply as a badge of authority.

dog basket. An old and leaky ship.

dog robbers. Tweed clothes worn by naval officers when ashore. From the type of check tweed worn by men who used to sell dogs at street corners. (Wardroom.) Cf. MALLABY-DEELEY'S.

Dogger Bank Dragoons. The Royal Marine Commandos. (A self-description: 1939–45. Cited in *The Awkward Marine*, by James Spencer, 1948.)

dogger. A two-masted Dutch fishing craft used in the Dogger Bank fishery. From:

Dogger, the. The Dogger Bank fishing grounds. Cf. BANK, THE.

doggo. Plain of features. (Lower-deck.) One who is modelled on the lines of Wallace Beery rather than of Stewart Granger. ' Nice looking piece, isn't she? But look at her old man, proper doggo, ain't he? ' (A face like a good-natured bulldog's.)

doggy. A Captain's or Commander's *doggy* is his Midshipman aide-de-camp.

dogs. Inflated bladders used to buoy fishing nets. A Moray Firth term.

Dogs, the. Dog Watches, which are said to be a corruption of *dodge* watches. A ship's company is divided into two watches, Port and Starboard, each doing alternate four-hour ' tricks '; and in order that the same men shall not always be on watch at the same time each afternoon the Dog Watches are split into two, which are called the first and second (usually called Last) Dog Watches, respectively from 4 p.m. to 6 p.m. and from 6 p.m. to 8 p.m. The classic description of a Dog Watch is ' a watch cur-tailed '.

dog's cock. A back splice. (Essex fishermen's.)

dogs of war. The gunroom ' pack ' of chuckers-out, picked by weight and ready to throw out an unpopular member or visitor. The order of ejectment is ' Dogs of war, out So-and-So! ' All this is carried out in the spirit of ' good, clean fun '.

dogsbody. A Cadet or Junior Midshipman; any very junior officer in the Royal or Merchant Navy. Of little importance to anyone but himself. We are all dogsbodies once in our Service career.

doing a never. Skulking, or shirking work. (Lower-deck.)

dollar bo'sun. A Warrant Writer, R.N. Cf. LEDGER BO'SUN.

Dolly. The nickname for Gray or Grey. From the title of an old music-hall ditty, *Goodbye, Dolly Grey.*

Dolly Mopp's garret. Any private lodging-house, as distinct from a ' Sailors' Home '.

Dolly Varden. A lower-deck rating who is particularly fastidious about his appearance; one who is prim to the point of effeminacy.

donkey. (1) A donkey-engine—a small steam engine used for a variety of purposes, e.g. driving the windlass, pumps, or derricks. (2) A sewing machine owned by the ship's JEWING FIRM. (Lower-deck.)

doo hicky. A mechanical device whose name one has forgotten or never knew. Cf. FOO FOO VALVE and WIFFLO GADGET. (Wardroom.)

doors. (1) The otter boards that, on a trawler, keep the mouth of the trawl net open. (2) The lock gates of a canal. (Marshland term.)

dopper. A very thick jersey worn by East Anglian fishermen. (A Norfolkism.)

dormies. Dormitories at the Royal Naval College, Osborne.

dotter. A gunnery device introduced by Admiral Sir Percy Scott; it enables ships to elevate their guns with the roll of the ship and to be laid on the target without wasting ammunition. See LINE THE PENCIL.

double. An unusually large catch of fish in a trawl net; *twice* as much as the net can hold with safety.

double-bottoms money. This is an allowance for men doing work ' of an unpleasant nature ' (to quote King's Regulations) in the bowels (the double-bottoms) of an H.M. Ship. Cf. the Merchant Navy's DIRTY MONEY.

double-enders. Boats that have bow and stern shaped alike, e.g. a naval whaler. Of larger types, the Portsmouth–Fishbourne ferry is an excellent example.

double Hunts, the. Large destroyers built almost on cruiser lines. Twice the size of the ' Hunt ' class destroyers, they are themselves ' Hunts ', for they have been named after famous packs.

double-red. ' Attack imminent.' In the 1939–45 War a system of colour warnings was used for the approach of enemy aircraft; ' yellow ' meant that the enemy were somewhere within a hundred miles; ' red ' that an attack could be expected within five minutes; and the ' double-red ' that attack was imminent. It was sometimes used slangily for the approach of a Senior Officer, especially in a bar where conversation was somewhat free. Cf. DOUBLE SHUFFLE.

double shuffle. The movement to action stations on receipt of a DOUBLE-RED air raid warning. (Lower-deck.)

dough boys. Suet dumplings boiled in sea-water. (Merchant Navy.) Kipling uses the term.

doughcock. A West Country term for a stupid, ' doughy ' rating. (Lower-deck.)

doughnut. A life-saving raft known officially as a Carley Float. It is shaped somewhat like this comestible.

doughy. Dim-witted, silly, ' not all there '. As soft as dough. Cf. DOUGHCOCK.

down along. Sailing the English Channel in the direction of Devon and Cornwall—i.e. westward—the reverse direction being *up along*. Both are West Country terms.

drabble-tailer. See SLAP-TAILER.

draft chit. Officially a *draft note*, which a man is given when he is drafted from naval barracks to a ship or from one ship to another. It enables him to be accepted in his new ship and to draw his tobacco and rum allowance, etc.

Draftie. The Drafting Commander in a naval depot. He is responsible for all the drafting arrangements, works out the rosters, etc., seeing that, as far as the exigencies of the Service allow him, men do not spend unreasonable time ' foreign ' or hold on to ' soft numbers ' at the expense of others.

drafting Jaunty. The Drafting Master-at-Arms in naval barracks. He issues the *draft* and tobacco chits, etc.

drainpipe. Nickname for an excessively thin man. (Lower-deck.) Cf. SNAKEY and TACKLINE.

draw. When a man joins the Navy he has to decide whether he will take a daily tot of rum or remain TEMPERANCE. If he decides to cast his lot with the drinkers he is said to *draw*, i.e. draw his rum ration.

draw (him) **off a lemon.** To punch someone on the nose, to ' fill him in '. (Lower-deck.) i.e. to hand him something bitter.

dreadnought or **fearnought.** A contraceptive which is obtainable free of charge from a naval sick bay. Another advantage the naval man has over the civilian.

Dreado, the. H.M.S. *Dreadnought*. (Lower-deck.)

drift capstan. In a herring drifter the steam capstan that works the drift nets. Now a technicality.

drill, the. The correct procedure or method of doing a job. ' What's the drill, mate?—I've forgotten.'

drill ships. Old sloops or wooden frigates used as R.N.V.R. training ships: H.M.S. *President* in London (the H.Q. of the London Division, R.N.V.R.); *Flying Fox* at Bristol; *Claverhouse* on the Clyde; and the old ' third-rater ', *Unicorn II*, at Dundee.

drink. The sea. Cf. 'OGGIN and DITCH.

drink, give a. To treat to a reprimand or BOTTLE. ' Jimmy the One gave me a drink this morning for not calling away the motor boat.'

drink at Freeman's Quay. To drink free liquor; to receive a ' treat ' generally. See HARRY FREEMAN'S.

drip. To complain, grumble, fault-find; be generally a ' fathom of misery ' and a pain in the neck to the mess: cf. *howl*, TOOT (2) and MOAN. (Lower-deck.)

drip pan. A perpetual grumbler; one who is for ever ' doing a tap '. (Lower-deck and old Royal Naval Air Service.) In R.N. Air Station hangars, drip pans were placed under aircraft oil and petrol tanks.

dripper. (1) = DRIP PAN. A naval parallel to the Air Force's ' binder '. (2) Planks of any desired length and about six inches wide on which haddocks are laid for DROUGHING.

driver, the. A barge engineer.

driving. Fishing. (East Anglian.) (Driving the herring into the nets?)

drogy. Short for hydrographer. (Wardroom and Admiralty.)

drop the hook. To anchor. Hence, to retire from a seafaring life, to SWALLOW THE ANCHOR.

droughing. The partial drying of haddocks on ' drippers ' preparatory to their being placed upon spits for smoking. (*Drough* is dialect for dryness.)

Drowning Flotilla, the. An ill-fated flotilla of German U-Boats that suffered grievous losses in the 1914–18 War. The Dover Patrol dealt with them very efficiently.

drummer, the. Paradoxically, the Royal Marine bugler.

dry hash. At sea this is simply minced meat and mashed potatoes served without gravy.

dry-land swimming. Instruction for non-swimmers. (Royal Naval College, Dartmouth.)

dry ship. See WET SHIP.

Duck Pond, the. The assembly place for ' ducks '—the amphibious motor vehicles used in the invasion of Normandy in 1944.

duck up. To clew up an area of a sail in order to give the helmsman a clearer view ahead. (Bargemen's.)

duck-tail stern. One so shaped. Not unlike a modern ' cruiser ' stern.

ducks. White duck suits worn in the tropics.

duff bag. That part of the sailor's black ' silk ' where the bight is tied in by the tapes of his jumper forming a loop wide enough to hold two fingers. Also known as the ' pudden '.

duff chokers. Lowestoft driftermen's nickname for Yarmouth men.

duff night. An obsolescent term for Guest Night in a naval wardroom. There is plenty of pudding. cf. FULL BELLY NIGHT.

Duffoes. Ratings of the Devonport Division or GUZ. (The eaters of duff.)

dug-out. A naval officer on the Retired List recalled for service in times of ' national emergency '. Cf. OLD AND BOLD and REPAINT.

dumb barge. A barge that has neither power nor sail.

dummy barge. A permanently moored barge, or ' hulk '.

dummy engineer. An Engineer Midshipman.

dummy run. Any exercise or rehearsal.

dummy week. Non-payment week in the Royal Navy. Men are paid fortnightly.

Dun Cow, the. The famous ship *River Clyde* of Gallipoli. Cf. HORSE OF TROY.

dun head, the. Those after-strakes of a barge which form its cabin.

dunnage. Luggage of any kind, trunks, suitcases, kit-bags, etc. ' Stow your dunnage and come below.' Ernest Weekley derives it from the Standard English sense, matting or brushwood used in packing goods for stowage.

duration hitch. A clumsy, unseamanlike knot made by a New Entry who has joined the Navy for the duration of the war. Cf. HOSTILITY BEND.

dustbin. The bridge of a Motor Torpedo Boat. From its shape.

duster. An ensign or flag of any kind. Originally it was humorous, with reference to domestic dusters.

dusting. A rough passage at sea. From civilian slang *dusting*, a thrashing: cf. *dust* (someone's) jacket.

dustman. Seamen's term for a stoker rating. Cf. DAB DAB and DAB TOE.

dusty boy. A Supply Assistant in the Royal Navy; particularly one employed in the stores—a very dusty job. Cf. JACK DUSTY.

Dutch parliament = PORTUGUESE PARLIAMENT.

Dutch pennants. Untidy ropes hanging from aloft; = IRISH PENNANTS.

Dutch red. A red herring cured in Holland.

Dutchify. To convert a square stern into a round one after the Dutch model.

Dutchman. Dutch or German merchant ship.

Dutchman's anchor. Anything left behind that is particularly essential. ' What! you don't know where it is? Left behind like the Dutchman's anchor, I suppose? ' A certain legendary Dutchman, when he ran aground, protested that he had a very good anchor—in harbour.

Dutchman's breeches. The blue patches in a stormy sky. Rather like a generously patched pair of trousers as worn by music-hall Dutchmen.

Dutchman's Cape. Such a bank of cloud as a look-out may mistake for land. Also known as CAPE FLYAWAY.

Dutchman's log. A piece of wood or other floating object thrown overboard as a means of judging the speed of the tide.

Dutchy. Any Dutch, German or Scandinavian seaman or vessel. Cf. DUTCHMAN and SCANDINOOGIAN.

Duty Boy. The Officer-of-the-Day or -Watch. (Wardroom.)

Duty Sub, the. The Duty Sub-Division of the Watch; it can be called upon to lend additional weight when necessary.

dyso. The lower-deck form of *dghaiso*, an Eastern craft.

E

E.G.O. The Canadian Navy's Long Service and Good Conduct medal. *E*verybody *G*ets *O*ne. Cf. BLUE PETER.

ear-puller or **ear-swinger.** An idle seaman who loafs at the dockside borrowing money from former shipmates—*pulling their ears down.*

earth chasers. Torpedo ratings, who spend most of their time looking for (electrical) earths and ' shorts '; S.T.s or Seamen-Torpedomen.

ease off a fish or **squeeze off a fish.** To fire a torpedo. See FISH.

easting or **running down her easting.** Making distance eastward.

eat the wind. To get to windward of an opponent in a race, and thus *eat the wind* out of her sails.

eating irons. Knife, fork and spoon. (Lower-deck colloquialism —common to all three Services.)

E-Boat Alley. That dangerous stretch of water between Great Yarmouth and Cromer along which convoys were frequently attacked by German E-Boats in the 1939–45 War.

ecclesiastical bricks. Holystones, used for scrubbing decks. (Wardroom.) Also known as *hand bibles*; cf. PRAYER BOOKS.

Edna. The inevitable nickname for anyone surnamed May. Miss Edna May was a favourite musical comedy star of the 1890's and early 1900's.

educated trimmers. Engineer officers in the Merchant Navy. Cf. DECK ORNAMENTS.

efficient ship is a happy ship, an. A naval truism and proverb.

egg. A mine or bomb. (1914–18 War slang, used in the 1939–45 War by REPAINTS.)

Egg Market, the. The Falkland Islands, in which wild birds abound.

egg on a raft. A poached egg on toast. (Lower-deck.)

eggo or **egg.** The nickname for any bald-headed messmate. Cf. SKATING RINK. (Lower-deck.)

Egg-shells. H.M.S. *Achilles.* By ' Hobson-Jobson ': from the lower-deck, not the Greek, pronunciation.

Egyptian A.F.O.s. Indecent literature sold ashore in Eastern ports. The pamphlets somewhat resemble the appearance of *A*dmiralty *F*leet *O*rders. (Lower-deck.)

Eighth, the Fighting. The 8th Destroyer Flotilla in the 1939–45 War: *Faulkner* (leader), *Firedrake, Forester, Fury, Fearless, Foxhound, Foresight, Fame* and *Fortune.* Its title was deserved.

Eldest, the. The senior Lieutenant or Lieutenant-Commander who is the ship's First Lieutenant. Cf. SENIOR. (Normally the *eldest* Lieutenant.)

electric cow, the. A machine for converting milk powder into ' milk '. A term in use in both the Royal and Merchant Navies.

electric fish. The bonito, because of its amazing muscular agility and lightning movements which make it a very difficult fish to catch.

elephant's part, the. That part of work which is done by a looker-on. (Lower-deck.)

Elsie. A special searchlight which worked in conjunction with the predictors in the Maunsell forts. *L.C.* (Light Control) = ' Elsie '.

end-for-ending. Changing the running or standing gear ' end for end ' to lessen the strain on vulnerable parts and thus obviate their carrying away in heavy weather.

end's a-wagging, the. The end of a job is in sight. From the wagging end of a rope when it is pulled inboard. (Lower-deck, obsolescent.)

Engineering pie. A particular brand of pie produced at lunch in the Engineering workshops at the Royal Naval College, Dartmouth.

entry, the. The shape of a ship's bows where they meet the sea.

Equality Jack. An Old Navy term for an officer who likes to ingratiate himself with the ' troops '; a ' Popularity Jack '. He seldom gains respect thereby.

'Ermy One. A jocular rather than illiterate name for H.M.S. *Hermione*.

Eskimo Nell. The title of a low ballad of interminable length; known, I should imagine, by all who follow the sea. Compare the exploits of Nell's male counterpart, MEXICAN PETE.

Evans of the Broke. Admiral Lord Mountevans, who as Commander Evans, R.N., distinguished himself as captain of the destroyer *Broke* which, in a Channel action with the destroyer *Swift*, routed six German destroyers after an old-fashioned hand-to-hand fight with cutlasses and revolvers.

every hair a rope yarn; every finger a marline-spike; every drop of blood Stockholm tar. A description of a tough sailor, a real dyed-in-the-wool mariner. (General nautical.)

everything drawing. All sails filled and the ship ' full and bye '.

everything on a split yarn, have. To be prepared to carry out an evolution; to be ready for any eventuality. ' We had everything on a split yarn and then the party was scrubbed.'

everything on top and nothing handy. The alleged state of a midshipman's chest. Cf. HURRAH'S NEST.

everything under control. Nothing to complain of; everything running according to plan. ' Is everything under control, Chief? ' ' Yes, sir, all can do.' (Wardroom.)

executive curl, the. The curl above the lace stripes of a naval officer's uniform. Originally this curl was worn only by officers of the executive branch, those officers who ' fought ' the ship; the Civil Branch—Paymasters, Surgeons, Engineers —having stripes without this curl. During the 1914–18 War the ' executive curl ' came to be worn, as it is now, by all officers. (Incidentally, until the curl became general, the anchor in a Civil Branch officer's cap badge was gold to distinguish him from an executive officer, whose badge-anchor was silver. Now all wear the silver anchor with the laurel leaves.)

eyes of the Fleet, the. The ratings on a ship's flag-deck. Cf. BRAINS OF THE NAVY.

eyes of the ship, the. The bows. The term may have been adopted from the early China Station days: Chinese ships used to have eyes painted on the bows.

Eye-ties. Italian naval or military forces. From the illiterate *Eye*-talian.

91

F

F.s, the. The ' F ' class destroyers. See EIGHTH, THE FIGHTING.

face like a churchyard clock, he has a. Said of an unsatisfactory rating. Churchyard clocks are notoriously unreliable.

face like a sea boot. A face that is habitually miserable; a long, doleful face. There can be few things uglier than a sea boot.

face like a scrubbed 'ammick. An expression as sour and pale as a newly scrubbed hammock. (Lower-deck.)

fair wind. To give anything a ' fair wind ' is to pass it to someone. ' Give the cruet a fair wind.' (Wardroom.)

fairy guns. The tracer fire of E-Boats seen at night—giving a particularly beautiful effect from the green, red and white tracing.

fake. A circle forming the coil of a rope; *faking down* means coiling rope. Cf. CHEESE DOWN.

false-nose party. A Royal Marine Commando or irregular naval unit which attacks a key position (e.g. a radio station or gun post) on enemy-occupied coast. The men usually attack under cover of darkness and their faces are blackened to render them invisible. Cf. CLOAK AND DAGGER MERCHANT.

false rope. A rope that is bearing a strain.

Famishing Fifty, the. See HUNGRY HUNDRED.

famous crimes. A man with a scowling face. (Lower-deck.) Prompted by the pictures of famous criminals in the now defunct Police Gazette, which specialized in the detailed and illustrated reports of murders.

fan. A ship's screw or propeller. Cf. WHIZZER.

fancy fish. Fish outside the usual categories sold by the fish-monger.

fancy frigate. A very TIDDLEY warship in which everything is 'Bristol fashion' with discipline to match. Somewhat of a strain to serve in.

fancy religions. Nonconformist creeds. 'Church of England fall in on the right; Roman Catholics on the left; fancy religions in the rear!' Cf. NON-CAN-GO-ISTS. (Lower-deck.)

fancy waistcoats. A mere nicety of detail; a punctilious accuracy of statement. (Wardroom.) 'Whether it happened on that particular day is simply a matter of fancy waistcoats, the fact remains he *did* break out of ship and that's all I am concerned about'; 'A few degrees out in reckoning is just fancy waistcoats, we'll get there all right'.

fancy work. Any 'tiddley' knotting or splicing; sennits; double wall and crown; the decorative work in the ship's bell-rope.

fang farrier. A Naval dental surgeon. Usually shortened to *fang*. (Lower-deck.) Cf. TOOTHIE, TOOTHWRIGHT.

fanny. A large mess kettle.

Fanny Adams. General nautical slang for stew. The gruesome story behind this term is that about 1862 a certain Fanny Adams was foully murdered, cut up and boiled in a copper. Cf. HARRIET LANE.

fantod. A ship's officer of a nervous, finicky disposition. Cf. civilian slang *the fantods*, 'restlessness; restless uneasiness', perhaps deriving from Kentish dialectal *fantod*, 'restless'.

Farce, Operation. See OPERATION FARCE.

Farewell Jetty. Portsmouth Railway Jetty, where the families of a ship's company proceeding on a foreign commission wave farewell to them.

farlands. The shallow, oblong boxes in which herrings are gutted by the fisher girls. They are from 25 to 40 feet long and from 6 to 9 feet wide; the sides and ends are sloped inward in order to make the work easier for the girls.

farmyard nuggets. Eggs. (Lower-deck.) Cf. CACKLE BERRIES and CHICKEN FRUIT.

Faroemen. Trawlermen who work off the Faroe Isles. Cf. ICELANDMEN.

fast. The catching-up of a trawl net in an underwater obstruction. From Standard English *fast*, firm, firmly held.

fat head. A condition induced by the ' fug ' 'tween decks when the ship is battened down in heavy weather. (Royal Navy.)

Fat Hen = GOOD KING HENRY.

Father. Captain Graham Edwards, R.N., one of the personalities of the Dover Patrol in the 1914–18 War. He commanded the flotilla leader *Hoste*. He was known as ' Farver ' by his flotilla and usually made the signal ' Follow Father ' when he led the patrol. He was a great wit; and many tales are told of his exploits.

fathom of misery. Any lean, lugubrious-looking type of rating. Cf. FAMOUS CRIMES.

Fear God and tip the crusher. An Old Navy motto dating from the ' bad old days ' when it was possible for ratings to get out of an unpopular job or a foreign draft by tipping the Drafting Master-at-Arms in naval barracks, and most Ship's Corporals (now called Regulating Petty Officers) could be made to look the other way when tipped by a man who went out of barracks during his duty watch. Such practices ceased long ago, after a disciplinary ' show-down '. See CRUSHER.

feather. The ' wash ' made by the periscope of a submarine. (Now accepted as a technicality.)

feather-white sea. A wind-whipped sea. Cf. IVORY.

feaze. To untwist cordage for making oakum. (Originally Standard English but now colloquial—when not dialectal. Cognate with German *fasen*, to separate threads or fibres.)

feeding part, the. (Of cordage) the part which runs through the block, as distinct from the ' standing part '.

female Lieutenant-Commander. A First Officer in the W.R.N.S. She wears two and a half stripes on her sleeves. (Wardroom.)

fetch bumf. A gunroom game which was very popular in the days when gunroom ' evolutions ' were more popular than they are today. On the cry ' Fetch bumf ' the midshipmen dashed out to the wardroom toilets (or ROUND HOUSE), and the first to bring back a sheet of toilet paper won. The last into the gunroom was also ' suitably rewarded '.

fiddle fish. A king crab, which, in shape, somewhat resembles a small fiddle.

Fiddler's Green. The final rest of old sailors; a sailor's paradise. There, fiddlers play all day and most of the night. Being Elysium, Fiddler's Green has lasses, suitably responsive, and glasses, suitably filled.

Fiddler's Race. A tricky stretch of water in the Solent off Yarmouth, Isle of Wight.

fifth pricker. One who signs on for a further five years' service after twenty-two years in the Royal Navy. He ' has a stab ' at a further five.

fifty north. Latitude fifty degrees north, the fishing grounds of the North Sea trawlers.

figgy dowdy. The West Country version of:

figgy duff. Any kind of suet pudding, whether or not it contains figs. (Lower-deck.)

Fighting Fifth, the. The Fifth Motor Launch Flotilla in the 1939–45 War. (Coastal Forces.)

fill in. To give (someone) a good hiding. ' The next time he says that to me I'll fill him in ! ' (Lower-deck.)

fire. The phosphorescence from the plankton in the sea. (Herring fishery term.)

fire in anger. To fire in action against the enemy, as opposed to practice shooting.

firm. A lower-deck partnership that runs a concern for the benefit of the messdeck; A DHOBEY, GOFFER or JEWING business run ' pro bono publico '.

first, the. The first watch, eight o'clock in the evening to midnight. (Colloquial.)

first and first, a. A rating who is first class for conduct and first for leave. A lower-deck paragon.

First Class rock. A Naval Boy, 1st Class.

first Dicky. A First Lieutenant. Cf. JIMMIE THE ONE, NUMBER ONE, and ONE.

fish. (1) A torpedo. Cf. KIPPER, MINNOW, MOULDY and TIN FISH.
(2) A fish-shaped type of hydroplane used at the end of the

1914–18 War for the detection of submarines; the precursor of the present-day Asdic gear.

fish holds. The stowage spaces for torpedoes in a submarine depot-ship.

fish pans. The coverings of the engine fittings in a submarine. They resemble the frying pans in a fish-and-chip shop.

fisherman's sauce. A fearsome mixture of salt water, vinegar, mustard and beaten eggs. (Trawlermen's.)

fishermen. Steam trawlers or drifters; vessels of any kind engaged in the fishing industry. In wartime trawlers and drifters are classed either as H.M. Ships (which are engaged in anti-submarine patrols or minesweeping) or as *fishermen*; the latter means that they have an Admiralty licence to pursue their peacetime calling. 'Was that a White Ensign trawler that bought it last night?'—'No! She was a fisherman.'

fishes' eyes. (Also *jerker*.) Tapioca pudding. (Lower-deck.)

fish-gunners. The Royal Marine Artillery. A term that was obsolescent at the beginning of this century. The implication was that they succeeded in shooting only fish; fish came to the surface when the shells burst under the water.

fishing fleet, the. Women who frequent the Ladies' Lounge at the Union Club, Malta, in peacetime, fishing for eligible males; known also as PERAMBULATING NAVY LISTS, for they know the seniority—and pay—of every officer of their acquaintance. Cf. SNAKE PIT.

fishing frog. An angler fish: a huge, ugly creature with large head and saw-like teeth. It lies on the bottom of the sea and preys upon any fish that stray near it. It is capable of swallowing a fair-sized cod.

fit double clews. To get married. A very old Service expression, scarcely ever heard today, deriving from the time when women went to sea in H.M. Ships. Double clews were fixed to the hammocks. Cf. GET SPLICED, JUMP OFF THE DOCK, and TIE-UP.

Fittie. The fishing suburb of Footdee, Aberdeen.

five and sevens. Men enlisted in the Royal Navy for a period of seven years with the colours and five on the reserve.

96

five-fingers. A star fish. (Fishermen's.)

five-oner. A naval officer who obtained all five First Class certificates in his examination for Lieutenant. A type who eventually attains Flag rank.

Fiver. A Fifth Officer in the Merchant Navy.

fix, get a. To obtain the ship's position on the chart. (Cf. COCKED-HAT.) Now a technical term.

flag Jack. A Flag Lieutenant. (Wardroom.) Cf. FLAGS.

Flag, the. The Flagship, from which all instructional signals emanate. ' Flag to So-and-So.'

flag, get one's. (Of senior naval officers) to become a Commodore or Rear Admiral and so be entitled to fly the flag of rank.

flag-flapper. A signal rating. He flaps the flags when making semaphore messages. Cf. BUNTS.

flags. Rushes used for tightening herring barrels.

Flags. The Flag Lieutenant, an officer who arranges most of the social functions on board. He is usually selected for his good looks, general smartness, and social graces. He is also, almost invariably, a superb dancer. (Wardroom.)

flamboy. A paraffin torch used to warn fishing craft on dark nights when there is a heavy sea running. A Cornish term, a dialectal form of *flambeau*.

flan. Short for:

flannel. Soft sawder; an ingratiating manner that enables a man to ' get away ' with much that would otherwise get him into THE RATTLE. Flannel is both soft and soothing.

flannel, full of. Up to all the lower-deck tricks and able to FLANNEL THROUGH circumstances that would land a less skilful rating ' in the report '. ' Nothing happens to *him*, he's full of flannel.' See preceding entry and cf.:

flannel through. To bluff one's way through an awkward situation. (Lower-deck.)

flannelette. ' A little bit of flannel '; a soft answer that turneth away the wrath of authority. (Lower-deck.) See FLANNEL.

flap. (1) Any confusion or ' panic '. The term was coined in the 1914–18 War—probably from the frantic flapping of signal

flags—and has become ' Standard Navy '. See FLAPPA FLOW
and cf. PANIC.   (2) The turn of a ship's propellers: ' Give her
a flap astern (or ahead) '.

Flappa Flow. Scapa Flow, where most of the ' flaps ' originate
in wartime. See FLAP.

flap around. To rush about with no apparent purpose. (Wardroom and lower-deck.) ' What is the matter with him, he's been
flapping around like a blue-arsed fly all the forenoon? '

flat as a dab. Said of a clock-calm sea. (Cf. IRISH HURRICANE.)
A dab is a flat fish.

flat top. Any aircraft carrier of whatever tonnage. Cf. WOOL-
WORTH CARRIERS.

flat-aback. (Of a naval cap) worn at the back of the head as a sign
of bravado. It should be worn straight, and it is a punishable
offence to wear it otherwise—especially in a naval port, where
patrols can ' pick up ' the wearers and charge them with being
improperly dressed.

flatfoot. A seaman of the Royal Navy. Cf. DAB DAB and SAND-
SCRATCHERS.

flat-head. A tope, a dog fish resembling a small shark. Also
known as *shovel-head.*

flatiron. A vessel lying low in the water, specifically: (1) A
Yangtse River gunboat.   (2) One of the ' Monitors ' that
bombarded the Belgian coast in the 1914–18 War. (3) The
L.C.S. (Landing Craft Support) used in the 1939–45 War.

flat-iron collier. A vessel of the Gas, Light and Coke Company,
Ltd.; very low in the water with the funnel set right aft.

flats. Mudbanks, saltings in a tidal estuary which dry out at low
water.

flat-sweeper. A man detailed to sweep the *flats* or alleyways in a
battleship.

flattie. (1) A type of shallow-draught sailing boat used in the
creeks and estuaries of Essex. (2) Any type of flatfish.

fleet. To pay out a line of nets; (noun) a trail of nets. (Fishermen's.)

Fleet in being. A nucleus fleet, though of sufficient strength for
defence.

Fleet sweepers. The Fleet Class minesweepers, the SMOKEY JOES.

fleeting. (Of a ship) working with a fleet of trawlers on the fishery grounds. Cf. SINGLE-BOATING.

flemish. To coil rope into figures of eight for a harbour store. Cf. CHEESE DOWN.

Flemish accounts. Pay accounts that will not balance. Cf. ALL PROVED, TEN BOB OUT?

flimsy. A form of testimonial given to an officer at the end of a commission or appointment. A sheaf of good ones has earned many a Lieutenant-Commander his promotion.

flither women. Winkle-gatherers in the Filey and Flamborough district, *flither* being a local term for a periwinkle.

float. A piece of mackerel bait at the end of a line dropped over the stern of a boat. (A Devon coast term.)

floater. (1) A floating mine. (2) A suet dumpling. (Lower-deck.)

floaters fish. Immature fish. (East Anglian fishermen's.)

floaters in the snow. Sausages and mashed potatoes. (Lower-deck.)

floating coffins. Unseaworthy merchant vessels.

floating Fifth Avenue. A transatlantic liner.

floating gin-palace. A passenger liner.

floating hell. A ' hell-ship ', such as the notorious German prison ship *Altmark* in the 1939–45 War.

floating island. Any large area of driftwood and earth that, having broken away during coast erosion, is adrift at sea.

Floating Skeleton, the. The Tsarist Russian battleship *Arkold*. Cf. PACKET OF WOODBINES.

flog the cat. To ' take it out of oneself ' for doing something idiotic. (Lower-deck.)

flog the bung. To use a mallet for drawing the bung of a cask instead of the tool issued for the purpose. The corks are usually damaged by this unorthodox method, hence the term. See JIMMY BUNGS.

flog the clock. To advance the hands of the clock surreptitiously for private reasons. Cf. BELL, WARM THE.

floggin' the 'oggin. Sailing the high seas. (Naval lower-deck.) 'OGGIN is a form of '*ogwash*.

floosie or **flooz(e)y.** A girl friend. (Wardroom.) Cf. POPSEY and PARTY. A corrupted or perhaps a deliberately perverted form of *Flossie*; adopted from U.S.A.—originally, an underworld term.

Florrie. The inevitable nickname for anyone named Ford or Forde, after the famous music-hall comedienne.

Flow, the. Scapa Flow, the Grand Fleet anchorage in the two Great Wars. (A colloquialism.)

flower of the winds, the. The compass ' rose ' on a chart. It helps the navigator to plot a course.

flunkey or **wardroom flunkey.** An officer's steward, or one who waits at table. Specialization of the civilian term.

Fly Martin. Admiral Martin, who commanded a Mediterranean Squadron and was noted for his ' fly ' manoeuvres.

fly to. What a sailing ship's head does when it comes suddenly into the wind.

flying bathtubs. The early type flying boats used by the R.N.A.S. in 1915.

Flying Horse. A Gloster Gladiator, a fighter aircraft used by the Fleet Air Arm.

flying shoot. A flying launch from the breakers. (Fishermen's.)

flying wombat. A flying bomb, later to be known as a ' doodle-bug '. From the Australian marsupial, shaped like a small bear.

fo'c'sle. The forepart of the ship; a colloquial shortening for *forecastle*. In the days of the old ' wooden walls ', raised platforms were built at either end of the ship, these being *castles*.

fo'c'sle wireless. Rumours started in the fo'c'sle. Cf. the Army's *latrine rumour* and the Air Force's *Elsan gen*.

fog watch. A watch kept at night in thick weather with the duty of ringing the upper-deck bell. (A term used on the training ship *Conway*.)

follower. A rating who is transferred from ship to ship with his captain instead of being paid off at the end of a commission. A good man whom his captain wishes to keep. Cf. OLD STANDER.

foo foo band. See SQUEEGEE BAND.

foo foo barge. A sewage barge on the Yangtse River. It was a good thing to be to windward of it. Probably *foo foo* is echoic: *phew! phew!*

foo foo valve. Like a WIFFLO GADGET, this is any piece of mechanism that one cannot name. (Wardroom.)

Footballers, the. Steam-trawlers named after famous Association Football Clubs: e.g. Hull City, Aston Villa, Blackburn Rovers, Grimsby Town. Several of these were sunk in the 1939–45 War when operating as Admiralty minesweepers.

fore-and-aft rig. The uniform worn by men ' not dressed as seamen '; Petty Officers, Writers, Stewards, Sick Berth Attendants and Engineroom Artificers. Suits of civilian cut (double-breasted doeskin for ' best ') worn with a peaked cap.

fore-and-after. (1) An officer's cocked hat worn on occasions of ceremony. (2) A schooner-rigged vessel.

forearm semaphore. See LOWER-DECK WIRELESS.

fore-bitters. Songs round the fore-bitts on the fo'c'sle head. (Colloquial.)

fore-ends, the. The foremost part of a submarine. Equivalent to the forecastle in a surface craft.

foreign, go. To proceed overseas. 'He's got a draft chit to the *Nonesuch*; she's going foreign.' (Lower-deck.)

foreigners. Naval ratings who do not live within easy reach of their Port Depot. Contrast NATIVE.

forenoon, the. The forenoon watch, 8 a.m. to noon. ' Who has the forenoon tomorrow? ' (All such terms are colloquialisms, not examples of slang.)

foretopman's lock. The ' quiff ' beloved of seamen at the beginning of the century which was still fairly popular in the Fleet at the end of the 1914–18 War and is still occasionally worn by Fleet Reservemen.

foreyard, sun over the. See SUN OVER THE FOREYARD.

fork in the beam. An old gunroom custom: to place a fork in the beam above the Sub-Lieutenant's head was a sign that he wanted to be left alone with his thoughts. The junior midshipmen took it as a sign for them to leave the gunroom and they had to wait outside until the Sub allowed them to return. ' Fork in the beam ' was merely an intimation that there was too much noise and the banishment was a hint for them to keep quieter in future.

fork tail. A skua. (Wildfowlers'.)

Formy. H.M.S. *Formidable*. (Lower-deck.)

forty pounds of steam. Anyone who gets a sudden draft is said to have *forty pounds of steam behind him*. From the old days when a safety valve would fly off under a pressure of forty pounds. (Naval lower-deck.)

foul. The opposite of ' free '. An ensign is being ' foul ' if it is wrapped round the halliard and not flying free as it should; a foul wind is one that is bad for sailing in a desired direction; a target is fouled when an object gets between it and the bombarding ship.

foul-weather Jack. A ' Jonah ' who brings bad weather or ill luck to a ship.

four-letter man. A particularly noisome or objectionable fellow, one who is detested by his messmates. There are two four-letter words notably applicable to this type of individual: you take your choice.

four-stackers. United States destroyers which formed part of the destroyer force of the British Navy in 1941. Cf. YANKEE. They had *four* smoke-*stacks* or funnels.

fourteen penn'uth. Fourteen days' cell punishment. (Lower-deck.)

Fourth. The Fourth Hand in a submarine.

fowl. One who is rather worse than a BIRD.

frapping lines. Wisps of hair across a semi-bald head. (Navy.) In nautical language, a *frapping* is a lashing that either binds something tightly or binds various things together.

Fred Karno's Navy. The auxiliary patrol of trawlers, drifters, armed yachts and the like. Discipline was said to be free, and routine run on music-hall lines. The term was coined in the

1914–18 War and was again used in the 1939–45 War. Cf. RAGTIME NAVY. (See *Forces' Slang* for several interesting sidelights. Fred Karno was a popular comedian of the early 1900's.)

free and blowing. A sailor's ' square rig ', with its blue jean collar that blows round his neck and the bell-bottom trousers that flap in the breeze.

Freeman, Hardy and Willis. The three 1914–18 War medal ribbons; 1914–18 Star, General Service, and Victory. From the name of a well-known firm of boots and shoes merchants; a name selected at random.

freezer. A refrigerator ship. (Merchant Navy.) Cf. FROSTY.

French heron. An East Anglian term for a bittern. Cf. BOTTLE BUMPER.

fretter. A beachcomber. This word seems peculiar to the Sussex coast and may derive from the little-used noun, *fret*, a channel or beach caused by the sea. *Fretting* is a common term in the Eastbourne district. Cf. the Yorkshire SCRATTING.

Friday while. Long week-end leave: Friday to Monday. The ' while ' element of the term is pure North Country for *until* and the term probably originated during the 1914–18 War when a large number of North-Country ratings were training in Chatham Depot; *Friday while* (Monday) means Friday *until* Monday. See SATURDAY WHILE.

fright. A passenger in a pleasure boat. See:

frighting. A Devon coast term for *freighting*, or carrying human cargo for pleasure trips in fishing boats.

'Frisco. San Francisco.

Fritz. A German (used during the 1914–18 War). From the very common German pet-form of *Friedrich*. Cf. HEINIE.

Froggy. A Frenchman. From his partiality to frogs.

frogman. Officers and ratings who work under water clearing obstructions, etc. They wear a rubber costume, the feet of which are shaped like a frog's. This enables the under-water workers to move speedily. (1939–45 War.)

frosty or **freezer.** (1) The maintenance engineer who attends to refrigerated cargo. (2) A nickname for anyone named Snow.

103

fruit machine. (1) The automatic calculator in a submarine which regulates the firing of torpedoes. From its resemblance to the fruit machines at fun fairs. (2) GOOSEBERRY, the code name for the merchant ships sunk off the Normandy beaches to form a breakwater during the Allied invasion of Normandy in 1944.

fry of fish. A present of fish, herring, plaice, cod or what-have-you.

frying pans. The Whitby collier brigs now obsolete, which had a wind vane so shaped.

fudge. To alter records, Service certificates, or in any way to tamper with documents. It may be a corruption of *forge* or a variant of the dialectal *fadge*; just possibly, however, *fudge* derives from one Captain Fudge, who was one of the most notorious liars in the history of the Old Navy and who rivalled the celebrated TOM PEPPER.

fu-fu. A species of treacle and barley pudding. (An arbitrary formation.)

fug pants. Naval winter-weight under-pants worn by ratings in severe weather. Comforting if ' fuggy '.

full Admiral. An Admiral. He wears one broad stripe and three thin half-inch stripes as distinct from a Vice-Admiral (broad and two thin stripes) and a Rear-Admiral (broad and one thin stripe).

full belly night = DUFF NIGHT.

full due. (Of an appointment) more or less permanent; for ' all time '. A ship ties-up for a ' full due ' when she intends being alongside for some time. An officer is appointed to a ship either for a ' full due ' or is merely ' lent '; the latter means that he is in his new appointment for a course of instruction or *vice* someone who is sick on shore and will return to his own ship when the man recovers. Cf. LENT.

full house. A mixed grill. (Lower-deck.)

full tops. Caps with full tops worn by senior cadets at the Royal Naval College, Dartmouth.

full-rigger. A full-rigged sailing ship.

funnel cover. A seaman's cap which is flat and resembles one. (Lower-deck.)

funny party. An official concert party in an H.M. Ship as distinct from the free and easy—and how easy !—SOT'S OPERA.

Furibox. H.M.S. *Furious*, the aircraft carrier.

furry things. Rabbits. Fishermen are very superstitious about these and never mention them except by this name.

G

G.s. ' G ' notes on the bugle, sounded as a warning that ' Divisions ' are imminent and that ratings must hurry themselves if they are not to be ' adrift '; three G.s is the final warning. ' You'd better smack it about, Nobby, two G.s have gone.'

gabby Dick. A chatterbox, one with the ' gift of the *gab* '. (Lower-deck.)

gadyang. A China coasting craft. (A *gad*der on the *Yang*tse River.)

gaff shandy (sic) **rig** = FORE-AND-AFT RIG.

gaff-topsail hat. A silk ' topper ' in which Masters of sailing ships were once wont to visit the owners.

gallers. The gallows on a steam trawler, used to pay out and rewind the net. They are shaped like an inverted *U*.

galley downhaul, the. A non-existent fitting. A time-honoured joke is to send a New Entry to look for it.

galley growler. A grumbler, SEA LAWYER, breeder of discontent.

galley stoker. An idler who pretends to stoke the galley fire in order to escape an irksome job of work on deck.

galley swab. A cook's steward in the training ship *Conway*.

galley wireless = FO'C'SLE WIRELESS.

galley yarn. A wildly improbable story told round the galley fire; a piece of unreliable information.

gangway for a naval officer! A traditional naval catchphrase requesting a *gangway* or passage through a crowd of men.

gannet. A man with a voracious appetite. (Lower-deck.)

ganzy. A corruption of *guernsey*, a thick sweater worn by fishermen and by deck-hands in the Merchant Navy.

Garden, the. A herring ground off the Leman Bank in the North Sea.

garnet. A gannet. (East Anglian fishermen's.)

garters on, have the. To be in irons in the ship's cells. Humourously euphemistic.

gas bag. An airship. Cf. AERIAL SAUSAGE and BLIMP.

gash. Left over; spare; superfluous. Also, any refuse. A *gash bucket* is a rubbish bin (cf. ROSY); a *gash hand* is a man without a job; a *gash boat* is a stand-by duty boat. ' Any gash plew loafing? '; ' I want a couple of gash hands to do a job '; ' He's coxs'n of the gash boat '. (Lower-deck.) Perhaps from French *gâchis*, a ' mess ', or *gâché*, done clumsily, spoilt. Hence the contraction:

gashions. Extra rations.

gate. Opening in a defence boom which allows ships to pass in and out. The gate is opened when a signal is made to the boom defence vessels.

Gate. A nickname for anyone inclined to loquacity. *Gate* is a lower-deck term for mouth. Cf. GATE AND GAITERS.

gate and gaiters or **gas and gaiters.** A Gunnery Instructor. (A Whale Island term.) *Gate* is the mouth, and *gaiters* are worn by the instructors and symbolize much squad drill.

Gateway, the. A passage between the Dogger Bank and the Yorkshire coast.

general service. Time spent at sea in ' ships of war ' rather than in Combined Operations and detached duty. ' I'm chokker with this commando stuff, I'm going to smack in a request to go back to general service.' (Lower-deck.)

gens. General leave. *Did you have good gens?* ' Did you have a good leave? ' (Lower-deck.)

gentleman bunts. An R.N.V.R. signalman. From the number of Public School men in the peacetime Divisions of the R.N.V.R.

gentleman, no sailor. A phrase born in the 1914–18 War and resuscitated in the 1939–45 War was: ' R.N.V.R.—gentleman, no sailor; R.N.R.—sailor, no gentleman; R.N.—neither the one nor the other '. The reference is to officers.

geological survey. The stony stare of disapproval directed at one who has made a *gaffe*. (Wardroom.)

George. Any enemy reconnaissance aircraft.

gerines. An Old Navy term for the Royal Marines.

get her cable. (Of a ship) to be riding to anchor with the cable stretched taut.

get spliced. To marry. Cf. FIT DOUBLE CLEWS; JUMP OFF THE DOCK; TIE-UP. (Lower-deck.)

Get your ears back! = DIG IN, FILL YOUR BOOTS. (Lower-deck.)

gharri. A Maltese cab; hence *gharri-wallah*, its driver. (From Hindustani.)

ghost. To sail the high seas at night without steaming lights. Fish-poaching vessels do this.

giggle-water. Cocktails, over-indulgence in which makes the girls giggle.

Gilded Staff. The members of the Flag Officer's staff, the wearers of gold aiguillettes. (Wardroom.)

gill net. The drift net used in the herring fishery. The one-inch mesh catches the fish by the gills and suffocates them immediately. An American term adopted by herring fishermen.

gilt poll. The gilt-headed fish. (Fishermen's.)

gimlet. A drink: gin and lime. (Wardroom.)

gin pennant. A green-and-white pennant run up as an invitation to a ' chummy ship ' to repair on board for a gin-drinking session. (Royal Navy.)

gin sweep. A process that takes place when a ship is out of gin a few days before the arrival of BOND; officers visit neighbouring ships to borrow odd bottles to tide them over.

ginger campaign. Any form of official shaking-up of a slack ship's company. A gingering-up of sluggards. ' You can take it from me, we're in for a ginger campaign; the Old Man's been pretty terse lately.'

ginger string. Spunyarn. From the colour. (General nautical.)

gingerbread work. Any fancy carving or paintwork on board ship. Hence the term, *gilt off the gingerbread*.

ginners. The gills of a fish. (Dialect and slang of the north-east coast.)

ginormous. Adjective for something really impressive—a brush with the enemy, a raid upon shipping by submarines, or a particularly heavy party in the mess. Telescopic: *Gi* (gantic) + (e)*normous.*

girls have the towropes, the. Said of a ship that is nearing her home port.

glass-house sailors. The men of the Royal Naval Division and the R.N.V.R. who were trained in the Crystal Palace, London, in the 1914–18 War. Cf. CRYSTAL PALACE ARMY.

Globe-rangers. The Corps of Royal Marines, which travels the world. A term seldom heard at the present time though fairly common in sea literature at the beginning of the century.

globe spanner. A bird like the curlew-sandpiper: an Arctic tern, which covers tremendous distances.

glop. An underwater explosion. Echoic.

glory hole. (1) A fo'c'sle in a tramp steamer. (2) Stewards' quarters in a passenger liner, hence:

glory hole steward. A ' stewards' steward ' in a passenger liner.

gnat. An acoustic torpedo. It buzzes towards its target.

Go back and cross the T's. Ironical advice to a learner-coxswain who has ' written his name ' in the wake of an erratic course. (Naval.)

go for a sailor. To adopt the sea as a career. ' Young man, if anyone had told me what sort of life it was, I would never have gone for a sailor! ' (Colloquial.)

go for an officer. To leave the lower-deck for a course as candidate for an R.N.V.R. commission. (Lower-deck.) On the analogy of GO FOR A SAILOR.

go foreign. To proceed to an overseas draft. (Lower-deck.)

go the wrong side of the buoy. To make a serious mistake in seamanship or conduct. ' Pity about old So-and-So! He was a decent bloke and I'm sorry for him; a brilliant career, then he suddenly goes the wrong side of the buoy and gets beached.'

Go Under, the. The *Gayundah,* a gunboat of the 1914–18 War. Of the FLAT-IRON type which is usually wet in a seaway.

goal posts, the. Twin masts in a turret steamer. They have a cross-piece that causes this appearance.

go-ashores. A sailor's best uniform; his TIDDLEYS or NUMBER ONES.

gob stick. A wooden spoon. Seldom heard today. From *gob,* mouth.

gobble bellies. Little gobies, small fish found in estuaries and often taken in shrimp nets. (Marshmen's.) The same nickname applies to the yellow-speckled goby. (Estuary fishermen's.)

gobby. A coastguard, hence:

gobby fleet. Any ships attached to the coastguard service—guardships, etc.

goffer or **gopher.** Any fizzy drink.

goffer firm. Purveyors of preceding. (Lower-deck.)

gold lace. The officers collectively. (Lower-deck.) Cf. BRASS.

golden-crested Wren. A blonde member of the W.R.N.S.

Goldfish Gang, the. The sea-going Navy's name for the Fleet Air Arm.

gong team. Any Fleet Air Arm 'plane crew (pilot and observer) who both have decorations.

gongoozler. A canalman's equivalent of DOCK WALLOPER. One who has time to ' stand and stare '. The term may derive from the nautical *goosing,* looking for a job, with the *gon* added in reduplication.

Good King Henry. The seaweed usually known as Mercury Goosefoot. The nickname is derived from the Latin name of the weed, *Chenopodium Bonus Henricus.* Also known as FAT HEN.

Good Ship Venus, the. A bawdy song known to most members of the Royal and Merchant Navies. Cf. ESKIMO NELL.

gooseberry. A shelter formed by the sinking of a line of block-ships—about sixty in number—in two-and-a-half fathoms of water. It formed part of Mulberry Harbour used in the invasion of Normandy in 1944. Cf. FRUIT MACHINE.

goose-winged. A yacht sailing with the foresail on one side and the mainsail on the other.

Gosport Liners. The tiny steam ferry boats that ply between Portsmouth and Gosport.

Gourock ham. Salted herring. (Gourock fishermen's.) Cf. ABERDEEN CUTLET.

grabbies. Soldiers. (Lower-deck.) Cf. PONGO and SWADDY.

grab-hooks. Fingers. (Lower-deck.)

Grable-bodied seaman. A Wren member of a trot-boat's crew. After Betty Grable, the shapely film star, with a pun on *able-bodied seaman*.

grain race. The race by sailing ships to bring grain from Australia to Europe.

Granny. The affectionate name given by her crew to the veteran Cunard White Star liner *Aquitania*, which has served under the house flag for over thirty-seven years and is still (1948) afloat as a transport.

granny bend. A slippery hitch made when another knot was intended.

grass line. Coir rope which floats on the water.

grasshopper. An Italian one-man submarine.

grave-digger. A naval rating who has been disrated and has never recovered status; an A.B. who was once a Petty Officer or Leading Hand. (He has dug his own grave.)

gravel-grinders. Gunners' Mates in R.N. barracks. They take the squad-drill, etc. Cf.:

gravel-grinding. Squad-drill on the gravelled parade ground in naval barracks. Cf. SQUARE-BASHING.

Gravesend nip. A quick clearance from an anchorage. Of barges which ' nip ' neatly from their mooring by luffing and filling until they are clear of other vessels. Gravesend stands opposite Tilbury in the Thames Estuary where there is considerable shipping traffic.

Gravesend sweetmeats. Shrimps—for which the town is noted.

graveyard. Any creek or basin in which old ships lie until they can be broken up. Cf. KNACKER'S YARD.

graveyard watch. The middle watch, midnight to 4 a.m. ' When graveyards give up their dead.'

gravy, the. The sea. Cf. DITCH, DRINK, 'OGGIN.

greaser. A Merchant Navy engine room hand. From his oily, greasy work.

greasy. A naval shortening of:

greasy neck. A Cook rating. Cf. SLUSHY.

Great Blizzard, the. This occurred during the evacuation of the British forces from the coast of Gallipoli during the 1914–18 War. A gale and blizzard raged for nearly a week causing great destruction ashore and sinking many ships off-shore with a large loss of men.

Great Flight, the. The strategic withdrawal of British naval forces from Alexandria and the threatened parts of the Mediterranean during the German advance in 1941.

Great Silent, the. The Royal Navy—the ' silent ' Service. A term used by journalists in the 1914–18 War.

green. The starboard side of the ship (right-hand side looking towards the bows). In action, enemy vessels or aircraft are given on a colour bearing thus: ' Two hostile aircraft bearing green o–five ', or ' Object bearing red four–five '. The use of colour bearings helps to avoid any confusion between a bearing and a helm order such as ' Starboard twenty ' which means that the helmsman is to steer twenty degrees to starboard.

green coat, wear the. To appear innocent; a ruse tried by New Entries who have broken one of the rules. ' He's not so dim as he looks, sir; he wears the green coat, that's all.' Cf. ACT GREEN.

green fish. Cod, haddock, herrings and the like, freshly caught and not yet salted. (Fishermen's colloquialism; *green* connotes freshness.)

green jacket. A variant of GREEN COAT.

green pennant = GIN PENNANT.

green rub. An undeserved rebuke. A BOTTLE ' stopped ' by oneself but intended for someone else. (Lower-deck.)

112

Green Sea, the. The sea in the Persian Gulf off the coast of Arabia. From the prevalent colour of the water.

green stripers. Officers in the Special Branch of the Royal Naval Volunteer Reserve, a branch instituted in 1941 to provide the necessary executive officers and ' specialists ' for Shore Establishments. These officers were those who fell short of the standard of physical fitness required for sea service, either through defective eyesight or by reason of age. They released younger and fitter men for sea. Many *green stripers* were first-class seamen, yacht owners, or ex-R.N., anxious to do some form of naval service. Their duties were multifarious: officers of the watch in harbour, bomb disposal, Intelligence and Security, salvage, etc. The green braid worn between the gold stripes on their sleeves is of an emerald shade, not the bottle-green as worn by Electrical Officers.

green 'un. A heavy sea which breaks over a ship. Cf. TAKE IT GREEN.

Greenland dove. An old whalers' term for the black guillemot.

grey. An immature saddleback gull. (Wildfowlers'.)

greyback. A heavy ' grey ' sea (wave) that threatens to break over a ship's gunwale.

greyhound. A hammock lashed thinly owing to its not having the full amount of bedding inside.

griff, the. Information. ' Give us the griff, Jack ', is the Navy's equivalent of the Air Force's ' What's the gen?' From the *griffin*, which is the stable information, as it were; reliable intelligence.

Grimmies. Grimsby trawlermen.

grippo run. Free treat or entertainment ashore.

grippos. Free entertainment of any kind. Concerts, free cinema shows and the like. (Lower-deck.) See preceding.

grocer's hitch. A lubberly knot that will not come adrift. Cf. SNOWBALL HITCH.

grog. The rum ration in the Royal Navy, allowed to all lower-deck ratings but not to officers. Before Admiral Sir Edward Vernon in 1740 introduced diluted rum in the interests of sobriety (and economy), rum was served neat. The ' two-water

113

rum' (grog) takes its name from the *grogram* coat which Admiral Vernon always wore; he was known throughout the Service as ' Old Grog '.

grog blossoms. Heightened colour round the nose resulting from much indulgence in rum. Cf. TODDY BLOSSOMS.

grog tub, the. That from which the rum is served. It is inscribed ' The King, God Bless Him' and at one time the ship's company used to assemble round it to drink the King's health.

gropers. Short for *Channel gropers*. See CHANNEL GROPING.

grounders. A full tot of rum, 'grounds and the lot', offered by a grateful pal in return for a special service rendered; it must indeed be a special service to warrant the surrender of a complete tot.

growl book. A suggestions or complaints book kept in a naval mess. Books are suggested for the wardroom library, complaints or ' moans ' are made about the monotony of menus, etc.

grub spoiler. A naval cook. (Lower-deck.) Cf. HASH WRECKER and SLUSHY.

grunter. Cf. PIG, NAVAL.

grut line. A long or ' great ' line used in cod fishing. (Dialect rather than slang; a common term.)

guarantee Chief. A shipbuilders' engineer who sails in a new ship to see that her engines run satisfactorily and economically.

guard-rail critic. One who leans over the rail offering advice to those doing the work. He can always do the job better than anyone else but is never seen to do any work himself.

gubb. A seagull.

gubber. A beachcomber. Like a GUBB he picks up all he can find. Cf. GUBBINS.

gubbing. Beachcombing. This term may spring from GUBB.

gubbins. Extra food or any free treat ashore. (Lower-deck.) Cf. preceding.

guff. Cheek or ' side '. (Royal Naval College, Dartmouth.) *Guff rules* are promulgated each term by the Cadet Captains and privileges and restrictions are formed for seniors and juniors. To be *guffed* is to be hauled up for any infringement of these rules. From civilian *guff*, empty talk.

guffy. Adjective = cheeky. (Royal Naval College, Dartmouth.)

Gulf, the. The Persian Gulf. (Colloquial.)

gull. A creek or estuary. Perhaps a form of *gulf*, an arm of the sea, but probably from obsolete *gull*, the gullet.

gull in night clothing. A crow. (Lower-deck.) See CROW IN WORKING RIG.

gulls live, they don't know where the. An expression of contempt for men of extreme stupidity.

gulpers. A taste of a messmate's tot of rum on one's birthday. See GROUNDERS, LIGHTERS, SIPPERS, for relative values in ' rum-ology '.

gum bucket. A tobacco pipe. (Wardroom.)

Gunboat. A nickname for Smith. It derives from the famous early twentieth-century English boxer ' Gunboat ' Smith.

gunboats, the. The motor gunboats of the Coastal Forces flotillas in the 1939–45 War. (Colloquial.)

gunfire. Early morning cups of tea. A term borrowed from the Army during the days of Combined Operations.

gunnel under, i.e. *gunwale under*. (Of a ship) experiencing heavy weather in seas level with her decks. (Colloquial.)

gunner. A wildfowler's gun punt used in East Anglian creeks and estuaries.

Gunnery Jack. A Gunnery Officer in the Royal Navy.

Gunroom. Collective noun for a Midshipman. Literally the Midshipmen's Mess in a cruiser or battleship. It is presided over by a Sub-Lieutenant whose word is law and who occasionally invokes the assistance of LITTLE BENJAMIN, OUR RULER to ensure that order is preserved. Cf. 'ORRIBLE 'OLE. (Technical, not unconventional.)

gunroom evolutions. The time-honoured games of the gunroom: ' Priest of the Parish ', ' Fetch bumf ', etc. In recent years gunroom ' evolutions ' have fallen off somewhat, maybe owing to the sterner realities of war.

Guns. Gunnery Officer. Wardroom nickname and vocative. ' Oh, Guns, will you make up a party for bridge tonight? '

Guns, Gaiters and Guff. The Gunnery Officer's motto. Cf. GATE AND GAITERS.

gurry. A hand barrow for carrying pilchards from the beach to the curing houses. (Cornish coast term.)

gussock. A sudden *gust* of wind. An East Anglian coast variant of ROGER.

Gut, the. A well-known street in Malta.

guts for a necktie, I'll have your (his). A picturesque naval threat by an officer or Petty Officer. ' If the Bloke sees this mess he'll have your guts for a necktie.' A variant is ' have your guts for garters '. (General naval slang.)

Guz, short for **Guzzle.** Devonport Barracks. So called because in peace-time there was an abundance of food and the lads were able to ' guzzle ' as much as they liked. Cf. DUFFOES and JAGO.

gypping. The gutting of herrings. This is performed with incredible swiftness by the fisher ' lassies ' of the east coast of Scotland. A Scotticism, perhaps from the Scottish dialectal *gype*, keen, energetic.

gyppo. (1) Gravy. (Lower-deck.) From dialectal *gipper* or *jipper*, meat-juice, gravy. (2) An Egyptian. (Lower-deck.)

gyvo. (Pronounced with hard *g*.) Unorthodox; not according to SEALED PATTERN, e.g. a seaman's TIDDLEY suit with extra wide bell-bottoms on the trousers. (Lower-deck.)

H

haddie. A haddock. (Fishermen's.)

hags. Women in general. (R.N. and W.R.N.S. officers' term.) 'How many hags will be at the party?' Ungallant perhaps, but nevertheless genuine Navalese.

hahnsey-gutted. Lean, 'skinny' (person or ship). East Anglian; from *hahnsey*, a solecistic form of *hernshaw*, a heron. (Dialect and slang.)

half a dog-watch. *He hasn't been in the Service half a dog-watch.*
—Used in extenuation when a New Entry rating does something notably stupid; or in reproof: 'Who are you to talk? You haven't been in the Service half a dog-watch.'

half curlew. A whimbrel. Cf. JACK CURLEW.

half marrow. A man in the Merchant Navy who, having served his time as an Ordinary Seaman, is not efficient enough to be rated Able-bodied.

half shot. Partially drunk; BONKERS.

half stripe. That thin gold ' ring ' between two thick ones denoting the rank of Lieut.-Commander, a rank that, up to the year 1914, was known as ' Eight-year Lieutenant '. Before the introduction of the new rank a Lieutenant in command of a Torpedo Boat or T.B.D. (Torpedo Boat Destroyer) was known as ' Lieutenant and Commander '. (Colloquialism.)

half whites. NUMBER SEVEN uniform, blue jumper and white trousers. Also known as MAGPIES. Used in tropical climates.

half-tide rock, like a. Said of a ship which is TAKING IT GREEN, her decks being partially submerged like a rock at half-tide.

haling way. A towing path. (Marshland term.) The boat is *haled* through the canals by horses.

hambone. A sextant (much the same shape). (Wardroom.)

ham-handed. Lubberly and unseamanlike. Like a *ham* actor.

hand out the slack. To answer back; to cheek one's ' elders and betters '; a New Entry habit that is quickly cured on the lower-deck. Cf. Dartmouth's GUFF.

handraulic power. Any work that requires ' beef ' and manual effort. Cf. JOHNNY ARMSTRONG. A sarcastic pun on *hydraulic*. (Lower-deck.)

hands, the. The working part of the Ship's Company. (Royal and Merchant Navies.) (A technicality.)

hands to dinner; C.W. candidates to lunch. An ironical ' pipe ' from a—perhaps jealous—Quartermaster. ' C.W.s ' spend three months as ratings in sea-going ships and are regarded with a mixture of envy and scorn by Active Service ratings.

handsomely. An official order to lower the boat's falls slowly and with care. It is included because the term is an unusual one and is intrinsically interesting. Cf. ROUNDLY.

handspike hash. A variant of BELAYING-PIN SOUP; rough treatment. (Euphemistic.)

handy Billy. A small tackle used for a variety of purposes—it is very handy indeed.

hang on the slack. To lounge about waiting for something to happen. ' I went to meet that party last night, but she kept me hanging on the slack for half an hour, so I got chokker and came back on board.' From *slack* as opposed to a *taut* rope.

hanging out the washing. Making sail. A very old term.

hank for hank. Sailing craft ' neck and neck ' in a race.

Hannah. A Marine Wren. After one Hannah Snell who, disguised as a man, served with the Royal Marines at sea in the eighteenth century. Cf. MAREN, MARINETTE.

happy ship. One in which officers and men work together in close harmony. (Colloquial.)

Harbours rot ships and men. An old Navy saying that is profoundly true.

hard. That hard ground in a marshy tract from which men can embark.

118

Hard, the. Portsea Hard, Portsmouth. (Colloquial.)

hard fish. Salted or dried fish, e.g. haddock or cod. (Colloquial.)

hard lyers. Hard lying money paid to officers and men in small craft where quarters are cramped and much discomfort results in bad weather. Only very small craft receive this nowadays, but up to the 1939–45 War men serving in the older destroyers had it; and there was a great 'moan' when the new destroyers were built with better quarters, for the crews were no longer 'entitled'. A shilling a day 'hard lyers' made a big difference to the men's pay and that was probably the reason for the great number of volunteers for the destroyer service.

Hardship, H.M.S. The conventional answer to the question, 'What ship are you *on*?' (instead of, correctly, *in*).

hardtimers. Poorly conditioned cod.

Harriet Lane. A Merchant Navy version of FANNY ADAMS. The two reputedly suffered the same fate.

Harry. Since the adoption of HARRY FREEMAN'S for any free treat, the Navy has prefixed Harry to several 'personified' nouns, e.g. Harry *Flatters* means a flat calm sea; Harry *Flakers* is a state of being flaked out after a party ashore. Harry *Crashers* is to be fast asleep, *crashing down the swede*. (Lower-deck.) See SWEDE.

Harry Freeman's or **Harry Free's.** Something for nothing. From one Henry Freeman, a City merchant who used to give free beer to the porters who worked for him. Cf. HARRY and ON THE BARON.

Harry Tate's Navy. The Auxiliary Patrol of trawlers, drifters, armed yachts and the like in the 1914–18 War. Said to be run on comic lines. Harry Tate was a noted comedian whose speciality was awkwardness and imbecility in doing a job of work. Cf. FRED KARNO'S NAVY.

hash wrecker. A cook. (Merchant Navy.) Cf. GRUB SPOILER and SLUSHY.

Haslar hags. The nurses at the R.N. Hospital, Haslar, Hants—the LIME TANK. (Old Navy term.) Cf. HAGS.

Hatchet. A nickname for any long-faced individual in the Royal Navy. (Lower-deck.) Short for *hatchet-faced*.

hate. Any demonstration of hostility. A bombardment or air raid. A ' down ' on somebody. ' The Bloke has a hate on me, I'm always in the blooming rattle.' (Lower-deck.)

H'attitude is the h'art of gunnery and whiskers make the man! An old Whale Island slogan of the pre-1914 Navy.

haul-down promotion. A Flag Officer's promotion on hauling down his flag on retirement.

Have got? ' Do you understand, have you got my drift? ' (Wardroom.) (Pidgin English: China-side influence.)

have one's back teeth awash. To be very drunk indeed.

haven screamers. Seagulls. They wheel and scream about the harbours.

hawseholers. Naval officers who have risen from the lower-deck. Equivalent to the peace-time Army's *rankers*. See AFT THROUGH THE HAWSEHOLE.

hayfork, the. A similarly shaped radar aerial used in H.M. Ships.

haystack. A sailing ship with an ugly suit of sails, which, when set, looks like a haystack.

hazing. The harassing of a ship's crew by her officers, a survival of sailing-ship days still current up to the 1914–18 War, especially in the Mercantile Marine in which there were still a few barques and brigantines in service.

head herrings. The two herrings placed across the heads of those in the tier below in packing a barrel. The first tier is laid, then two *head herrings* laid across the heads, a second tier laid and so on. (Technicality.)

headfast. Head rope. (Bargemen's.)

heading. The beheading of a fish. (Fishery term, verging on jargon.)

heads. Ratings' lavatories, situated in the beak-heads in the ship's bows. Cf. ROUNDHOUSE.

heads, captain of the. A rating responsible for keeping the HEADS clean. ' My son's getting on so well in the Navy, Mrs Jones; he says he is captain of the heads.' (Old Navy ' crack '.)

heart of the wind. The strength of the wind.

heart yarn. The centre yarn in a strand of rope. Cf. ROGUE'S YARN.

heart yarn of the mainbrace. A really tough seaman.

heave small. To take things easy. (Colloquial.)

Heavy Reach, the. A stretch of water in Fareham Creek, Portsmouth.

heavy weather, to make. To find difficulty in doing a job. ' Old Nobby seems to be making heavy weather of that splicing.' (Colloquial: from a ship *labouring* in a heavy sea.)

Heinie. The 1939–45 War nickname for a German. From Heinz, a common German name. It was used more often than the *Fritz* or *Hun* of the 1914–18 War. (Wardroom.)

Helen's Reef. A range of submarine rocks of which Rockall is the summit and the only reef that appears above the water. It is about 300 miles off the west coast of Scotland and well-known to the Royal Navy and the fishing fleets. From the brig *Helen* which was wrecked on the reef about 1824.

Hell's corner. Any crowded mess-deck of ' transit ' ratings in naval barracks with no room to 'sling' and chaos at meal-times.

Hell-bent for election. Steaming at full speed; cf. RATE OF KNOTS.

Hell-fire Corner. The Straits of Dover in the 1939–45 War. Much shelling and bombing took place there. Borrowed from the Army.

Herbaceous Borders. The ' Flower ' Class sloops. Cf. MR MIDDLETON'S LIGHT HORSE.

herring hog. A porpoise. It is a *hog* for *herring*.

herring moon. The October moon, during which the best herring catches are made. (East Anglian fishermen's colloquialism.)

herring spink. The golden-crested wren. (Fishermen's term.) In English and Scottish dialect, a *spink* is a chaffinch.

herring-bone. To repair sails with herring-bone stitches.

high drieds. Red herrings, which are cured by drying on high spits in the curing houses. (East Anglian term.)

Hinder, the. The Noord Hinder Light Vessel. (Colloquial.)

Hindrance, the. An old Dover paddle-tug, the *Aid*, whose engines always failed at awkward times. So named by the Dover Patrol to which she was attached in the 1914–18 War.

hip hip hurrahs, the. Engine-room Artificers of the Royal Navy. Cf. TIFFY. A rather subtle pun: *the E.R.A.s—the E.Ra's.— the Hurrahs*—by elaboration, *the hip hip hurrahs*.

hit the beach. To go ashore. (An Americanism very common on the lower-deck in the Merchant Navy.)

Hitch. The late Lieutenant-Commander Robert Hitchins, D.S.O. and two bars, D.S.C., R.N.V.R. A Coastal Forces ' ace ', he was killed in an engagement with German E-Boats. A grievous loss to the Navy and an inspiration to all who followed him. An oil painting of Commander Hitchins is in the headquarters of the R.N.V.R. Club, London.

hitcher. A boat-hook. (Bargemen's.)

Hitler's doorstep. The area of the North Sea and the English Channel exposed to attack by shore batteries, E-Boats, aircraft, etc. From the Wash to Dover. Cf.:

Hitler's graveyard. The stretch of water between the Thames Estuary and Harwich, the ' graveyard ' of so many fine ships sunk by E-Boat, aircraft or mines.

H.O. A '*H*ostilities *O*nly' rating—one of the ' Militiamen ' or temporary R.N.V.R.s, or the conscripts enlisted for the period of the war—as distinct from the ' Active Service ' (i.e. regular R.N.) personnel.

hobbler. One of the men who tow barges from the tow-paths of canals.

hoggin. See 'OGGIN.

hog's wash of the fo'c'sle head, the. Deck-hands of a tramp steamer in the early days of steam—and, indeed, until about 1910.

holiday. A space left when painting the ship's side or scrubbing the decks. ' Get on with that job and, mind, no bloomin' 'olidays.' Also a gap in a line of caps on the hooks in a cloak-room of a training establishment.

holiday cutter. This is a form of punishment in the training ship *Conway*, the victim pulling in the cutter instead of ' holidaying ' on shore leave. Cf.:

holiday messenger. A cadet in the training ship *Conway* acting as lower-deck messenger as punishment for some misdemeanour. He works when others are ashore.

HOLLAND. One of the many initialled messages on the envelopes of sailors' letters. It means, according to a Wren Censor Officer of my acquaintance, ' hope our love lasts and never dies '. The matelot's version—quoted by Charles Graves in his book, *Life Line*, 1941—is ' have on less lace and no drawers '. See SWAK.

hollow meat. Rabbits or poultry, as opposed to solid meat like beef or lamb. (Lower-deck.)

Holloway's Unfinished Symphonies. The Maunsell Forts in the Thames Estuary to which constant improvements were being made. A good-natured ' libel' on the excellent firm that erected them.

holy ground. (1) That portion of the deck of the training ship *Conway* which was consecrated by the Bishop of Liverpool and is used for Divine Service. (2) That part of a warship's quarterdeck used for the Divine Service.

Holy Joe. A naval chaplain. (Wardroom and lower-deck.) Cf. SKY PILOT, SIN BO'SUN, etc.

Holy of Holies, the. The Admiralty Buildings, Whitehall, London.

holystones. Soft sandstone slabs used for scrubbing and whitening the decks of His Majesty's Ships and Vessels. There are several supposed origins of the term, the most popular being that the decks are stoned for Divine Service on Sunday. I believe that there may be some truth in the idea that they are so called because the stones came from St Nicholas' Church, Great Yarmouth. Being porous, they are also *holey*. Cf. ECCLESIAS- TICAL BRICKS.

homer. A large skate (the fish). (East Anglian fishermen's.) With a pun on *get one's skates on*, to act promptly, to go fast.

homeward-bound stitches. The stitches used in sewing up a dead seaman in the hammock in which he goes to his final home. See LAST STITCH.

homework. Women generally. ' I saw Nobby Clark with a nice piece of homework last night.'

Hong Kong dog. Tropical fever.

honk. A Fleet Air Arm variant of TOOT.

honkey donks. Royal Marine's feet. (Lower-deck.) There is a well simulated ' hatred ' between the matelot and the ' Royal '.

hoodoo ships. Those associated with bad luck. Cf. ROGUE SHIP. *Hoodoo* is a variant of *voodoo* (Negro witchcraft.)

hoody. The hooded crow. (Wildfowler's.)

hook. An anchor or KILLICK, hence:

hooking-up party. Men who seem to be always absent from Divisions.

hooky. (1) A Leading Hand who wears the ' hook ' or anchor as badge of rank. (2) A nickname for anyone surnamed Walker: cf. *sling one's hook*, to walk rapidly away, to decamp.

hooligan. An Oerlikon gun. (See LOBSTER POT.) By ' Hobson-Jobson '.

horizontal champ. A rating with a great sleeping reputation. (Lower-deck.) i.e., *horizontal champion:* from boxing, where it has been applied especially to twentieth-century British heavyweights.

Horn, the. Cape Horn. (Colloquial.) Cf. *Cape Stiff.*

horse box. The mess of the Royal Marine sergeant-majors.

horse marines. Contractors who haul boats by horse through canals.

Horse of Troy. The famous steamer *River Clyde* which landed troops on the Gallipoli Beaches in 1915. She lay off Cape Helles, the most southerly point of the peninsula of Gallipoli that guards the entrance to the Dardanelles.

horse's neck. A wardroom drink: brandy and ginger ale.

hostile ord. A *hostil*ities only *ord*inary seaman. (Lower-deck.) *Ord.* is the official abbreviation of *Ordinary Seaman.* Cf. H.O.

hostility bend. A lubberly knot made by an ordinary seaman enlisted for the period of ' hostilities only '. Cf. DURATION HITCH.

hostility men. Men enlisted in the Royal Navy for a period of ' hostilities only '. Cf. H.O.

hot gunroom. One in which discipline is very severe, the Sub-Lieutenant has the reputation of being a ' taut hand ', and ' evolutions ' are frequently held. See GUNROOM EVOLUTIONS.

hot stuff, to. To ' wangle ', ' unhook ' or purloin gear or articles of clothing from naval stores. (A term used by the Royal Naval Air Service, 1914–18.)

hot walls. The sea-front or parade which runs from Portsmouth to Southsea, probably so called because it is usually exposed to the blazing sun.

house lighter. A lighter with a cabin (house). (A Fenland term.)

House that Jack built, the. ' The first permanent building in the Whale Island Gunnery School ' (Frank C. Bowen, *Sea Slang*).

hoveller. A Thames-side salvage worker; also a beachcomber who retrieves wreckage from stranded vessels.

huddy. The wider part of a sprat net. (Fishermen's.)

hugger-mugger. A bungled, unseamanlike job. Special application of an archaic Standard English term.

hulked, be. An old-time Gunnery School punishment: to be sent as a delinquent on board one of the Establishment's hulks lying in the stream. This precluded any chance of breaking out of barracks.

human minesweepers. Naval bomb-disposal parties trained to render mines safe under water.

humid. Dim-witted. A refinement of WET. Cf. the R.A.F.'s *soggy*.

Hunger, Famine and Starvation line, the. The nickname for the old Henry Fernie & Sons ships, from the initials H.F. & S. on the firm's house flag.

Hungry Hundred. The first batch of Royal Naval Reserve officers to join the Fleet (about 1911) from the Mercantile Marine. A further batch of fifty which joined later were dubbed ' the Famishing Fifty '.

hunting flotilla. A flotilla of destroyers engaged in anti-submarine patrols in the 1914–18 War.

Hunts. The ' Hunt ' Class of destroyers which take their names from the famous packs of hounds, e.g. *Pytchley*, *Quorn*, *Cleveland*. Cf. DOUBLE HUNTS.

hurrah cruise. A ' showing-the-flag ' cruise round the British Isles by H.M. Ships which anchor off seaside resorts to allow civilians to visit them.

hurrah boat. A paddle steamer with trippers visiting the Fleet at anchor during a Navy Week. The trippers usually cheered wildly as they approached the ships.

hurrah's nest. The state of confusion that characterizes a Midshipman's chest. Any state of untidyness.

husband's packet. The paddle steamer that used to leave London at week-ends to take excursionists to Margate. Husbands used to take passage in this paddler to visit their families on holiday there.

hush-hush. Most secret. Applied to signals, orders, weapons and so forth. (Wardroom and Lower-deck.)

hush-hush ship. (1) = Q-SHIP. (2) One of the cruiser-sized craft of bizarre design built during the 1914–18 War. They were built in great secrecy and their oddity of appearance gave rise to such nicknames as H.M.S. *Spurious, Outrageous* and *Unspeakable.*

I

Icelandmen. Trawlermen who fish the Iceland Banks. Cf. FAROEMEN. Hull trawlers fish either the one or the other area.

idle rich, the. (1) Men who try to dodge work, either by ' going sick ' or by skulking in the ' heads '. (Lower-deck; sarcastic.) (2) Officers who do not keep watches. (Wardroom.) Cf. IDLER.

Idle Women. The women who worked the canal boats during the 1939–45 War. Self-applied, the nickname derives from the initials *I*nland *W*aterways.

idler. An officer or man who does not keep night watches at sea: a Paymaster, Surgeon, etc. (Wardroom.) Cf. IDLE RICH.

I'll take the strain. It is on record that an Admiral, on seeing one of his officers ' snatching a lean ' against a stanchion, leant behind him and told him to relax saying, ' It's all right, I've got the strain '. The sarcasm is frequently used in naval barracks when a rating is seen to be taking it a little too easy.

Immediate Reserve. The Royal Fleet Reserve, which can be recalled to the Navy without the formality of a Royal Proclamation. R.F.R.s are men who have done their ' twelve ' and receive a ' retainer ' from the Admiralty; they do a week's or a fortnight's training a year. When called up for service in an emergency they are summoned by telegram. (A notable technicality.)

Imshi! Clear off! Scram! (Lower-deck. Arabic word borrowed from the Army.)

in. Inside the Navy. ' How long have you been in, chum? ' ' You can't tell me anything about that, I'm ten years in.' Cf. OUTSIDE. (Lower-deck.)

In-and-Out Club. The Navy and Army Club in London, so named because of the *in* and *out* signs on the pillars in the forecourt.

in bad. The state of being a defaulter or of undergoing punishment.

in irons. (Of a sailing boat) unable to tack owing to being head to wind.

in soundings. Nearing the land; within the depth of the sounding lead.

in the house. Doing duty as cook of the mess. Confined to the house for the day.

in the rattle. See RATTLE.

in the stream. Lying off shore in the roadstead. Said of a ship lying at her buoy as distinct from being warped to a quay. (Colloquial.)

inboard. On board a ship, over the gangway. ' Come inboard and have a gin.' (A colloquialism verging on jargon.)

inboard, I'm. See SOT YOU, JACK, I'M INBOARD.

Incubator, the. The training establishment, H.M.S. *King Alfred*, at Hove, Sussex, where hundreds of R.N.V.R. officers were given courses of instruction during the 1939–45 War. The establishment ' paid off ' at the end of the war, but it retains the name; the King Alfred restaurant is very popular with holiday-makers and is often revisited by old ' K.A.'s; cf. K.A.

indiarubber man. The Physical Training Officer. He of india-rubber flexibility. Cf. BUNJE.

inky-fingers. A term applied collectively or individually to the members of the Accountant (now Supply and Secretariat) Branch of the Royal Navy.

Inland Navy, the. British and Canadian troops using ' Ducks ' and 'Buffaloes' for fighting in the flooded areas between Nijmegen and Cleves in 1945.

inshore heroes. The crews of the small Auxiliary Patrol Vessels which ' policed ' the three-mile coastal belt in the 1939–45 War. They had a multiplicity of duties and, in bad weather, life was far from pleasant in small craft of the type used for this patrol. A good-natured rather than disparaging sobriquet: the term *hero* was used with justification.

inside-walkee. See OUTSIDE-WALKEE.

inspection fever. Tension caused by the imminence of the C.-in-C.'s inspection.

insult, the. The matelot's pay. (Lower-deck.)

interview, the. That first terrifying interview before the selection board for naval cadets. (Colloquial.)

into the fish. Into abundant shoals on the herring grounds. ' We ran into the fish off Tea Kettle Hole and we couldn't get 'em inboard fast enough.' (Fishermen's colloquialism.)

Inver Gee. Invergordon, the scene of a naval mutiny in 1931.

ipe. A rifle. From the order *Slope ipe*, all that can be understood of the strident sound that is meant to be *Slope Arms*.

Irish hurricane. A flat calm; PADDY'S HURRICANE.

Irish lantern. The moon = PADDY'S LANTERN.

Irish mail. A sack of potatoes. (Lower-deck.)

Irish man-of-war. A Thames or Medway barge.

Irish moss. The edible seaweed commonly called *Carrageen*.

Irish pennants. Untidy ropes' ends hanging from aloft = DUTCH PENNANTS.

iron duck = TIN DUCK.

Iron Man. The Gyro Pilot, an automatic steering device used in liners = METAL MIKE.

iron polisher. An engineroom artificer.

Island, the. (1) Whale Island, the Royal Naval Gunnery School at Portsmouth. (2) the Isle of Wight. (3) the Island Sailing Club, Cowes, Isle of Wight.

Island jetty. The landing jetty near the headquarters of the Island Sailing Club, Cowes, Isle of Wight.

Island of the Saints. Caldey Island near Tenby, South Wales. It has a community of Benedictine monks.

Isle of Wight parson. A shag, a species of diving bird.

Is-was. An indicator fitted to the gyro repeater in a submarine. It shows the amount of ' throw off ' on the periscope when the target is in the cross wires on the glass. If a torpedo is fired at that moment it would proceed in the direction of the target which will arrive at a set position for a direct hit—if the estimation on the ' Is-was ' has been accurate. (Submariners'.)

It isn't (or **wasn't**) **funny.** A wardroom description of feelings during, or after, an air raid or surface action. It wasn't funny in Plymouth during the 1940–41 blitz days, neither was it funny at Dunkirk, Salerno, Malta, nor at any of the landings on enemy-held territory.

It's not my end. The Navy's refusal to accept responsibility. It is not his end of the rope.

ivory. A wind-whipped sea causing white horses. (An East Anglian term.)

J

' Ja ' for ' Yes ' men, the. German or Dutch seamen. The term was current at the beginning of the century but, like many such phrases, then fell into desuetude. SQUAREHEADS seems to be the predominant nautical twentieth-century term.

Jack. The universal name for a bluejacket. Short for *Jack tar* (*pot*). At one time the sailor wore a tarred pigtail.

Jack Curlew. A whimbrel. Cf. HALF CURLEW.

Jack Dusty. A Supply rating in the Royal Navy. He usually works in the ship's stores, and it is a very dusty job. Cf. DUSTY BOY.

Jack Hern. A heron. (A longshoreman's term peculiar to the south coast of England.)

Jack in the Basket. The last ' mark ' in the river at Lymington, Hampshire, well known to yachtsmen.

Jack-me-hearty. A boisterous, devil-may-care type, a roarer-up of authority ashore, but a more reasonable type to deal with than a JACK STROP.

Jack Muck. A seaman in the Merchant Navy, one who does all the ' mucky ' work.

Jack Nasty. Any unpopular seaman. He is a ' nasty piece of work '.

Jack Shalloo. An officer whose aim is to be popular with ' the troops '. A corruption of John Chellew, a naval officer who earned himself the name ' Popularity Jack '.

Jack Strop. A truculent, trouble-making type of rating, a SEA LAWYER. See STROPPY.

Jack Strop's old woman. A mess deck know-all; one who acts like a tiresome old woman who is never wrong and backs up her arguments with an arms-akimbo truculence. A fit consort of JACK STROP.

jackass. Heavy, cumbrous type of craft seen on the New-foundland Banks.

jackdaw. To purloin paint or any material from dockyard authorities. To ' scrounge '. From the jackdaw's acquisitiveness.

Jacker. All Cornishmen are so nicknamed on the lower-deck. From JAGO.

jackers. Boys undergoing training in Boys' Establishments or training ships.

jacks. Short for *jackdaw*. (Cornish fishermen's.)

Jack's delight. A ' lady of easy virtue ' in a dockyard port.

Jacky. Admiral Sir John (' Sack the lot ') Fisher, a firebrand who walked out of the Admiralty Board Room because Their Lordships could not see eye to eye with him on a matter of policy. He was First Sea Lord from 1904 to 1910, when he resigned. He was recalled in October 1914, finally resigning in 1915. See X-SHIP.

Jacky's Yacht. The old *Renown*, which was Admiral ' Jacky ' Fisher's flagship. From her very smart appearance. See JACKY.

Jacob. A starling. (Fishermen's.) No doubt because of their variegated Jacob's-coat breast-feathers.

Jago. A nickname for a Victualling Paymaster. (Devonport Division.) *Jago* is a common Cornish name.

Jago's. The mess in Devonport Barracks, named after the officer who introduced the better messing conditions therein.

jam. To stop, cancel or otherwise impede progress. Leave can be ' jammed ' at the last moment. Probably from the jamming of wireless signals.

jam bo'sun. A victualling warrant officer.

Jam Jug, the. The Russian warship *Zhemtchug*. A lower-deck ' Hobson-Jobson ' nickname. (1914–18.)

Janc, the. An initials-formed name for the Junior Army and Navy Club.

Jane. The current edition of *Jane's Fighting Ships*, a book of reference on the world's navies with photographs, details, etc., and published periodically by Messrs. Sampson Low, Marston & Co., Ltd.

Jane Shore. The same as FANNY ADAMS or HARRIET LANE. She is immortalized in Nicholas Rowe's tragedy, *Jane Shore*, 1714.

jankers. Punishment of any kind. A term borrowed from the Army, which took it from the underworld, which thus corrupted *janglers*—in reference to the jangling of fetters and chains in prisons.

Jaunty. A Master-at-Arms, a ship's policeman. He is to the Navy what a Chief Constable is to the Police Force. (See CRUSHERS.) Probably from *gendarme*.

jawing tackle. The tongue. (Lower-deck.)

jean. The blue jean collar with its three rows of white tape worn by ' men dressed as seamen '.

Jellicoe Express, the. The night train from King's Cross to Thurso with officers and men drafted, or returning, to the Fleet at Scapa Flow. The term was born in the 1914–18 War and revived in 1939, when this famous train started to run again. A term that honours Admiral of the Fleet (later Earl) Jellicoe (1859–1935).

Jellybelly. The nickname of a naval tailor in Hong Kong who used to make a suit for an officer within twenty-four hours of the order.

Jenny Spinner. A cockroach. (Lower-deck and Merchant Navy.) By personification.

Jenny Wren. (Usually shortened to *Jenny*) a rating member of the Women's Royal Naval Service (' Wrens ') in the 1939–45 War. Cf. JILL TAR.

Jerry. A German aircraft or the Germans collectively. ' You New Entries had better find where the shelters are in case Jerry comes over to-night.' Originally *Gerry*: from *Ger*man.

Jew's harp. A shackle that joins a cable to the anchor. Shaped like the musical instrument so named.

jewer. One who runs a:

jewing firm. A ship's tailoring firm run by the men. It repairs or makes clothes. Any man who owns a ' donkey ' or sewing machine is always asked to start a jewing firm and there are usually a couple of ' sew-sew ' boys who join him. Like all ship's ' firms ', jewing firms are very cheap and popular.

jigamaree. Anything new-fangled. (Lower-deck.) A re-shaping of that linguistically ubiquitous term, *jigger*; influenced by *thingummy*.

Jill tar. A Wren rating. A term that was never popular and died almost at birth. A too obvious pun on *Jack tar*.

Jimmy, or **Jimmy the One.** The First Lieutenant. He runs the hands, arranges the working parties, etc. Cf. NUMBER ONE and ONE.

Jimmy Bungs. A cooper rating who is responsible for the drawing of the bungs of rum casks, making and mending barrels, etc. The rate is now practically extinct in the Royal Navy, although there are plenty of coopers engaged in the fisheries.

Jimmy Bunts. A signalman. An obsolete term, superseded by the shortened form, BUNTS.

Jimmy Ducks. A ship's poulterer. Like the two preceding terms, a personification.

job number. A shipbuilding term for a naval vessel in the process of being built. The vessel remains *Job Number* — until she is launched and commissioned.

jobation. A BOTTLE couched in solemn and lengthy terms. From *Job* of the Bible, perhaps with a pun on *jaw*, for *jawbation* is a folk-etymological variant.

jobber. A Thames waterman in irregular employment; he sometimes ships on board a barge when an extra hand is required.

jobble. Any ' confused ' sea that causes a ship to pitch. (Cf. POPPLE and LOP.) From the Irish and Lincolnshire dialectal *jobble*, restlessness, uneasiness, tremulousness; ultimately echoic.

Jock. The generic name for all Scotsmen in the Navy or elsewhere. Scottish form of *Jack*: cf. *John Bull*, a typical Englishman.

Joey Major. A Major of the Royal Marines.

Joey, the. A Royal Marine. (Cf. JOLLIES, ROYAL, LEATHERNECKS, etc.) Perhaps from JOLLIES.

John and Joan. A herring that contains one hard and one soft roe. (Driftermen's.)

John Cocking. A Cornish coast name for the cormorant or shag. Cf. ISLE OF WIGHT PARSON.

Johnny Armstrong. Any hard work that involves pulling or hauling—HANDRAULIC power: use of the strong right arm.

Johnny Dory. A marshmen's colloquialism for the fish *John Dory*, which personifies *dory* (or *doree*), a common food-fish. *Dory = doree = doré = poisson doré*, literally ' gilded fish '. Strictly not gilded but merely coloured yellow to olive, with a dark spot on each side.

Johnny Newcome. A green hand; a new-comer. (Merchant Navy.)

joiners. Ships that join a convoy *en route*; for example, from the Tyne or Humber.

Jollies. The Corps of Royal Marines. ' Taken from the nickname of the City Trained Bands ' (Frank Bowen, *Sea Slang*, 1925): perhaps *les Jolis*, the *Jolis*, the handsome fellows, *the Jollies*.

jolly boat, take the. To break out of ship, to go on leave without permission.

Jolly Roger, the. The pirate's flag depicting a white skull and crossed bones on a black background.

Jonas. A lower-deck variant of *Jonah*, a man associated with bad luck. ' We don't want that ruddy Jonas with us.'

jonnick. Correct in procedure; according to naval etiquette; the right ' form '. Adoption of a dialectal word.

Jonty. Another shape of JAUNTY.

Jordan Queen, the. An improvised armoured train run by the Navy during the Palestine ' trouble ' in 1935. The ' Queen ' operated on the Haifa-Samakh line and was in action several times.

Jose. The name for every Maltese rating in the Royal Navy; or a Maltese ashore. *Jose* is a very common Maltese front-name. Also *Malts*.

Josher. A canal boat owned by the firm of Fellows, Morton and Clayton, Ltd. The founder's name was Joshua Fellows.

joss. A Chinese household god. Used slangily in the Navy thus: 'It was pure bad joss his being scuppered. If he'd been on the upper deck he'd have got away with it.' The word *joss* is a Pidgin English form of the Portuguese *deos* (Latin *deus*), a god.

joss-house. A temple or church. (China-side.)

joss-house man. A parson. (China-side.) See JOSS and JOSS-HOUSE.

joss-man. (1) A measure of Plymouth gin. From the picture of the monk on the bottle label. All holy men are *joss-men* to the Chinese. A naval officer will frequently ask the mess steward for a 'double joss-man'. (2) The Master-at-Arms. (Lower-deck.) Cf. JAUNTY.

joss-piece. A mascot. (R.N.) See JOSS.

jowder. A Cornish coast term for a man who hawks his catch of fish in the outlying districts. In Devon a *jowd* is a jellyfish, so the Cornish term may be jocular.

Judy. A policewoman. Perhaps from *Punch and Judy*.

juicey. A telegraphist. From the electricians' slang term, *juice*, electricity.

Jumbo. A large haddock, an 'elephant' of the species. (Trawler-men's.)

jump off the dock. To get married. To leap into deep water. (Lower-deck.)

jump the ship. To desert her. Cf. RUN.

Jumper. The traditional nickname for Collins.

Junior Nelson. A Lieutenant-Commander, R.N. (Lower-deck ironic.)

junket bo'sun. A ship's steward; a wardroom 'flunkey'. He carries junket to the officers.

just awash. Having a hangover from the binge of the night before. (Submariners'.)

just made. Newly promoted.

Just Party, the. Those men who are always 'just about' to do this or that but never actually do anything. The skulkers of the lower-deck.

jute-box. A gramophone, or any mechanical musical instrument. (Lower-deck.) Probably a corruption of the American *juke-box*.

K

K.A. Short for H.M.S. *King Alfred*, the training establishment for embryo R.N.V.R. officers. ' Did you go through K.A., or were you pre-war V.R.? '

K.R.s. See NAVAL BIBLE.

kagg. To argue; to go into conference (e.g. on mess matters or sports fixtures). Hence (n.) a Service argument; a noisy all-talk-at-once discussion. (From the long-established civilian slang *kagg* or *cag(g)*, ' to anger, irritate, render sulky ', itself probably echoic.)

Kaiser ships. The *liberty ships* constructed during the 1939–45 War by Henry J. Kaiser. They were built in one piece and designed for utility, not beauty.

K-block. Sick Quarters for nerve cases in a naval hospital.

kedge off. To pull a boat off the mud by hauling on a kedge anchor. A favourite pastime of estuary yachtsmen.

keep a weather-eye lifting. To be circumspect, to keep an eye on authority, especially when nearing promotion. To be observant (in a general sense). (Ward-room.)

Keep it on the deck! Naval football supporters' cry when the ball comes too often into ' touch '. Cf. :

Keep it on the island! ' Keep the ball in play! ' When football matches were played on Whale Island, Portsmouth, the ball occasionally went into the sea when it found ' touch '.

Keppel's Nob, stay at. To be ' high hat ', snobbish. A pun on Keppel's *Head* Hotel, Portsmouth. Only ' the best people ' (the NUT) stay there. Cf. also MA SCULLARD'S.

kettles. (1) A ship's boilers. By humorous meiosis. (2) Steam ships generally. A name bestowed originally by sailing-ship sailors.

key of the starboard (port) watch, the. Like the GALLEY DOWN-HAUL, this is a traditional ' catch ' for a young apprentice in the Merchant Navy. He may discover the *long stand*, but never this key.

K.G. Five (written *K.G.5*). H.M.S. *King George the Fifth*. (General naval slang.)

Khaki Marines. The Royal Marine Commandos. They wear khaki uniforms. Cf. BLUE MARINES and RED MARINES.

kicking strap. A brail used on a Thames barge to secure the spritsail and prevent its creeking during the night. It stops the sail from ' kicking '. (From the *kicking strap* attached to obstreperous horses and cows.)

kill. The sinking of an enemy ship or destruction of an enemy aircraft.

killick. An anchor (old naval term); hence a Leading Hand, who wears the anchor as symbol of his ' rate '. From the Erse *killech*, a wooden anchor? Cf. UP-KILLICK.

King, the. The drinking of His Majesty's health at dinner in a naval wardroom. ' The King, God bless him! ' The toast is drunk seated in the Royal Navy.

king crab. A species of shallow-water crab that has the outline of the Royal Crown on its back. Inedible, but good for bait.

King of the Sea, the. The herring, which roams at will: cf. ATLANTIC RANGERS.

King's Bencher. A sea lawyer. (Old Navy term.) In reference to the *King's Bench* Division of the High Court of Justice.

King's hard bargain. A BIRD; a naval nuisance. A habitual leave-breaker and skulker. One whom the Service could well do without.

King's Parade, the. The quarter-deck. (Old Navy term.)

King's pardon, the. The pardon granted to all peace-time deserters from the Royal Navy if they give themselves up in a national emergency or on the declaration of war. An announcement reading thus: ' His Majesty the King has been graciously pleased to approve of pardons being granted to all deserters from the Royal Navy and Marines who surrender themselves forthwith ' appears in all the principal newspapers.

kipper. A torpedo. (Submariners' term.) Cf. FISH, MINNOW and MOULDY.

kipper kites. A 1939–45 term for those aircraft of the R.A.F. Coastal Command which undertook the protection of the East Anglian fishing fleet. They looked after the ' kipper ' boats.

kippers, a pair of. To *get a pair of kippers* is to receive PENNANTS from a Flagship for some such offence as bad station-keeping. Pennants are hoisted in pairs denoting a ship's code number. ' Captain " D " gave her three pairs of kippers in one day.'

kiss the gunner's daughter. To receive corporal punishment while bending over the breech of a gun.

kitty. A kittiwake gull. (Wildfowlers'.)

Kitty Witch. A crab. (East coast term.) There is—or was—a Kitty Witch's Row in Great Yarmouth—a *crab-seller's* row?

Klondike. To ship fresh herrings to foreign countries.

knacker's yard, the. A ship-breaking yard attached to a naval depot. See ROTTEN ROW.

knitting. (1) A girl friend; one's girl friends. (Lower Deck.) (2) A minesweeper's gear. ' Don't get too close to her, she has her knitting out.'

knittles. The reef points on a sail.

Knock, the. Kentish Knock, in the Thames Estuary. (Colloquial.)

knock-knock. An acoustic mine. Cf. CAUSTIC.

know the ropes. To know one's way about a ship or be master of one's trade. Literally, to have a knowledge of the ship's rigging. A relic of the ' masts and yards ' era.

Knuts, the. Officer members of the Dover Patrol in the 1914–18 War. A (*k*)*nut* was one who prided himself on his smartness of appearance. The term arose from the music-hall song of the period, ' I'm Gilbert the filbert, the King of the Nuts '.

kye. Navy cocoa, which used to be issued in slabs. (See BUG JUICE.) A perversion of *cocoa* itself.

L

L's, the four. Lead, log, latitude and look-out: the naval ' safety first ' code.

L.D.A. The ' lower-deck attitude ' possessed by the non-ambitious. Cf. O.L.Q.S.

lace. The froth on a rough sea which, in appearance, resembles lace.

laddering. In gunnery, a method of firing with an increase of range until the target is crossed, then a decrease until the shells fall short of it. This method is used when the target is zig-zagging to evade hits.

lady's ladder. Ratlines that are shrouded so close together that a woman could climb them with ease.

lagger. One of the men who pilot canal barges through tunnels. They lie on their backs and propel the barge by working their feet on the head of the tunnel arch. (Probably an ironically humorous reference to *lugger* = luggard = lazy fellow.)

lairy. Smartly turned out and sophisticated; the complete ' blood '. (From the training ship *Conway*.) Cognate with the Cockney *leary*, ' smart; stylish; showy '—itself from the at first underworld sense, ' alert '.

lammy. A duffel coat. A cowled overcoat made of lamb's wool and worn by men in severe weather.

lammy suit. A complete suit of duffel issued to officers and men serving in torpedo boats at the beginning of the century. These craft had little freeboard and were extremely wet in a seaway; there was hardly any protection on the upper deck.

lamp-post. A lightship or light-buoy, the responsibility of the Brethren of Trinity House.

lamp-post navigation. Proceeding from buoy to buoy on a very dark night. (The reference is to *light* buoys.) From:

Lamps or **Lampy.** The ship's lamp trimmer. (Merchant Navy.) Also known as a *bati-wallah*, *bati* being a Hindustani word for ' light '.

Land of Hells, Bells and Smells, the. The Navy's name for Malta. (Cf. BATH BRICK.) In its terminologies, the Navy occasionally exaggerates.

landlubber. The seaman's name for a SHORE-LOAFER.

land-swab. A useless hand on board a merchant ship. A LAND-LUBBER who has shipped on board in return for food and drink but is quite incompetent as a seaman.

lanyard knot, tough as a. Extremely tough. Applied to Navy beef or men. A lanyard knot is designed to prevent unreeving.

lash-out. A sudden burst of energy from a working party on the approach of the First Lieutenant or any other officer.

lash up. To stand treat. Literally, to lash up someone else's hammock; hence, to grant any favour to a messmate. ' If you come ashore to-night, I'll lash you up to a couple of pints.'

lash-up. General confusion caused by a misunderstood order or a bungled job of work. Cf. the Royal Navy's lower-deck term, COCK-UP.

last bucket, the. *I didn't come up in the last bucket* is a lower-deck catch-phrase equivalent to the civilian's ' Do you see any green in my eye? ' It is a challenge to a person who attempts to impose on or make a fool of one. (The speaker is far from being WET.)

last stitch, the. A man buried at sea is sewn into his hammock, and the rule is that the sailmaker should put the last stitch through the dead man's nose to ' make assurance doubly sure '.

late night final. The last drink before the wardroom bar closes. (With reference to evening newspapers.)

laugh like a Chief Stoker. To laugh with a loud cackle like that of a seagull; the seagull is said to be the embodiment of a Chief Stoker. To emit a raucous belly-laugh of appreciation.

laugh like a drain. To chortle; chuckle. (Wardroom.) ' I had to keep a straight face but inwardly I was laughing like a drain.'

lavatory brushes. The cut of beard popular with submarine personnel. (Submariners': 1939–45 War.)

lay. To come, go or put, as in ' Lay aft the duty watch '; ' Lay me across her bows '.

lay Lords. The Civil Lords of the Admiralty.

lay on. To arrange (a programme), to organize (something). One *lays on* a party. (Either from the gunnery sense of laying on a target or from plumbing—laying on water, gas, etc.)

lay up. A Yorkshire beach-combing term. Any firewood found is *laid-up* above the tide-line and a stone placed upon it; etiquette renders it sacrosanct until the *layer-up* collects it at his convenience.

layings. Cultch beds for oyster breeding.

lazy. (Of a person or object) serving no useful purpose. A *lazy guy* or *lazy painter* is a rope that bears no strain but is there simply to use if needed; usually it is idle, hence the term.

leading strings. A rudder's yoke lines.

leaf. The matelot's pronunciation of *leave*. ' It's time we had a drop o' leaf.' It may have arisen from the *leaf* that was torn out of the railway warrant book or leave-pass book; the rating proceeds *on leaf*, i.e. the railway warrant. More probably, however, *leaf* comes from the widespread adoption of *leaf*, the Essex dialectal form of *leave*.

Leather-necks. Royal Marines. (See BOOT-NECKS.) They're tough.

leave the sea and go into steam. To leave the sailing ship for a steamer. Coined during the transition period during the latter part of the last century.

ledger bo'sun. A Warrant Writer, R.N., in charge of the ship's ledgers and pay accounts.

lee boards. Side-whiskers. Lee boards are placed on the hulls of shallow-draught vessels, especially Thames barges and Dutch eel-schuytes, galliots and barge-yachts. When these craft reach deep water they drop their lee boards, which enable them to sail closer to the wind by reason of the increased resistance under the water. Cf. the shore synonym, *side boards*.

lee line. See WEATHER LINE.

leeward, get to. To get or be on the wrong side of someone. To incur the displeasure of Authority.

143

leeward, go to. To place oneself in a disadvantageous position. TO CARRY THE CAN back for someone.

leeway, give. To allow freedom of speech or movement to a person.

left hanging Judas. Left in the lurch, let down by a girl friend. Specifically, of a rope hanging over the side of a ship. (Lower-deck.)

leg. A board or tack in the course of a sailing vessel.

legging. The work done by a LAGGER.

legs of, have the. (Of a ship) to outdistance another. ' She had the legs of us and we lost the range.'

lengthman. A man in charge of a stretch of canal water. (Colloquial.)

lent, be. (This term, though strictly not slang, is included for the enlightenment of the layman.) An officer or rating may be sent to a ship as ' additional ' for duty or a course of instruction, and when his course of duty is ended he will return to his own ship or port depot. He is said to be *lent* because he has not been transferred to the temporary ship's ledger for payment. Unless he is appointed permanently, or for a FULL DUE as they say in the Navy, he is merely *lent* and in the column of his ship's ledger will be found the letter ' L ' against his name. This does not affect his pay but is simply an indication that he is being victualled out of his ship. In Accountant parlance, he is *checked* as *lent*.

let out a reef. To unbutton a jacket after a hearty meal. The term had become definitely obsolete by 1948.

Let's call it eight bells! A naval officer's phrase when drinking earlier than the conventional time: mid-day, when ' the sun is over the foreyard '.

liberty boat. A boat taking LIBERTY MEN ashore; a leave boat. In shore establishments the buses from barracks to a town are also known as *liberty boats*, so sensitive is the Navy to ' atmosphere '. See:

liberty men. Those proceeding on leave either for the evening or the week-end. *Furlough* is a term not used in the Royal Navy.

lice. L.C.I.s, i.e. Landing Craft (Infantry), which were used for beaching troops in all the important Allied landings on enemy territory in the 1939–45 War.

lid. A submarine hatch.

lie like a flat fish. To romance in a big way. To emulate TOM PEPPER. (Lower-deck.)

lie on the knuckle. (Of a ship) to wait at the harbour mouth for a tug.

lifeboat V.C., the. Coxswain Blogg of Cromer, who served fifty-three years with the Lifeboat Service and helped to save 873 lives. He was particularly busy in the 1939–45 War, for Cromer was near the most dangerous part of E-BOAT ALLEY.

lighters. Lightly wetting the lips in a pal's tot of rum. (Lower-deck.) Cf. SIPPERS, GULPERS and GROUNDERS.

lighthouse. The similarly-shaped pepper pot. (Lower-deck.)

lighthouses. Clyde Shipping Company vessels, which used to have very high funnels.

lightning conductors. The broad gold stripes on the trousers of naval officer's full dress.

lily. A floating runway for aircraft used by the Fleet Air Arm.

Lime Tank, the. The Royal Naval Hospital, Haslar, Hants.

Limejuicer. See:

Limey. A British seaman. (American term.) Short for *Lime-juicer*: from the old nautical practice of drinking much lime-water, as a preventive against scurvy.

line, up the. See UP THE LINE.

line the pencil. To make a bee-line for anywhere, especially the beach. The phrase was born when Admiral Sir Percy (Guns-before-ceremony) Scott introduced his DOTTER device.

lined-up. Paraded in front of the Commander as a defaulter. Cf. TROOPED.

liner. An inshore fishing boat—coble, smack, etc.—employed in long-lining.

links of love. A bunch of sausages. (Lower-deck.) Cf. BAGS OF MYSTERY and MYSTERY TORPEDOES.

listening trawler. An Admiralty trawler used for anti-submarine detection. She is fitted with Asdic gear and ' strange devices '. In the early months of the 1939–45 War many of these trawlers were not armed but merely passed on information to ships which were equipped for dealing with U-boats.

little Benjamin, our Ruler. The cane kept by the Sub-Lieutenant in charge of the gunroom for the preservation of order.

little stink. A small motor boat. (The training ship *Conway*.)

Live Bait, the. The Harwich Cruiser Force in the 1914–18 War, which drew the enemy battleships.

liver money. A share paid to the crews of trawlers from the money taken for fish liver, which is used for the manufacture of cod-liver oil.

Liverpool weather. Exceptionally bad or ' dirty ' weather. (Merchant Navy.)

Lizzy. The Cunard White Star liner, *Queen Elizabeth*. (Merchant Navy.)

loader. A red-gilled herring, believed by driftermen to be lucky. It loads one's craft with good luck.

loaf. To idle, DODGE POMPEY, or be otherwise slack. Men's belongings found *loafing* on the mess deck are impounded by the Petty Officers and placed in the SCRAN-BAG; cf. also LAZY, SOFT NUMBER and SCULL.

loafing number. A nice, soft job in a shore base—the smaller the base, the better. (Lower-deck.)

lobbo! A training-ship synonym of the Public School *Cave! Lobbo! crusher*—' Beware of the ship's policeman.' (Perhaps on the analogy of the Army's *dekko!* (more usually, *take a dekko!*), ' Look! ')

loblolly boy. A Merchant Navy steward. He serves *loblolly* or porridge. Cf. LOLLY-BANGER.

lobster pot. The Oerlikon gun platform in a submarine. From its appearance.

lobster soldier. A Royal Marine Light Infantryman. Rather because of his (former) red tunic than because of his weathered complexion?

locked doors. A term descriptive of a trawling mishap when the otter-boards lock and thus cause much inconvenience and profanity. (Trawlermen's.)

loco. 'Daft', lunatic. (Merchant Navy.) Synonymous with the Royal Navy's BATCHY. Adopted from the U.S.A., it is simply the Spanish *loco*, mad.

loco da poco. A fanciful elaboration of LOCO.

Lodge and Comp. Lodging and Provision (previously Lodging and Compensation) Allowance given to officers and men in a shore base where no Service accommodation is provided. See COMPO.

Lofty. The inevitable name for anyone over six feet high.

Log, a. A 'programme' or account of how an afternoon of energetic exercise is spent at the Royal Naval College, Dartmouth. A book is kept in each dormitory and everyone puts down what he did during the afternoon. Some forms of energy constitute only 'half a log' and, therefore, the other half must be made up.

logie. Calm and still. (Devon fishermen's.) Provincial slang, *logie* or *logy* is a variant of dialectal *loggy*, 'like a log'—hence, 'dull, slow-moving'.

Logs, the. The timber pond in Portsmouth dockyard.

lolly-banger. A ship's cook. (Merchant Navy.) A maker of *loblolly*; cf. LOBLOLLY BOY.

London, the. The Royal London Yacht Club, Cowes, Isle of Wight.

Loneliness of High Command, the. A phrase descriptive of a captain's life on board. He dines alone and is not a member of the wardroom except by courtesy of his officers.

long book, the. A book issued to naval cadets in a training cruiser. It is about three feet long and contains skeleton plans of the ship's decks and compartments, etc., the cadet being responsible for completing the picture to scale.

long-distance men. Those who, living a long distance from their naval port, are allowed extra time for travelling when on leave. (Colloquial.)

147

long glass. A telescope. (Merchant Navy.)

long-haired chum. A girl friend (until the introduction of shingling). Cf. PARTY and DOBASH.

long hundred. In the herring fishery, 132 fish; elsewhere, 120. (A technicality.)

long-jawed. Worn-out cordage so stretched and untwisted that it coils both ways. Cf. MAGGED.

long leave. The Navy's annual leave, as distinct from week-end and evening shore leave.

long-legged. (Of a ship) drawing a lot of water.

long ship. An Old Navy expression meaning that there is a long interval between the first drink and the OTHER HALF. (i.e. a long way from the wardroom to the pantry.)

longshore butcher. A coastguard.

long tripper. A trawler which fishes off Iceland, the Faroes and Shetlands, a ' long trip ' from its home port. Cf. SCRATCHER.

long week-end, the. The period between the 1914–18 and 1939–45 Wars. A ' breathing-space '.

look out for. To relieve (a pal during his watch). ' Look out for me for ten minutes, there's a good fellow.'

look-see. A check-up or look round; a cursory inspection. Pidgin-English.

look-stick. A LONG GLASS or telescope; a ' bring-'em-near '.

Loony-Bin. The Royal Naval Auxiliary Hospital, Barrow Gurney, near Bristol. It was originally built as a mental asylum and requisitioned by the Admiralty in the 1939–45 War.

Lootenant. The lower-deck pronunciation of *Lieutenant.*

lop. A ' bit of a sea ', a JOBBLE; choppiness caused by tide-rips or a CAPFUL OF WIND.

lop-eared. A term of abuse on the lower-deck. ' Get out of the way, you lop-eared ullage! '; ' Of all the lop-eared, lubberly sons of sin, you're the perishing limit.'

Lord's Own, the. H.M.S. *Vengeance.* (' Vengeance is Mine, saith the Lord.')

148

lorker. A seagull. An East Anglian term, probably a corruption of *Glaucus* (*gull*).

lose the bottom. (Of a leadsman ' in the chains ') to be unable to make contact with the bed of the ocean.

lose the number of one's mess. To ' shuffle off this mortal coil '; to be either killed or drowned at sea.

Lossie. A steam drifter registered at Lossiemouth.

Lot's wife. Salt. (Lower-deck.) From the Biblical story; cf. the low civilian simile, *as salt as Lot's wife's backbone*.

Lover's Leap. The first train from Waterloo to Portsmouth in the morning. (Wardroom.)

loves. Wooden splines in a herring-curing loft on which the fish are hung to dry. The term is probably a corruption of *louvre*, a ventilating shaft.

Lower-deck, the. Generic term for all non-commissioned officers and men in the Navy. ' It's all right for officers but not so good for the lower-deck.' Cf. TROOPS and WARDROOM.

lower-deck wireless. Messages from signalman to signalman made in semaphore, using the wrists only, with hands substituted for flags. A strictly unofficial procedure.

Lowerdeckese. The slang of the mess-decks and training establishments, i.e. of naval ratings.

Lowestiff. The Scottish herring driftermen's form of *Lowestoft*.

lubberly. Unseamanlike or slovenly. From nautical *lubber*, an inexperienced or clumsy seaman—a special application of *lubber*, a big, clumsy man, a lout, itself cognate with the synonymous *looby*, a term cognate with—perhaps derived from—*lob*, a dull, heavy person, something heavy and thick; itself from, or at least akin to, Frisian *lob* or *lobbe*, a short, thick, pendent lump or mass. (*Webster's New International Dictionary*.)

lubber's hole, the. The square opening in the mainmast of a sailing ship through which the ' funks ' crawled, instead of climbing over the futtock shrouds to square the yard-arms. Only lubbers would go through the hole.

luffed in. Detailed for (an unpleasant job); LURKED. ' I got luffed in for the side party yesterday, and was I chokker? ' (Lower-deck.)

lug. The shoulder of a salmon. (Almost a technicality; cf. *lug*, now Scottish and dialectal for ' ear '.)

lump. A heavy lighter or harbour punt used for carrying heavy gear such as anchors, anchor cables and buoys. (Pejorative: they're lumpish craft.)

Lundy Island. Meat baked with potatoes round it. (Cf. *schooner on the rocks*.) Precipitous Lundy Island, which has two lighthouses, stands in the mouth of the Bristol Channel.

lurked. Chosen for an unpopular job of work with no means of getting out of it.

lush. Short for *luscious*. Infinitely desirable, a *lush thrush* being a very pretty girl. This adjective is, in the Navy, as popular as SMASHING, which took hold of the Services in 1939–45.

lush up. A variant of LASH UP.

luverly grub. A large, satisfying meal. (Lower-deck.) Cf. BIG EATS.

M

Mac, the. H.M.S. *Maguire*, which trained cadets in sail.

Macaronies, the. Italians generally. (Lower-deck.) Cf. EYE-TIES. From their addiction to macaroni.

machiowler. A jelly fish. (A Cornish vernacular term, of obscure origin.)

Mad House, the. The Admiralty. Cf. WESTMINSTER PALACE OF VARIETIES.

maddie. A mussel. (Fishermen's.)

magged. (Of cordage) worn or stretched. Cf. LONG-JAWED.

maggie. A magnetic mine. (Lower-deck.) Cf. SAMSON.

Maggie May. An improper but amazingly popular nautical ballad. Cf. ESKIMO NELL.

Maggie Miller. Washing clothes by the simple method of towing them over the stern when the ship is under way. (Lower-deck.) Was Maggie any relation of ANDREW MILLER?

magpies = NUMBER SEVENS, HALF WHITES.

main-drain rangers. Fish of an indeterminate species served at dinner in the wardroom. A pejorative term, formed on the analogy of ATLANTIC RANGERS.

make. To promote: ' He's just been made a killick.' (Lower-deck.)

Make an evolution of it! An exhortation to the hands to get on with a job. In the naval sense an evolution is a smart and seamanlike piece of drill or work. On the other hand, if an officer says, ' All right, don't make an evolution of it,' he means that the job can be done in one's own time—that there is no urgency.

make and mend. A half-holiday in the Navy, given originally for the purpose of making and mending clothing.

make-and-mend pudding. A baked jam roll, a heavy helping of which would induce sleep on a sailor's half-holiday or ' make and mend '. See ZIZZ PUDDING, and cf. STEERAGE HAMMOCK.

make one's number. To report for duty or introduce oneself to a new mess. From H.M. Ships hoisting their pennant numbers when approaching harbour.

makee learn. A naval novice, a learner. (China-side influence.)

Mallaby-Deeley's. Plain clothes; after the very elegant Sir Harry Mallaby-Deeley (1863–1937), a Member of Parliament from 1910 to 1922. (Wardroom.) Cf. DOG ROBBERS.

Maltese fashion. (Of boats) propelled with the rowers facing forward instead of sitting back to bows in the orthodox way.

Maltese lace. The frayed edges of well-worn bell-bottoms; frayed shirt-cuffs, etc.

Maltese shuffle. A shambling gait that is supposed to pass for a march. ' Smartly now, no Maltese shuffling! ' (Lower-deck.)

Mammoth. GINORMOUS. (Wardroom). Compare the contemporary journalistic abuse of *giant* as an adjective.

manany. One who procrastinates; putting off until *tomorrow* (Spanish, *mañana*) what he ought to do today. (Merchant Navy.)

man o' fight. A variant of *man o' war*. (Lower-deck.)

march past, the. Roast beef served with vegetables. (Lower-deck.) Spectacular and inspiriting.

Maren. A conflation of *Marine Wren*: one employed in the Royal Marine Barracks in much the same duties as the Wrens in naval shore establishments. In place of the H.M.S. ' tally ' on her cap she wears the globe and laurel of the Royal Marines. Cf. HANNAH and MARINETTE.

Margaret Hakon. A mistake. ' He made a proper Margaret Hakon of the job.' But who was Margaret Hakon? Some East Anglian girl who had herself made a mistake would seem to be an obvious guess, for the term is used on the East Anglian coast, and occurred as recently as 1947 in George Goldsmith Carter's fine novel, *The Smacksmen*.

marine casualty. Shipwreck or damage sustained by a vessel from ' natural causes ' rather than enemy action. If a ship runs aground in a fog she would be classed as a *marine casualty*. If she were run ashore by enemy craft that would be *enemy action*. A technicality of interest to landsmen.

marine officer. An empty bottle. See DEAD MARINE.

Marinette. A Marine Wren. Cf. HANNAH and MAREN.

Maritimes. Gunners of the Royal Artillery serving in *D*efensively *E*quipped *M*erchant *S*hips; also known as DEMS GUNNERS.

market ranger. A fish-wharf thief; a ' spiv ' of the fisheries.

marks of the beast. The patches worn on the collar of a Midshipman's uniform. R.N. Midshipmen wear white ones; R.N.R., royal blue; and R.N.V.R., maroon. See *Revelation*, xvi. 2.

marline-spike seamanship. Instruction in the art of splicing, knotting, etc.

marmalade boat. A Thames sewage-barge. (Bargemen's.) Ironic. Compare the Canadian soldiers' (1914–18) *honey-bucket*, a latrine bucket.

married man's trade, the. Ships in the Port Nolloth copper-ore trade, so called because the crews were seldom able to get ashore and spend money. (William McFee, *In the First Watch*, 1947.)

masby. A *M*otor-*A*nti-*S*ubmarine *B*oat, formed from the initials, with a ' y ' added for euphony.

Ma Scullard's. The NUT, after its one-time proprietress.

maskee. ' It doesn't matter', ' It is of no account '. Pidgin-English. Used on informal occasions for the more Service-sounding *Belay!* ' You can maskee that, Bo'sun, we shall not need it after all.' Skeat has most ingeniously derived it from Portuguese *mas que*; but the Spanish *mas que* is equally probable. Most probable, however, is the Mexican Spanish *masque*, ' it doesn't matter '.

Master. Short for *Master-at-Arms*, it is the formal mode of address: ' Master! have you got the list of the draft that came this morning? ' Cf. JAUNTY.

mate of the beer cask. A junior Midshipman who is told off to see that the gunroom beer barrel is properly stowed and not leaking.

matelot. The self-adopted nickname for all bluejackets. A typical SOD'S OPERA story begins: ' 'Ere, did you ever 'ear that yarn about the matelot wot . . .?' Pronounced *matlo*, it is French for ' sailor '.

maternity home, the. Nickname of the Liverpool Naval Head-quarters in the 1939–45 War. From the storks or *livers* on the roof of the Liver Building. Cf. SALIVA, H.M.S.

Matty Walker. The Matthew Walker ' knot ' used for the shroud lanyards. The answer to the old Navy riddle, ' What is forrard on the starboard side, aft on the port side, and inside on both sides? ' Matthew Walker, the originator, lived in the eighteenth century; the earliest mention of his knot occurs in 1808.

maund. A large wicker basket used in the herring fishery. (A dialect term.)

Maunsells. ' The " forts " erected on the principal sandbanks in the Thames Estuary during the Hitler War to form an anti-aircraft/E-boat defence. They were invented and designed by G. A. Maunsell, the brilliant engineer who constructed the Storstrom Bridge in Denmark. Built in sections, the forts were towed out to their positions and sunk; they were well armed and manned by Royal Navy and Royal Marine per-sonnel.' (*Forces' Slang.*) Cf. HOLLOWAY'S UNFINISHED SYM-PHONIES.

Max. Admiral Sir Max Horton, the submariner V.C. of the 1914–18 War.

May bird. The whimbrel, which makes its appearance in Britain in the month of May.

maze. A measure of five hundred herrings. A dialectal variant of *mease* (from Old Norse *meiss*, a basket).

mazey or **mazy.** Weak or sickly, as of herring about to shoot their roes. (Common in East Anglia and chiefly applied to herring.) From *maze*, a state of bewilderment.

meal. A sand-dune or ' dene '. (Norfolk coast.) (Dialect rather than slang, but included as interesting. Cf. Icelandic *möl* and Old Norse *melr*, a sandbank, a dune.)

meal ticket. A naval officer or other ' boy friend ' who does a Wren proud when dining her ashore. ' What's he like? '— ' Well, he's a good meal ticket.' (Wrens'.)

mechanized dandruff. Head lice. (Lower-deck.)

Med, the (Wardroom); **Meddy, the** (Lower-deck). The Mediterranean.

medico. A Medical Officer. Adoption of the civilian colloquialism for a physician.

Merchant Jack. A Merchant Navy rating; a member of the Mercantile Marine or Merchant Service, now known as the Merchant Navy.

Merchant Service, the. The name by which the Merchant Navy was known until fairly recently.

merchantman. A merchant cargo-carrying ship. A RED ENSIGN SHIP. A colloquialism that has become Standard English.

Merely Fooling About. A libellous term for officers and men serving in Merchant Fleet Auxiliaries in the war of 1914–18. Recorded by William McFee in *North of Suez*, 1930. From the initials.

merry men of May, the. Currents caused by an ebb tide: tide-rips.

mess clouts. Dusters supplied to the messes in the training ship *Conway*.

mess traps. All Crown-supplied cooking utensils in a naval mess.

mess treat. A tip given by an 'Old Conway' to his former mess. It stands them a good tea.

messenger. A heaving line. Cf. MONKEY'S FIST.

messman's horror. A rating with an enormous appetite.

Metal Mike. The gyro pilot, an automatic steering device used in liners. Also known as the IRON MAN.

mewsy. Stormy. (East Anglian fishermen's.) ' That look mewsy, bor, fare to me we'll have some wind.' From the *mewsing* or screaming of the seagulls at the approach of, and during, such weather.

Mexican Pete. The lover of ESKIMO NELL.

'mick. Short for '*ammick*, the lowerdeckese for *hammock*.

Mickey Mouse. A Motor Mechanic. (Lower-deck.) From the character in Walt Disney's cartoons. Cf.:

Mickey Mouse diagrams. Charts used for plotting positions of convoys and bombarding forces during the Allied invasion of

Normandy. These charts were made hourly and there were so many that, if turned over quickly, they had a Walt Disney cartoon effect. Cf. preceding.

Middle, the. The middle watch, midnight to 4 a.m. Cf. GRAVE-YARD WATCH.

middle-watcher. A snack taken during the middle watch. See preceding.

Mids. Midshipmen. Either this term or SNOTTIES will be tolerated by the YOUNG GENTLEMEN: but never *middies*, please!

midshipman's muffin. A hard-tack biscuit soaked in water until comparatively soft, then baked in the galley. (Merchant Navy apprentices'.)

midshipman's roll. A hammock hurriedly and carelessly lashed up.

Midshipmen have guts; wardroom officers have stomachs; and Flag Officers have palates. An old naval catchphrase which survived the nineteenth century.

miker. A work-dodger, a lazy type. (Lower-deck.) From *mike*, to hang about idly; cognate with *mooch*.

milk a cow with a spanner. To open a tin of milk. (Lower-deck.)

millionaire ship, the. The Cunard White Star liner s.s. *Franconia*, used principally for taking the wealthy and leisured for world cruises. It is one of the most beautifully appointed ships afloat.

Mincing Lane. The alley-way in a ship where the Purser's staff have their being. After Mincing Lane, London.

Mind your helm! 'Look where you are going!' (Wardroom.)

mine bumpers, the = BEHEMOTHS.

mine-layers. Men who drop cigarette ends from their hammocks. If they are seen by Authority there is an explosion.

minnow. A torpedo. (Lower-deck). Cf. FISH, MOULDY, and KIPPER.

Misery, the. H.M.S. *Mersey*. (Lower-deck.)

miss stays. Literally, to fail to go about when sailing a ship's boat. Colloquially, to fail to 'register', to miss a signal, or in any way to miss the point. A relic of the sailing days in the Royal Navy.

Mist, the Isle of. The Isle of Skye, because it is frequently shrouded in mist.

Mister. The mode of address to the First Mate in the Merchant Navy.

moan. A mess-deck grumble: a *growl, bleat, drip, howl.* (General Navy slang.)

Moaning Minnie. The ululating Air Raid Warning siren used in naval ports, as elsewhere, in the 1939–45 War.

mock-turtle squadron. A fleet of dummy ships in an anchorage as decoy to enemy bombers.

moke. The mesh in a herring net. A dialectal word, cognate with *mesh* itself.

Mole, the. Zeebrugge Mole, which was stormed by a naval party under the command of Captain Carpenter, R.N., in H.M.S. *Vindictive* on Saint George's Day (April 23) 1918. Block ships were sunk in the entrance to the harbour and a storming party landed to demolish and generally ' clean up ' harbour defences. There was a gallant sacrifice of lives and many acts of individual heroism.

money for old rope. The Navy's version of *money for jam*, something cheaply and easily acquired. A ' dead-easy ' job of work: ' It's money for old rope, old boy.'

monkey. An adjective of diminution in the Navy. Cf. DICKY.

monkey and the nut. The house flag of the Cunard Steamship Company. From the monkey-like lion and nut-like globe of the flag design.

monkey boat. (1) A small boat used for ferrying about a harbour. (2) A *narrow boat* used on canals. It is longer than a barge and from seven to eight feet in beam, which allows it to pass through the narrowest channels of Britain's inland waterways.

monkey boats. Ships of the *Elder Dempster Line*; they often carry nut kernels in their cargoes.

monkey island. A ship's upper bridge. Also known as *Mount Misery*.

monkey jacket. A naval officer's ' reefer ' coat.

monkey motions. The Navy's name for Swedish drill, which became the rage just before the 1914–18 War.

monkey piss. Lime juice. (Merchant Navy.)

monkey's fist. A knot on the end of a heaving line the weight of which makes the line easier to throw. Cf. MESSENGER.

monkey's orphan. A term of abuse for a lubberly seaman. (Merchant Navy.)

Monty's Own Navy. The minesweeping craft that, based along the East African coast, kept the fairway swept for transport carrying the Eighth Army, which was commanded by Field-Marshal *Mont*gomer*y*.

moon-box. The lantern in a lightship.

moon-raker or **moonsails.** *Sky*-sails in a full-rigged ship.

more than that. A lower-deck catch-phrase implying a fabulous quantity. 'What a party! There was more wallop than that'; 'You ought to have been in Plymouth in '41, more bombs than that!'

morfy. A vehicle of hybrid design (half cart, half wagon) used in the East Anglian herring industry, especially in Great Yarmouth. A local term, probably a shortening of ' her*moph*rodite ', a solecism for *hermaphrodite*.

morning red, the. A presage of bad weather. From the weather-lore rhyme, ' Red in the morning, sailor's warning; red at night, sailor's delight '.

mother and baby. A term used by the Germans for their human torpedo.

Mother Cary's chicken. A stormy petrel, a small black and grey sea bird, the harbinger of stormy weather. (Colloquial.) *Mater cara*, the Virgin Mary.

Mother Cary's goose. A larger type of petrel than a MOTHER CARY'S CHICKEN.

Mother of the Navy, the. The philanthropist Dame Agnes E. Weston, who founded the Sailors' Homes. Cf. AGGIE'S.

mother ship. A depot ship attached to a flotilla of destroyers or submarines. She is usually a converted cruiser or merchant ship; or, as were the submarine depot ships *Maidstone* and *Forth*, she may be specially built for the job. She provides cabins, sick bay, wardrooms and messes for the crews of the vessels attached to her, workshops for carrying out minor repairs, etc.

mothers' meeting. A lecture given by the Captain for which the lower-deck has been ' cleared '.

motor mech. A motor mechanic. See MICKEY MOUSE. (Lower-deck.)

motoring. Yachting under power instead of sail. (Yachtsmen's.)

mott. A girl. (Merchant Navy.) Adopted from the underworld, the term represents a thinning of the very old underworld *mort*.

mouldy. (1) A torpedo. From dialectal *moudie* or *mouldy*, a mole. (2) (adjective), miserable, down-hearted and habitually gloomy; also a nickname in this sense. (3) A confection sold in the STODGER at the Royal Naval College, Dartmouth.

Mountbatten pink. The colour suggested by Lord Louis Mount-batten, Chief of Combined Operations, as being the most serviceable for landing-craft. It was also known as BARMAID'S BLUSH.

mouse-trap. Cheese. (Lower-deck.) See BUNG and cf. SOAP AND FLANNEL.

movies. Motor launches of the Auxiliary Patrol. (1914–18.) Because they moved quickly. The term was coined by the Canadians.

Mr Johnson. The name to which H.M. King George VI answered during his midshipman's time in H.M.S. *Collingwood*. (*The King and the Navy*, by ' Taffrail ', 1937.)

Mr Middleton's Light Horse. The flower-named corvettes. After the late Mr Middleton, the B.B.C. gardening expert, who broadcast weekly to amateur gardeners. Cf. HERBACEOUS BORDERS.

M.R.U. *much regret unable*. See N.C.D.

muck. A trawlerman's term for all inedible, unmarketable fish. Originally slang, it has become a technical classification.

Muckle Flugga Hussars. The Armed Merchant (10th) Cruiser Squadron of the Northern Patrol in the 1914–18 War. See A.M.C. Muckle Flugga is the name of a rocky, lighthouse-bearing islet in the Northern Shetlands.

mucko. A stoker. (Lower-deck.) He has a ' mucky ' job.

muckstick drill. Rifle drill in naval barracks. Muckstick is an inverted form of *musket*, a rifle.

Mud Island. Southend-on-Sea, in the Thames Estuary, the popular week-end holiday resort to which Londoners flock in thousands to disport themselves on the estuary mud. Also applied to Canvey Island, Essex.

mud-fish. Fish served at breakfast in the messroom of Osborne College. Cf. MAIN-DRAIN RANGERS.

mudhook. An anchor. Often shortened to *hook*. ' I'll be jolly glad when we drop the hook, it's been a hell of a trip.'

Mulberry. One of the two prefabricated harbours erected on the coast of Normandy when the Allied Forces invaded Europe in June 1944. So called because the operation was code-named *Mulberry*.

mule. A double-ended craft of hybrid design. As the mule is a cross between a horse and a donkey, so is this craft a cross between a coble and a keel, which may account for the term. It is in use on the Yorkshire coast.

multiform. Any unorthodox uniform—part civilian, part Service —worn by the men in minesweepers at sea. (1914–18.)

Mumble Bee. A Brixham sailing trawler. With a pun on *bumble bee*.

mundungus. Rubbish. A lower-deck corruption of the Spanish *mondongo*. It is applied to tobacco dust or any unserviceable odds and ends.

mun fish. Inedible fish used as *man*ure. (West Countrymen's.)

mungy. Food of any kind. (Lower-deck.) Either a corruption of the French *manger*, to eat, or a shortening of *mungaree* (or -*y*), a tramps' word for ' food, a meal ', derived from Italian *mangiare*, to eat. MUNGY is less used than SCRAN on the lower-deck.

muscle banging. Any kind of heavy manual work. Cf. ARM-STRONG'S PATENT.

muscle bo'sun. A physical training instructor. (Lower-deck.) Cf. INDIA-RUBBER MAN.

muslin. Sails. Also, colloquially, *canvas*. (Yachtsmen's.)

mussel duck. The scoter, a bird that thrives on mussels. (Wild-fowlers' colloquialism, verging on Standard English.)

Mutt and Jeff. The Jubilee and Coronation medals (of the 1914–18 War) worn together. From a famous pair of comic figures.

mutt house. A cadet's former Preparatory School. (Royal Naval College, Dartmouth.)

my dear. This seemingly effeminate idiom of address is peculiar to the men of Devon and ratings of the Devonport Division of the Royal Navy. ' If I have any more " lip " from you, my dear, I'll give you a clip over the 'ear 'ole.'

My Lords. The Lords Commissioners of the Admiralty. (Ward-room.)

mystery torpedoes. Sausages. (Lower-deck.) Cf. LINKS OF LOVE; BANGERS.

Mystery Towers. Concrete erections built in the Straits of Dover which were to be heavily armed and to act as anti-submarine/aircraft defences. This 1914–18 idea was improved upon in the 1939–45 War and several forts were built in the Thames Estuary and did very valuable service against E-boats and aircraft. See HOLLOWAY'S UNFINISHED SYMPHONIES.

N

N.A.A.F.I. rating. One with *no a*im, *a*mbition or *f*urther *i*nterest. A play on the initials of the *N*avy, *A*rmy and *A*ir *F*orce *I*nstitutes.

N.C.D. An informal reply to an invitation to a party when it is not possible for the invited to accept. It means ' no can do '. Acceptance is, *W.M.P.*—with much pleasure. Both replies are to a CHUMMY SHIP's signal, *R.P.C.*—request the pleasure of your company. The formal reply is M.R.U. = much regret unable.

N.O. Short for Naval Officer. (A naval colloquialism.) Cf. WREN O.

nail-sick. Said of a ship whose nails and fittings are corroded with rust.

narrow boat. A long barge-like craft used for carrying merchandise along the canals.

Narrow Seas, the. The English and Irish Channels, the seas round the coasts of Great Britain.

Narviks. A powerful class of German destroyers used in the 1939–45 War. From the name of the first of the class to be put into commission.

native. One whose home or ' other interests ' lie in his Port Depot. See:

native leave. Leave granted to a native.

Nav House. The Royal Naval School of Navigation at Portsmouth. Cf. WRECKER'S RETREAT.

Naval Bank Holiday. Coaling ship. (1914–18 War.)

Naval Bible, the. That ponderous and terrifying tome, ' King's Regulations and Admiralty Instructions ' (otherwise K.R.s), the tripper-up of the unwary.

naval warm. A naval officer's overcoat of blue fleecy material cut on the same lines as an Army officer's *British warm*.

Navalese. The idiom, slang and jargon of the Royal Navy, known only to those who are serving, or have served, under the White Ensign.

Navy, tot of. A measure of Navy rum offered to a guest by one who has BOTTLED THE TOT.

Navy House. The Sailor's Rest House in Chatham, run on the same lines as AGGIE WESTON'S, of which there is no branch at Chatham.

Navy time. Five minutes before the stipulated time for duty, or an appointment.

Navy Week. A selected full week each year, when, as on Bank Holidays, His Majesty's Ships and Dockyards are open to the public—the OWNERS of the Navy—for inspection. They are allowed on board and shows are put on for their entertainment. These weeks are valuable as an incentive to recruiting. (A colloquialism that has become Standard English.)

Navy's Fledgling, the. H.M.S. *Gosling*, a Fleet Air Arm training establishment in the 1939–45 War.

Navvies. Ships of the General Steam Navigation Company.

Navvy. The Navigating Officer. (Lower-deck.) See PILOT.

neap. Neap tides. (Colloquial.)

neaped, be. Caught in such a position off shore as to be aground on a neap tide.

neaters. Undiluted rum, or any strong drink taken *neat*—without water. (Lower-deck.)

necky. Cheeky, ' sidey '. (A *Conway* term.) Cf. GUFF.

negative. Without. Night clothing is *negative jean collars*. On October 1 the RIG OF THE DAY is *negative white cap-covers*.

Nelson's blood. Royal Navy rum, so named because of the belief that Nelson's body was brought back to England pickled in rum.

Neptune's Bodyguard. The Corps of Royal Marines.

Neptune's sheep. The white crests of short seas. Also known as *white horses*.

nesting box. A cabin in a WRENNERY.

net-eye. A herring. (Fishermen's.)

nettle stuff. Rope yarns used for making hammock clews.

nettings. The rack upon which hammocks are stowed during the daytime.

never a barrel the better herring. As good—or bad—as each other. (An old herring-fishery saying.)

never a dull moment. A catch-phrase used ironically in the midst of an air raid or such-like ' panic '. Cf. ARE YOU HAPPY IN THE SERVICE? (1939–45 War.)

never at Sea. A 1917–18 Wrens' motto. Probably a journalistic coinage. The W.R.N.S. was a very small service and most of the work was clerical or domestic.

never explain and never apologize. The maxim of the naval officer.

New! The *Britannia* equivalent to the Public School's ' Fag! '—a fagmaster's call for his fag. *New* cadets were fagged by the Seniors.

New Entry. A recently joined naval rating. Equivalent to the Army's ' recruit '. Cf. SPROG.

New Navy. This term was applied to the Navy about 1907, when Lord Selborne's scheme for increasing Naval Reserves was supported by improved messing conditions and general amenities on the lower-deck. See OLD NAVY.

Newfy. Short for *Newfijohn*, i.e. St John's, Newfoundland. (Royal Canadian Navy term.)

nibble. To fine as a punishment for being absent over leave. ' Two days' pay stopped and get your hair cut.' (There is a scale of fines in King's Regulations.) The Paymaster has a *nibble* at the man's pay. (Lower-deck.)

nibby. A ship's biscuit. Something to *nibb*le at.

niffle. A smoke or ' draw '. (Used in the training ship *Conway*.) Cf. the naval lower-deck's BURN.

Niffy Jane. *Iphigenia*. (Lower-deck.) By 'Hobson-Jobson.'

Nigger. Nickname for any dark-featured or dark-haired man.

nigger's spit. The hard, brown knobs found in brown sugar. (Lower-deck.)

niggly gouger = FANTOD.

night hawk. A liner's steward who keeps night watches.

ninny cock. A small lobster. (Yorkshire coast term. The lobster is also known as a *nancy* on this part of the coast.)

nippers. Strong yarns taken from teased-out cordage and marled together.

nissack. An Orcadian nickname for a porpoise. (Wright in his *The English Dialect Dictionary* spells it *nisik* or *nissac*, says ' Shetland Islands ', and derives it from Old Norse for a dolphin.)

Nix! The warning of the approach of Authority in the training ship *Conway*. The term is not exclusively *Conway* as several Public Schools and Grammar Schools use it, though *Cave!* is the general equivalent.

no wanchee. ' I don't want it, thank you.' (China-side; Wardroom.)

Noah's Ark. Marshman's or wildfowler's hut built on the hull of an old fishing smack or ship's lifeboat. Many are to be seen in the creeks and estuaries of Essex and, especially, on the Norfolk Broads.

Nobby. The nickname for all men surnamed *Clark*(*e*) or *Clerk*(*e*) and of H.M.S. *Niobe*. The nickname for men has been adopted from civilian slang. In the old (i.e. pre-1914) days many chief clerks, especially in London, wore *top* hats, as did the *nobs*.

Noisy. The ironical nickname for any quiet, retiring type of rating.

Non-can-go-ists. Naval nonconformists. Cf. FANCY RELIGIONS.

non-sub. A sounding on the Asdic which is caused by the proximity of a submerged object, e.g. a wreck.

nooner. A midday drink in the wardroom. Cf. SUN OVER THE FOREYARD.

Norie. *Norie's Nautical Tables.* In the earlier half of the nineteenth century John William Norie wrote many books on navigation.

Norskers. Norwegian ships or seamen. (Cf. DANSKERS and SCOWEGIANS.) From Scandinavian *Norsk*, a Norseman or Norwegian.

north-easter. What a man gets when he has no pay to draw. From the initials *N.E.*, meaning NOT ENTITLED; with an allusion to the cold blast of the north-easterly wind of Great Britain.

norther. A treacherous north wind peculiar to the Northern Hemisphere. (Colloquial.)

Northo. H.M.S. *Northumberland*. (1914–18.) (Lower-deck.)

nosebag. An anti-gas respirator or gas-mask. (Lower-deck.) See WINKERS.

nose-ender. A wind from dead ahead. (Blowing into one's nose.) Cf. DEAD MUZZLER.

Nosey. The inevitable nickname for anyone surnamed Parker.

not entitled. When a man, by reason of advances or ' mulcts ', has no pay to draw, the letters *N.E.* are written against his name in the Ship's Ledger; he is *not* entitled to receive pay until his debt to the Crown is cleared. As a colloquialism it is used for any restrictions in the Navy. ' Only officers are allowed in the *Black Swan*; matelots are not entitled'; 'She's a nice bit of stuff, but we ain't entitled, she's for export only '—said of a girl with a penchant for Americans or Poles. Cf. NORTH-EASTER.

nozzer (boy). New Entry boy at the training establishment at Shotley known in the Navy List as H.M.S. *Ganges*. These boys have been called *nozzers* and their mess *nozzers' lane* because, when the establishment opened, their Petty Officer in charge was nicknamed ' Noser '. Maybe his name was Parker?

nucloid. A ship of the Reserve Fleet in peacetime carrying a nucleus crew.

Number One. The First Lieutenant of one of His Majesty's Ships. (Wardroom.)

number one pash; number two pash. See PASH.

number one piecee. China-side for first class, ' the tops '. (Wardroom.) Cf. PIECEE ONE.

number ones. (1) The sailor's best uniform with gilt badges, worn at Sunday Divisions or for shore-going. (2) Canal boats owned by the men who work them.

number twos. The second best uniform with red badges; wartime NUMBER ONES.

number threes. Working rig; old NUMBER TWOS.

number fours. Night clothing, the same as NUMBER THREES, NEGATIVE jean collar.

number fives. White working rig.

number sixes. A uniform of drill material with jean collar and cuffs.

number sevens. Tropical rig, blue jumper and white trousers. Known also as MAGPIES and HALF WHITES.

number eights. Same as NUMBER SEVENS.

number nine. A pill, the naval surgeon's panacea for all ills.

number nine bo'sun. A Warrant Wardmaster in a naval hospital.

number nine locker. A scuttle or port-hole through which a NUMBER NINE pill is thrown.

number nines. Blue working overalls.

number tens. White uniform worn on foreign stations.

number seventeens. Any unofficial, but comfortable, working rig worn by members of the R.N. Patrol Service in the 1939–45 War; indeed the term was coined by them.

Nut, the. The famous Keppel's Head Hotel on the Hard, Portsmouth. A pun on *head*. (Wardroom.) Cf. KEPPEL'S NOB, MA SCULLARD'S.

nuts and bolts. Stew. (Lower-deck.) A steak and kidney pie is described as *nuts and bolts with awning*.

nutty. (1) Chocolate, whether or not it contains nuts. (Lower-deck.) (2) Any large-headed person. (Lower-deck.)

O

O.D. An Ordinary Seaman. A naval colloquialism, *O.S.* or *Ord.* being the official abbreviation. *O.D.* is never permitted on documents but is used by officers and men alike when referring to a New Entry. See HOSTILE ORD.

O.L.Q.s. Officer-like qualities. These must be possessed by candidates for commissioned rank in the Royal Navy or the Reserves. Cf. L.D.A.

O.O.D. Officer-of-the-Day. (Colloquial: wardroom.) See DAY ON.

O.O.W. The Officer-of-the-Watch. (Wardroom.) See DUTY BOY.

ocean greyhounds. Fast ocean liners. (Journalistic rather than nautical.)

ocean ramblers. Herrings. Cf. ATLANTIC RANGERS and SEA ROVERS.

ocean's gift. Any kind of flotsam found on the tide-line; yours if you can get it before the coastguard sees it—or you.

ocean-going grocers. The N.A.A.F.I. staff on board H.M. Ships.

Ocean Swell, the. Admiral Sir C. G. Ramsey. From his immaculate appearance. (Wardroom.)

odds and sods. *Hoi Polloi* of the lower-deck, the rank and file of the Navy. Also the miscellaneous ships of the auxiliary patrol.

off caps! This is sometimes murmured when a famous name is mentioned or reference is made to a departed shipmate: ' This is our new cat; he relieves " Ginger " (off caps!) lost overboard last trip.' (Lower-deck.)

office copy. The return drink. See OTHER HALF.

official cuts. Ceremonial punishment at a Royal Naval College or training ship, justified by exceptionally bad conduct.

'oggin. The sea or DITCH. A perversion of *'ogwash* (*hogwash*). See FLOGGIN' THE 'OGGIN.

oggy. (Short for TIDDY-OGGY.) Cornish pasty. (Originally a Devonport ratings' term, it has become general Navy slang.)

oh, Miss Weston! 'Language, please!' An expression of simulated horror when bad language is being used on the mess-deck. Dame Agnes Weston was a great stickler for propriety.

oil spoiler. A stoker rating. (Lower-deck.) Cf. PIPE SPOILER.

oiler. An Admiralty oiling vessel, a fleet tender. ' What time is the oiler coming alongside, Number One? ' (Colloquial.)

oily. An oilskin jacket or coat; not to be confused with OILER.

oily wad. One of the first type of oil-driven torpedo boats.

Old and Bold. A naval officer brought back into the Service during wartime. Cf. REPAINT and DUG-OUT.

Old Blue Lights. The Warrant Gunner, R.N., whose job was to attend to rockets, etc., and who occasionally treated the ship's company to firework displays.

Old Brit, the. The Royal racing yacht, *Britannia*.

Old Close-the-Range. Admiral of the Fleet Lord Cunningham, from his ' engage the enemy more closely ' policy. Cf. A.B.C.

Old Conway. A man who has gone through the course in the training ship *Conway*.

Old Girl, the. The crew's affectionate term for their ship—if it's a happy one. If not, she is usually referred to as the *old bitch*.

Old Glory. The United States flag. (Cf. STARS AND BARS.) A colloquialism adopted from the U.S.A.

old hues. Barking or tanning water that has been previously used. (Fishermen's.)

Old Jamaica. The sun. A general nautical term of long standing; see the *Introduction*. Also applied colloquially to Navy rum, Jamaica rum being famous the world over.

Old Lady of Canvey. A leading mark off Canvey Island in the Thames Estuary. In outline it somewhat resembles a bonneted lady of the Victorian era.

Old Lady of the Navy, the. H.M.S. *Warspite*, which fought in the 1914–18 War and was almost continuously in action in 1939–45. Cf. STODGER.

Old Man, the. See OLD 'UN.

Old Navy. The Navy in the transition period from sail to steam. The Navy was tough at that time and lower-deck personnel regarded with suspicion and contempt the introduction of better living conditions which greeted the arrival of TICKLERS and dubbed such signs of decadence NEW NAVY. Cf. SELBORNE'S LIGHT HORSE.

Old One-Eye. The veteran submarine depot ship *Cyclops*. The Cyclops were the one-eyed giants of Greek mythology.

old salt. A brine-steeped seaman, who has spent his life at sea.

old ship. A former messmate.

old stander = FOLLOWER.

Old 'Un or **Old Man.** The ship's Captain. ' Don't let the Old 'Un see them tapes or he'll have your GUTS FOR A NECKTIE.' (Lower-deck.)

Old Vet. A Royal Fleet Reservist, a pensioner recalled to the Navy in time of war. *Old* is a relative term in the Royal Navy, where men are said to be old at forty.

oldster. A senior cadet, or apprentice, in the Merchant Navy.

olive. An oyster catcher. An Essex wildfowler's term. According to Saxon mythology this was *St Olaf's* bird. Cf. SEA PIE.

Oliver. A West Country name for an eel. From the Standard English *elver*, a young eel, and probably influenced by *eel-fare*, a brood of eels.

on a ship. This is not slang but a popular error made by land-lubbers in reference to ships. One serves *in* a ship in the same way that one lives *in* a house rather than on it. ' My boy likes the Navy ever so much, he is serving on a torpedo.'

on dags. On leave, an obsolete term now displaced by UP THE LINE or GENS. ' *On* so-many *days*' leave '?

on service and **off service.** It is possible in the Navy for a senior officer to administer a reproof to a junior *on service* but later to share a bottle of beer in the wardroom *off service*, there being no ill-feeling.

on the roof. On the surface. (Submariners' term.) Humorous.

One. A form of address to a First Lieutenant. (Wardroom.) 'Oh! One, did you get my message about the new draft?' Usually NUMBER ONE is the style, but quite often this is abbreviated to *One.* Cf. ONE O.

One for the gangway. 'Will you have another drink before you depart?' A last drink before a guest leaves the ship. (Wardroom.) Cf. the shore-going *one for the road.*

One O. A First Officer in the Women's Royal Naval Service.

one-gun salute. The salute of one gun that is fired at COLOURS ceremony on the morning of a naval Court Martial. Cf. ROGUE'S SALUTE, and see COURT MARTIAL JACK.

onion. A fraction of a knot. (Naval engineering term.) 'We managed to get back at about six and an onion, but we were darned lucky.'

oosh-me-gosh. Sliced beef and vegetables. (Lower-deck).

Operation Farce. 'Operation Fabius', the rehearsal for the landing of the Allied forces on the Normandy coast in 1944. *Fabius* refers to the Roman general Quintus Fabius Maximus, nicknamed *Cunctator*, 'The Delayer', because in the Second Punic War he foiled Hannibal by his masterly avoidance of decisive battles.

oppo. A man's opposite number on the Watch Bill, one who does the same job in another watch. Used colloquially for pal or even a wife or girl friend.

Ops. The Operations Division, Admiralty.

opt landing. Short for *optional landing*: when on a rainy day there is no 'clear college' at the Royal Naval College, Dartmouth, a cadet may go ashore or stay 'on board' as he desires.

ormolu. Expensive, 'posh', smart, or in any way out of the ordinary in quality. (Wardroom; born in the 1914–18 War.) *Ormolu* resembles gold—in appearance.

'orrible 'ole, the. The Gunroom, the home of the YOUNG GENTLE-MEN. Also known as *the 'orrible den*. (Wardroom.)

other half, the. Drinks are served in half measures in the Navy. In returning a drink one asks one's companion to *have the other half*. Also known as the OFFICE COPY.

ounce of uranium, to feel like an. To feel very full of life and energy; on top of the world. A Royal Marine officer's coinage in reference to atomic energy.

Our Lady's Port of Grace. Newhaven, a fishing village on the Firth of Forth between Leith and Granton, mentioned by Peter F. Anson in his *British Sea Fishermen*, 1944.

outside. The lower-deck's idea of paradise. Civilian life generally. ' Once I get outside they'll never get me in this REGIMENT again '; ' I should think twice before you leave the Navy, son, things aren't so good outside these days.' Cf. IN.

outside tiffy. That engine-room ar*tific*er who is responsible for all machinery outside the engine-room.

outside-walkee. A paddle-steamer. (China-side.) The paddles ' walk ' outside. A screw ship is an *inside-walkee*.

over the side. Being absent without leave; breaking out of ship. Cf. YACHTING.

over the wall. Serving a sentence in detention barracks. Adopted from the underworld.

'Ow Dare She. H.M.S. *Audacious*. (Lower-deck.) By ' Hobson-Jobson '.

Owner, the. The Captain of the ship. (Wardroom.) See OLD MAN and SKIPS and cf.:

owneress, the. Wife of a Merchant Navy Captain. She usually sails with her husband. Cf. preceding.

owners, the. The British public, who ' own ' the Navy.

oxometer. A mythical instrument for measuring *bull*. (Lower-deck.)

P

P.A. A *P*ersonal *A*ttachment, or *P*leasing *A*ppendage—referring to the officers' womenfolk who stay in the ports to which their husbands' ships are attached. With a pun on *P.A.*, Personal Assistant.

P.G. H.M.S. *Prince George*.

P.M.O. The vocative for Principal Medical Officer. (Wardroom.) ' How about a game of Bridge, P.M.O.? '

P.Z. A tactical exercise in the Fleet at sea in peacetime. So called from the Code flags P.Z. which are run up when the exercise starts.

pack. In Naval Accountant circles, a file. ' Start a pack for this case—it's going to be tricky; the man's been in RED INK for a year and something must be done about it with D.N.A.' The *pack system* is the naval equivalent of the business filing system.

Pack, the. H.M.S. *Pactolus*.

packaging. The sealing, in protective cocoons, of all vulnerable equipment in a battleship that is laid up in reserve. The process is simple. A light framework of metal strips, tape, gauze or similar material is built round the guns, torpedo tubes, delicate wireless gear, and the like, and a coating of latex is sprayed over the cocoon. Before sealing, the moisture and air are extracted so that the equipment in the cocoon cannot rust. Several coats of plastic are applied and seal the cocoon so that the ship can lie up for twenty-five years without the efficiency of her fighting material being impaired. The cocoon can be broken in a matter of minutes. This process is also known as PICKLING.

packet. A ship of any kind; a *merchant packet*; an *excursion packet*.

packet, catch a. To be wounded; to contract an unpleasant disease. (Lower-deck.) Cf. BUY IT.

Packet of Woodbines, the. The five-funnelled Tsarist Russian Cruiser, *Arkold*—built in a spirit of emulation after our four-funnelled cruisers had paid a courtesy visit to Russia?

paddle sweeper. A pleasure steamer used by the Admiralty for mine sweeping in war-time. Because of their shallow draught these vessels were admirably suited for this work and did splendid service in both the 1914–18 and 1939–45 Wars.

paddler. A paddle steamer, such as is used for pleasure trips round the south coast or the Isle of Wight ferry services, e.g. *The Royal Eagle, Brighton Belle, Solent Queen.* Several such ships were lost in the evacuation of Dunkirk.

paddy boat. A rice-carrying craft. (China-side.)

Paddy Doyle. Detention Barracks or cells. (Cf. COOLER.) Perhaps from the name of a notorious defaulter.

Paddy's hurricane. A flat calm = IRISH HURRICANE.

Paddy's lantern. The moon = IRISH LANTERN.

Paddy's Milestone. The island of Ailsa Craig in the Firth of Clyde, half-way between Greenock and Belfast.

paid hand. A competent seaman employed professionally in a private yacht as distinct from the unpaid amateur members of the crew.

Painted Hall. The magnificent mess at the Royal Naval College, Greenwich, perhaps the finest naval or military mess in the world. It was designed by Sir Christopher Wren and painted by Sir James Thornhill, who took nineteen years over the task. The oak tables and chairs are designed ' in period ', and some of the chairs were made from the timbers of pre-Trafalgar ships supplied from the old Boat House in Portsmouth Dockyard. The silver candelabra are copies of Queen Anne candelabra and are spaced along the hall-length tables: and the effect in this Painted Hall with the electric candles, silver, and polished oak and the heightened colours of the mural and ceiling paintings is really magnificent.

pairoins. See STEEROINS.

panic. Excitement or bustle. 'What's the panic?' When the Commander-in-Chief is expected on board there is, in Lowerdeckese, 'more panic than that'. Cf. FLAP.

panic helm. The wild course steered by a MAKEE LEARN coxswain. See GO BACK AND CROSS THE T'S.

panic party. See Q-SHIPS.

panic stations, at. Prepared for any eventuality. At Action Stations; to have everything on a SPLIT YARN.

Pans, the. Prestonpans, the fishing village in the Firth of Forth.

panther piss. A brand of beer similar to TIGER PISS.

pantiles. Hard tack. (Merchant Navy.) With a pun on *pantile*, a roofing tile; *as hard as bricks*.

paper bag. A ship sailing in ballast.

paper shower. A false claim to have taken a shower-bath. A record of how many shower baths a cadet has in a week is kept in a Log Book at the Royal Naval College, Dartmouth, and the person in charge of it has to ask each cadet if he has had a shower that day. There is, of course, no real check, for anyone can say 'shower' whether or not he has had one.

parchment. A naval rating's Service Certificate, on which his character and abilities are assessed by the Commanding Officer of each ship he has served in. It is made of parchment to prevent erasures. See CLIPPED CORNER, and DISCHARGE.

Parliament heel, a. The careening of a ship in order that her hull be scraped or painted. Parliament-ordained.

Parrots. Ships of the Ellerman's Wilson Line, so called from their green hulls and red funnels.

parson's yeoman. The rating who volunteers to play the organ at Divine Service.

part brass rags. To quarrel. 'What's up with you, Jack? You look pretty chocker.'—'My missis and I have just parted brass rags.' Cf. RAGGIE.

part one's cable. See SLIP ONE'S CABLE.

party. (1) A brush with enemy surface vessels or aircraft or a sortie against enemy-held territory. Hence by understatement: (2) A girl friend. (Lower-deck.) (3) A TOOT or drinking session. ' Were you in the Walcheren party? '; ' Did you see that lush party Dusty Miller was with last night? '; ' My Lord! What a party last night; I've got a throat like the bottom of a parrot's cage.'

pash. A letter, graded according to its importance to the recipient, hence a girl friend. *Number One pash*, a man's best girl or STEADY; *Number Two pash*, ' just a little PARTY I know ashore '. Cf. YUM YUM.

pass the can. To shift responsibility on to someone else. Cf. CARRY THE CAN.

passed Boy. One who has passed through a training ship or Boys' shore establishment. (Colloquial.)

passed-overs. Those Lieutenant Commanders, R.N., who have failed to secure promotion to Commander.

passing-out number. A second-year cadet in H.M.S. *Britannia.*

passion killers. A variant of BLACK-OUTS.

Patch. Nickname for anyone who has a bald patch on his head; one who is ' a bit thin on top ' and does not quite merit the sobriquet, EGGO or SKATING RINK. (Lower-deck.)

pattern seaweed. The Admiralty design of the wardroom carpets supplied by the stores.

pawler. (1) The last word in an argument which, like a pawl in machinery, ' stops the works '. *Paul* is an old nautical verb for ' check ' or ' stop '. (2) A difficult question—something that one has to stop to think about.

Pay. The wardroom vocative for an Accountant Officer.

pay down. The quarterly settlement of pay to men in the Royal Navy. Payment is made fortnightly to the nearest shilling, the balance being given at the *pay down*.

pay off. Colloquially, to scrap anything: ' It's time you paid off that hat.' From the ' paying-off ' of a ship at the end of a commission. (2) The merchant seaman's money at the end of a trip. ' Look at old Jock, spending his pay-off on booze and women.' (3) (Of a ship's head) to move to port (left) or starboard (right). In the sailing ship days it meant, to fall off the wind.

176

paybob. The Senior Accountant Officer in an H.M. Ship or shore establishment. Cf. PUSSER and TIZZY SNATCHERS.

paying-off pennant. The long pennant with a gold bladder at the end which is flown by a ship returning from ' foreign ' to be paid off.

pea crackers. Yarmouth fishermen's nickname for Lowestoft men. Cf. DUFF CHOKERS.

pea doo. Pea soup. (Lower-deck.)

peedee. A ship's boy serving in a North-Country ship. Origin obscure: but cf. Greek '*paides* ', children.

Peggy. (1) The odd-job man in a ship; one who acts as waiter in a mess. The name derives from his ' maid-of-all-work ' duties. (2) H.M.S. *Pegasus*; cf.:

Peggy's guns. The guns of H.M.S. *Pegasus*. They were used on land in the German East Africa campaign in the 1914–18 War.

pelican = BIRD.

Pelorus Jack. A dolphin that, for years, met and accompanied ships through the Pelorus Pass, New Zealand and was protected by law. He disappeared during the 1914–18 War.

Penang lawyer. A bamboo cane used for punishment. (Ironic.) A cane from Penang: cf. *malacca* = *Malacca* cane.

pennants, get. To receive a rebuke from the Flagship for bad station-keeping, e.g. forging ahead or lagging astern; and generally for behaving in such a manner as to earn the displeasure shown by the Admiral or (if in a Destroyer flotilla) by Captain 'D'. The leading ship hoists the offender's pennant numbers. A sailor (overhearing a remark about himself) will sometimes say, ' Here, who's hoisting my pennants? ' Cf. KIPPERS, A PAIR OF.

penny reds. Coloured drinks of the ' fizzy ' kind sold in the canteen at the Royal Naval College, Dartmouth.

pepperpot. (1) A lighthouse, at sea or ashore. (From the shape.) (2) H.M.S. *Penelope*, which was so damaged from shell splinters that she resembled a pepperpot.

perambulating Navy Lists. See FISHING FLEET.

Periscope Course. The Commanding Officer's course for submariners. Cf. THE PERISHER.

periscope eye. An optical strain suffered by submariners in the early type of boats. It disappeared with the introduction of better periscopes.

Perisher, the. The stiff PERISCOPE COURSE for officers selected to command submarines. A ' perishing difficult ' examination.

permanent winds. The trade winds, which are constant, as opposed to ' periodical ' winds such as monsoons.

Peter, the. The Blue Peter, International Code flag ' P ' flown by ships in harbour as a warning that they are about to sail.

Peter boat. A small double-ended sailing boat used for smelting or similar fishery on the London River. Named after St Peter, the patron saint of the fisheries.

Peter Scott camouflage. A clever blend of off-white, pale blue and green which proved so effective in its ' invisible ' properties that two of H.M. Ships collided in mid-ocean, neither seeing the other. Designed by Lieutenant-Commander Peter Scott, who may have had the idea from his painting of wildfowl.

Phoney Quid, the. The late Admiral Sir *Dudley Pound*. Cf. TIDDLEY QUID.

Piccadilly Circus. The area of mine-swept water south of the Isle of Wight, from which the ships of the invasion forces set off along the swept channels to the Normandy landing beaches in 1944.

pick up. To obtain promotion or increase of pay. ' I'll pick up my HOOK next month '; ' At least you'll pick up HARD LYERS in destroyers.' (Lower-deck.)

picked up, be. To be charged as a defaulter. ' Don't wear your cap flat-a-back when you're ashore or you'll be picked up by the crushers.'

pickling. See PACKAGING.

piece. (1) A ship's gun. (Colloquial.) (2) An article of clothing on a ship's DHOBEYING line.

piecee one. See NUMBER ONE PIECEE. (Wardroom.)

pier head jump. A sudden draft to sea from barracks.

piffing. Sub-calibre firing. Echoic of the sound. (Naval gunnery slang.)

pig, naval. A naval officer. (Lower-deck.) Cf. GRUNTER.

pig, small. A Petty officer. (Lower-deck.)

pigstye. The Wardroom. (Lower-deck.)

pigs aft. Naval officers. A lower-deck traditional pejorative phrase.

pigtail. Navy ' perique ' tobacco. It is wrapped in canvas and lashed with spunyarn into a cylindrical shape tapered to a point at both ends. Perique, or ' prick ', as the sailors call it, is sometimes soaked in rum to give it a ' bite '.

pig troughs. Weapons used in merchant ships as protection against attack by low-flying aircraft or surface raiders.

pile up. To run a vessel aground. To put her ON THE PUTTY.

pile up points. To curry favour; to ' crawl '. To strive for advancement by constantly and ostentatiously thrusting oneself forward when any work is to be done that is likely to yield good results, and so get one's name to the fore.

Pilot. The Navigating Officer, R.N.

Pilot Jack, the. A small Union Flag flown as a signal for a pilot.

pill. (1) A Customs and Excise official. He is a 'searching' character. (2) A creek or estuary in the West Country. (Dialect.)

pill yawl. An old term for a Bristol Pilot ' cutter '. At one time these craft may have been yawl-rigged; cf. PILL (2).

pillar box. That two-inch projector containing ten rockets on each side which was used for the protection of merchant ships in the 1939–45 War.

pinch-gut. A niggardly victualling officer. (Old Navy term.) Hence a *pinch-gut ship*.

Pincher. All naval Martins are so named after an Admiral Martin of evil legend. He delighted in *pinching* or running in defaulters.

Ping. Wardroom vocative for the Asdic Officer. Echoic of the instrument he works.

ping, get a. To make contact with an enemy submarine. Cf. preceding.

pink. (1) Angostura bitters added to gin. The naval officer's favourite drink. From the resulting colour. (2) A Dutch ketch-rigged fishing vessel. Standard English. Its diminutive, *pinkie*, is eligible as a colloquialism.

pink bumf. Confidential signal-pads. Flag-deck term in H.M. Ships. *Bumf* is short for *bumfodder*; *pink* the colour of the pads.

pinuptuous. An adjective descriptive of feminine beauty. From *pin-up* girl and volup*tuous*. (Wardroom.)

Pip, Squeak and Wilfred. (1) The War Medals of the 1914–18 War: the 1914 Star, General Service, and Victory medals worn together. From the characters famous in a newspaper's series of cartoons. (2) A gun unit mounted on a lorry used by naval shore-parties. *Pip* is a two-pounder gun; *Squeak*, a three-pounder; and *Wilfred*, a searchlight.

pipe down! The Navy's ' Lights out! ' It is an official order to be quiet: ' Pipe down, you men.' Lower-deck: ' Why don't you pipe down?—you're always dripping about something.' Perhaps it is short for ' Put your pipe down and go to sleep '; probably, however, from the piping.

pipe spoiler. A plumber, R.N. Do not confuse with PLUMMER. Cf. also OIL SPOILER.

Pipes. An old term for a Bo'sun. The lower-deck term is BOSE.

pipey. A kind of sand containing small transparent tubes about half an inch long. A favourite food of plaice. (Fishermen's.)

pipped. (Of a ship) torpedoed or sunk; (of a man) killed in action. ' Did you know old So-and-So? He got pipped at Salerno during the landing.'

pirates. The Navy's name for officers and men serving in submarines and small craft in which any unorthodox rig is worn and a free-and-easy discipline prevails.

Piss Harder Club. The Pesada Club in Plymouth, a drinking haunt of naval officers.

piss-pot jerkers. Cabin stewards in passenger liners.

pitching and rolling grounds, the. Areas of tumbling seas in the Thames Estuary which cause a small yacht to be very lively indeed.

pitiful objects. Petty Officers. (One of those convenient initial-forming terms.)

planter. One of those officers who were in charge of the sinking of blockships which formed the GOOSEBERRIES in a MULBERRY Harbour. Their job was to see that the blockships were *planted* in the right positions.

plastered. Extremely drunk, though not quite incapable. Hence the traditional couplet:

> *If you come on deck well plastered,*
> *Steer by some more sober bastard.*

Plates. Nickname for the plate-washer in a liner.

play lively. To work smartly and cheerfully. ' Come on, play lively; the sooner we get the job done, the sooner we get a break.' Cf. SMACK IT ABOUT!

Player's Please! Whiskers and moustache like those of the Victorian seaman depicted on the Player's Navy Cut cigarette cartons. Few men achieve this magnificent effect. Cf. BUG WHISKERS and SET.

please! This is the traditional Navy way of granting a favour or request. If an officer wishes to leave the Wardroom before the end of a meal he will approach the Mess President, who will usually reply ' Please! ' In answer to a tap at the door the Navy uses ' Please! ' instead of ' Come in '.

plew. Tea. (Lower-deck.) ' Who is running the plew boat? ' (Cf. TEA BOAT.) A perversion of *brew*?

pluck. A tug or tow. (Fishermen's.) Cf. SNATCH.

plug mush. A ' free-for-all ' fight. (Merchant Navy.) Literally, a punch-face, *mush* being low civilian slang for *mouth*, hence *face*.

plumber or **plummer.** A naval engineering officer. The latter form has been influenced by PLUMS, engines; *plumber* is humorously pejorative.

Plummy. Nickname for a ship's plumber, whether Royal or Merchant Navy.

plums. A warship's engines. Cf. PLUMBER (or *plummer*), an engineer.

plussers. Sur*plus* rum. Ironic; the rum is poured into the ship's scuppers.

Pluto. From the initials *Pipe Lines Under The Ocean*. The code name for the wonderful operation carried out by the Navy during the first month of the Allied invasion of Normandy, 1944—the laying of fuel pipes under the sea from England to the continent. The term very soon became official. See CONUN.

Pneumonia Bridge. A bridge at Gosport, exposed to every wind that blows.

pneumonia rig. A tropical suit. (Lower-deck.)

pocket handkerchief, the. The small Union Flag worn as a battle-flag by H.M. Ships.

Point Beacher. A Portsmouth prostitute. (Old Navy term.)

poison on armour-plate. Ship's biscuits dipped in beef tea. (Lower-deck.)

poke Charley. To treat anything or anybody with derision. Why *Charley*, nobody knows. The phrase, obviously, is formed on the analogy of *poke fun at*.

poker. A pochard. (East Anglian dialect.)

poker pusher. A stoker rating in a coal-burning ship.

poltering. Beachcombing. (East Anglian, from *polt*, a thump or knock: cf. FRETTER, SCRATTING and the underworld *knock off*, to steal.)

Pompey. Portsmouth town and dockyard, and the Royal Naval Barracks known as H.M.S. *Victory*. There has never been a satisfactory derivation of the nickname; but one suggestion is that in the old days life was much freer at sea than in Portsmouth, where much *pomp* and circumstance reigned, and the port was known amongst the men as *old Pompey*. I admit that this seems a very feeble origin but I know of no other. (W.G.) Portsmouth was perhaps named after its naval prison, for in Yorkshire, *Pompey* is—or was—a house of correction; the term may well have travelled to the South. In its Yorkshire sense, *Pompey* is, I suspect, a folk-etymological corruption or perversion of *Pontius Pilate*, governor of Judea at the time of Christ's imprisonment and crucifixion. (E.P.)

Pompey Chimes, the. A lively air played by a ship's band when she is returning into Portsmouth after a foreign commission. See POMPEY.

pongo. A soldier. Naval nickname dating from before 1914, when the Navy and Army joined forces in annual landing exercises. (Cf. GRABBIES and SWADDY and the 1939–45 BROWN JOBS.) Perhaps ultimately from *pongo*, a large anthropoid ape native to Africa.

poodle-faker. One who pays polite calls ashore: one of the SOCIAL TITS. (Wardroom.) With a sly allusion to *gay dogs*.

poop off. To fire guns. ' We were pooping off at 'em for hours.' (Gunnery slang.)

pooped, be. To be caught by a following sea that breaks over the poop; hence *pooper*, a sea that does this.

poor as piss and twice as nasty. A lower-deck pejorative phrase, literally reflecting on the quality of the beer ashore but, in practice, levelled against anything inferior.

poor view of, take a; or **take a dim view of.** To regard a situation, person or thing with disfavour. To disapprove strongly. In general to deprecate and condemn. (Wardroom.) Also intransitively: ' He can be counted upon to take a poor view.'

Pope, the. A puffin. Cf. TOMMY NODDY. (Wildfowlers'.)

popple. A short, confused sea which causes a yacht to jump about. Cf. JOBBLE and LOP.

popsey, popsy, popsie. A girl friend. In the plural, generic for women. See COMMISSIONED POPSEY. (Wardroom.) A diminutive of *Poppy* (the girl's name): cf. FLOOSIE.

Porcupine, H.M.S. The cruiser *Penelope* which had her shell-splinter holes plugged with wooden pegs. Cf. PEPPER POT (2).

pork-bolter. An old term for a Worthing fisherman; hence, *pork-boat*, a Worthing fishing boat. From some old piece of folk-lore.

porous. A polite form of the lower-deck phrase, POOR AS PISS.

porpoising. (Of submarines) undulating on the surface when cruising with engines at full power, much like porpoises travelling at full speed.

port. A scuttle or port-hole. *Scuttle* is the usual term in the Royal Navy, but *port* is also used, though not as generally as in the Merchant Navy. (Technical.)

Port Mahon sailor. A lubberly, inefficient seaman. Cf :

Port Mahon sodgers. Royal Marines, from the fact that in the eighteenth century the ' Royals ' were garrisoned at Port Mahon in the island of Minorca. This term went out of fashion at the beginning of the twentieth century.

Port of Brighton. Shoreham-by-Sea, which is the harbour nearest to Brighton.

Port of Many Ships, the. The bottom of the sea, where many sunken vessels lie.

Port Winston. The prefabricated harbour at Arromanches erected during the invasion in 1944. See MULBERRY. Named after the Rt. Hon. Winston Churchill.

ports. Boards fastened ski-wise on a man's feet to enable him to walk on oozy marshland or the mud in harbour. A shortening of *supports*.

Portuguese men o' war. A species of acalephae; jelly fish. Cf. BY-THE-WIND SAILOR.

Portuguese parliament. A rowdy discussion, a ' natter party '—all talking; few listening. (Wardroom.) Cf. DUTCH PARLIAMENT.

Postie. The rating doing duty as ship's postman. Adopted from civilian speech.

pot-mess. A species of hot-pot very popular on the lower-deck. Cf. NUTS AND BOLTS.

potted air. A fug; stale air in a ship which has scuttles closed to keep out heavy seas.

Potter. Potter Heigham on the Norfolk Broads, a haunt of yachtsmen.

poultice walloper. A sick berth attendant, who ' wallops on ' the plasters. Cf. SICK BAY TIFFY.

pozzie. Jam or marmalade. (Lower-deck.) Origin still obscure, despite the numerous guesses made by scholars, sailors, soldiers and citizens.

pram cox'n. A sailor's firstborn. (Lower-deck.)

prayer books. Holystones, used for scrubbing decks. Cf. ECCLESIASTICAL BRICKS.

Press. Press Division, Admiralty.

press the tit. To press the wardroom bell for the steward to order a round of drinks. ' Press the tit, Guns, it's my turn to PUSH THE BOAT OUT.'

Pretty Royal. H.M.S. *Princess Royal*, a graceful ship which was at the Battle of Jutland in 1916.

prewell. A short gaff. (Norfolk Coast term.) (Cf. the blacksmith's *pritchel*, a term cognate with *prickle*.)

price of Admiralty, the. Death, a price which is high. Anyone killed in action is said to have paid the price of Admiralty.

prick. See PIGTAIL.

prick a chart. To mark a ship's course upon it.

pricker, Chief. See CHIEF PRICKER.

prickly heat. *Lichen Tropicus*, a papular eruption of the skin which causes itching and prickling and the sufferer much discomfort and irritation.

Pricky. A lower-deck nickname for anyone not possessing a traditional nickname. (Mainly Active Service ratings.) Compare the Cockney's favourite vocative, (*old*) *cock*.

pride of the morning. A sea mist at sunrise in summer. (Verging on Standard English.)

Priest of the Parish. A traditional Navy game of the hearty kind.

private rig. A Captain's sailing boat, rigged with his own suit of sails.

private ships. Battleships other than Flagships.

private till. An oblong deal box in which a cadet's private papers, etc., are kept. It is in the top of a chest. See 'BRITANNIA' SLANG (*Till Rux*).

private truck. A specially carved crown or similar object for an ensign-staff; used only on very special occasions of ceremony. Literally, a *truck* is a circular cap on the top of a mast or flag-staff.

prize firing. Fleet gunnery exercises in peace-time, prizes being given for the best shooting. (Colloquial.)

Professor. Nickname for anyone who talks in a high-falutin' or pedantic way. Any rating with intelligence above the average;

a rating with a university degree—there were many such in the Service in 1939–45. More of a B.A. than an A.B. (Lower-deck.)

promotion fever =:

promotionitis. Nervousness displayed by naval officers at the time of the Half-Yearly Promotion announcements by the Admiralty. The dread of becoming PASSED OVER. A humorous formation, on the analogy of *appendicitis*.

Public Room Men. Stewards on duty in the Lounge or Smoke Room in a passenger liner, the *public rooms* of the ship.

pudding. (1) A join in an electric cable. From the bulge caused by the insulating tape. (2) = DUFF BAG.

pudding, Tom. See TOM PUDDING.

pudding fender. A large, round rope fender.

puffer. (1) Motor fishing vessels. (Navy.) Echoic. (2) A type of small coal steamer peculiar to the Clyde.

pump ship. To urinate. (Nautical slang which has become very general among men.)

punka wallah. The native seaman whose job is to create a draught in the saloon of a liner that is not fitted with a mechanically driven punka. (From Hindustani *pankah*, a fan.)

pup. A young *dog*-fish. (Trawlermen's.)

purchase, have. To have 'pull' or influence. A purchase is a tackle for hoisting gear.

purple green. Purple laver, an edible marine plant.

push the boat out. To stand a round of drinks in the wardroom.

pushing water = FLOGGIN' THE 'OGGIN.

pusser. Name for all members of the Supply and Secretariat Branch. (A corruption—perhaps originally a dialectal pronunciation—of *purser*, an Accountant Officer in the Royal Navy.) 'I must touch the pusser for a fiver, I'm flat broke.' Hence (adj.): Strictly disciplined; one hundred per cent. ' Service '. A *pusser* ship is one which is run by a Captain who is a stickler for naval etiquette and ceremony. ' Give me destroyers every time, battle-wagons are far too pusser.'

pusser's bank. The savings bank run by the Accountant Officer in an H.M. Ship.

186

pusser's Condy. Soap, after 'Condy's Fluid' of shore use. (Lower-deck.)

pusser's crabs. Heavy regulation boots issued to ratings for squad drill, marching, etc.

pusser's dagger. A seaman's knife.

pusser's dip. A candle.

pusser's dirk = PUSSER'S DAGGER.

pusser's duck. A Supermarine Walrus aircraft.

pusser's grey. Admiralty grey paint. Cf. CRAB FAT.

pusser's grins. Sneers from officers; sarcasm of any kind directed at lower-deck ratings.

pusser's halo = CANE; cap grummet.

pusser's issue. Slops, food, tobacco, etc., issued by the Crown.

pusser's key. A marline-spike. Also known as a BO'SUN'S KEY.

pusser's lisle. The regulation black lisle stockings supplied to, but seldom worn by, Wren ratings.

pusser's pack. The SLOP CHEST.

pusser's pound. Fourteen instead of sixteen ounces. Contrast the shore-going term *baker's dozen*.

pusser's tally. A false name given by a rating when picked up by a naval patrol for being improperly dressed or committing a breach of peace or order; also the false name for oneself given to a girl friend ashore when her intentions seem dangerous.

pusser's yellow. Navy soap.

pusser's Vinolia = preceding.

Putty. The inevitable name for a ship's painter rating.

putty, on the. Hard and fast aground; on the mud. (General nautical.)

Q

Q.D. Short title for the *q*uarter-*d*eck, so called because it originally ran a quarter of the ship's length.

Q.E., the. The Cunard White Star liner *Queen Elizabeth*.

Q.M., the. (1) The battleship *Queen Mary*, which blew up at the Battle of Jutland in 1916. (2) The Cunard White Star liner *Queen Mary*.

Q-ship. One of the innocent-looking merchant ships, also known as *mystery ships* and *hush hush ships*, used by the Royal Navy in the 1914–18 War to tempt German submarines to attack. Her guns were concealed under dummy hatches and deckhouses. When a U-Boat signalled her to stop and abandon ship, a boat with a PANIC PARTY left the ship and rowed off to a safe distance. On board remained the guns' crews, closed-up, waiting the order to open fire on the U-boat, when—as usually happened—she came nearer. When the submarine presented the right target position, she was usually sunk or severely damaged by the Q-ship's gunfire. (From *Q.*, the abbreviation for Latin *quaere!*, inquire!)

quack, the. The ship's surgeon in the Royal Navy. (Lower-deck.) Cf. *pills*, SAWBONES, CHEMIST, etc.

quarterdeck, the. The collective noun for the officers in an H.M. Ship. Cf. WARDROOM.

Queen Anne's Mansions. The superstructure round the foremast of a modern battleship which somewhat resembles that London block of luxury flats.

Queen Bee. The radio-controlled target aircraft used for anti-aircraft gunnery in the Fleet exercises.

Queenie. The naval equivalent of the Army's *Archie*, an anti-aircraft gun of the 1914–18 War.

Queen's, the. The famous Queen's Hotel at Southsea, a popular haunt of naval officers.

Queens, the. The liners *Queen Mary* and *Queen Elizabeth*.

quid. A piece of chewed tobacco. (Lower-deck.)

quirk. A MAKEE-LEARN airman. A pilot under training in the old Royal Naval Air Service. From the unexpected *quirks*, turns and twists he made in the air.

R

R, pawn an. To desert or RUN from the Navy. The letter ' R ' is written against a deserter's name in the Ship's Ledger and on his ' S.161 ' sheet in the Drafting Office of his Port Division. He *pawns an R* with the Paymaster.

rabbiter. One who makes a habit of smuggling RABBITS ashore. (Lower-deck.)

rabbits. Illicit goods, smuggled ashore by naval ratings proceeding on leave. At one time men were allowed to take food with them, ' top pieces ' of prime meat, and rabbits—which, with their insides removed, made excellent hold-alls for (say) tobacco, which men were not allowed to take out of the ship.

Race, the. Portland Race, dreaded by small craft. (Colloquial.)

Racecoursers, the. A class of paddle minesweepers which were named after famous racecourses: *Epsom, Goodwood, Ascot,* etc.

Rag, the. Short for *Rag and Famish,* the Army and Navy Club. See especially, C. W. Firebrace, *The Army and Navy Club,* 1934.

rag-tearer. A signalman. Cf. BUNTS and FLAG-FLAPPER.

rag wagon. A sailing vessel. Cf. BATTLE-WAGON. (Merchant Navy.)

raggie. A companion; *raggies* are men who share cleaning rags when polishing brightwork. Cf. PART BRASS RAGS.

Ragtime Navy, the. A 1914–18 sobriquet for the Auxiliary Patrol. Cf. FRED KARNO'S NAVY.

Railway jetty, the. The South Railway jetty at Portsmouth where battleships lie before their departure on foreign commissions and where they usually moor on their return. (Colloquial.) Also known as FAREWELL JETTY.

Rainbow Bar. A stretch of mud near the entrance to Portsmouth Harbour on the Titchfield side, so named because of the colours from the oil deposits.

rainbow fashion. Dressing ship all over with the multi-coloured Navy or International Code flags.

rain goose. The red-throated diver whose call is said to portend bad weather. This bird is known in East Anglia as a SPRAT LOON.

raked fore and aft. Knocked silly by love. From the damage done to a ship when she is battered fore and aft by accurate gunfire.

raking. (Of a sea) breaking on a shingle beach and receding, with a sound reminiscent of the raking of gravel. (Coastal dialect.)

Ral, the. The Commander-in-Chief. Short for Admi*ral*.

ram's head. The rudder post on a canal barge. In many of these craft the ram's head is adorned with rope FANCY WORK and has a horse's tail attached.

Rampiles. H.M.S. *Ramillies*. A lower-deck rhyming on the solecistic pronunciation of the name. *Ramillies* was reputed to be a ' Jonah ' and *ram piles* may be reminiscent. She was paid off and sent to be scrapped in 1948.

range. A harbour swell. Cf. dialectal *range*, a clattering sound.

rank. A row of lighters moored afloat. These rows are numbered first rank, second rank, etc. Cf. BOTTOMS.

rasher-splasher. A cook rating. He splashes the rashers with fat. (Lower-deck.)

rat's tail. A short length of rope with an eye splice which allows it to run the length of a ship's rail. In bad weather a man is able to make his way along the deck using the rope as a life-line.

rate. The Leading Rate. ' Jones should be picking up his rate this year, he's a good man at his job.' Cf. KILLICK.

Rate or Rater. A term used in classifying wooden-hulled warships. Several of these grand old ' Wooden Walls ' are now used as Headquarters Ships for R.N.V.R. Divisions and for training purposes, and I think it therefore not out of place to explain the term. A *First Rate* carried over 800 officers and men and had 100 guns, ranging from 42-pounders on the lower-deck to 6-pounders on the quarter-deck. A *Second Rate* carried 90–100 guns; a *Third Rate*, the smallest line-of-battle ship, 80–84 guns; a *Fourth Rate*, 60–74 guns; a *Fifth Rate*, 32–40 guns. A *Sixth*

Rate carried any lower number. An excellent example of a *Third Rate* is the Headquarters of the East Scottish Division of the R.N.V.R., H.M.S. *Unicorn II*, which lies in Earl Grey Dock at Dundee.

rate of knots. To move *at the rate of knots* is to CRACK ON the utmost speed. Used throughout the Navy for any swift movement. 'If they give us a boiler leave, I'll be out of this ruddy harbour at the rate of knots.'

rattle, the. Any form of trouble with Authority; the defaulters' table, whether the Commander's 'petty sessions' or the Captain's 'assizes': there, they receive a severe *shaking*-up.

rattle, in the. Before the First Lieutenant or Commander as a defaulter.

rattle, score a. To place oneself in the RATTLE by defaulting.

Ratto = DOGGO. Having unprepossessing looks; with a face like a rat's. (Lower-deck.)

Ray, the. Hadleigh Ray, a channel that runs between Leigh and Southend, Essex, and thence inside Canvey Island to Benfleet. A useful anchorage for small craft and well known to Estuary yachtsmen. (Colloquial.)

Raysun, the. The Ray Sand in the Thames Estuary. (Yachtsmen's.)

Really not a Sailor. A member of the Royal Naval Air Service in the 1914–18 War. A play on the initials R.N.A.S.

rec room. The recreation room at the Royal Naval College, Osborne. Cf.:

rec space. The recreation space on board ship. (Lower-deck.)

recco. An enemy reconnaissance aircraft. E.g., the Blohm and Voss 'plane which used to spot Russian convoys two hours before the main attack by Stukas.

recliner. The Admiralty-issue arm-chair for the wardroom and Petty Officers' messes.

red. (1) The port side of the ship, which is on your left hand when you are looking dead ahead. Cf. GREEN. *Port* (the drink) is *red*-coloured. (2) A red herring. (East Anglian fishery term.) Contrast REDSPOT.

red ensign club. One of those ' Royal ' and ' private ' yacht clubs that wear the red ensign plain or defaced because their warrant is a Royal one issued by the Home Office and not an Admiralty one. The blue ensign takes precedence of the red: see BLUE ENSIGN CLUB. Cf.:

red ensign ship. Any vessel not commissioned by the Admiralty in wartime. Only H.M. Ships are allowed to wear the white ensign; others, unless they have an Admiralty warrant permitting them to wear the blue ensign, must wear the red ensign of the Merchant Navy.

red ink, in. In debt to the Crown by reason of advances of payment or ' mulcts '. All debts are entered in red ink against the man's name in the Ship's Ledger.

red lead. Tinned herrings in tomato sauce. Also fried tomatoes. (Lower-deck.) Cf. TRAIN SMASH.

Red Marines. The Royal Marine Light Infantry, so named because of their red tunics. Cf. BLUE MARINES and KHAKI MARINES.

Red Navy, the. The fleets of the U.S.S.R. (Colloquial.)

red recommend. A recommendation in red ink on a Service Certificate. This means that a rating is exceptionally efficient and is recommended for accelerated promotion. (Lower-deck.)

Red Squadron, the. The Royal Victoria Yacht Club, Ryde, which is the only ' Royal ' club to be so from its inception. Its yachts wear the red ensign defaced by the Club's device, in the fly: the letters VR in gold surmounted by a Royal crown. The burgee is red with a gold anchor between the letters VR and surmounted by the crown.

Red Wings. The red-sailed yachts of the Bembridge, Isle of Wight, Sailing Club.

redspot. Plaice. (Fishermen's.)

reefer. A Cadet or Midshipman in the Merchant Navy. The wearer of a reefer jacket.

Regiment, this. The Royal Navy. A variant of ANDREW on the lower-deck. ' Once I'm out of this perishing Regiment, there'll be no more sea for yours truly.'

relief. An officer or rating who takes the place of one appointed to another ship. ' Before you go, Pay, you'd better have some TALKEE TALKEE with your relief and put him wise to the snags.' (Technical.)

Remember your next astern! ' Do unto others as you would have them do unto you.' A good look-out will always keep his eye on both the ship ahead and the one astern and so avoid collision.

repaint. Any naval officer called back for service in time of war. In the 1914–18 War such an officer was known as a DUG OUT. Cf. also OLD AND BOLD.

repeat not. A term of emphasis borrowed from signalese. Any negative signal that requires emphasis has the insertion *repeat* or *repetition*, thus: ' Ships must not, repeat not, fire without permission from Captain "D".' Colloquially it is used throughout the Navy: ' Some blokes are going on leave this week-end but not, repeat not, you.'

re-scrub. To do any kind of job over again. (Lower-deck.)

Reserves, the. The Royal Naval Reserve and the Royal Naval Volunteer Reserve. (Colloquial.) Cf. ROCKY and SATURDAY NIGHT SAILOR.

resurrection pie. Any made-up dish, such as cottage pie or fish pie, served on board ship. Adopted from civilian slang.

revolver brand. A brand of beer which takes effect with the suddenness of a pistol shot. (Navy.) After a number of drinks— according to one who has sampled the stuff—there is a ' bang ' in one's head followed by a black-out.

Rezzo, the. H.M.S. *Resolution*. (Lower-deck.)

rib and trunk grounds. A fishing area in the North Sea, so named because trawlers occasionally bring up bits of wreckage in their trawls. Many ships have come to grief in the area.

rig of the day. The uniform to be worn for the day. This is ' piped ' each morning over the ship's loudspeaker.

ring number. The number on a table napkin ring at the Royal Naval College, Greenwich. Each member has his napkin which he takes from the rack each time he enters the Mess for a meal. He orders drinks in the wardroom by giving his *ring number*, and anything ordered is by number, the bill being presented at the end of the month.

ringer, two; two-and-a-half r.; three r.; four r. A Lieutenant; Lieutenant-Commander; Commander; and Captain. On the lower-deck, officers are known as ' ringers '; on the quarter-deck they are referred to as ' stripers '. ' That two-striper R.N.V.R. played a fine game last week; he is one of the best scrum halves I've seen for a long time.'

riser. A canal lock arranged in ' staircases ', the top gates of each lock forming the bottom gates of the lock above. There are examples of such locks at Newport, Mon., and a particularly notable example at Bingley on the Leeds and Liverpool Canal.

River, the. (1) The Yangtse Kiang. (Navy.) (2) The Thames, the ' London River '. (Merchant Navy.)

Rivers, the. A class of destroyers named after the principal rivers.

rixy. A small seagull. A dialectal term of uncertain origin.

roar up. To attack. Of destroyers and motor torpedo boats which ' roar in, roar 'em up and roar out again '.

roaring forties. The rough seas in latitude 40°–50° N. Hence, a slang name for those taut-handed Lieutenant-Commanders in their forties who are always ' roaring-up ' the hands.

roast-beef dress. Full-fig mess uniform in the Royal Navy.

rock chasing. Navigation exercises.

Rock Scorp. Short for *Rock Scorpion*, a policeman or male civilian at Gibraltar. From the *Rock* of Gibraltar.

rocket = BLAST or BOTTLE.

Rocky. The traditional wardroom vocative for a Royal Naval Reserve officer and, in the plural, generic for all R.N.R. officers and ratings. In peacetime, submarines carried ' Rocky ' navigating officers.

Rocky Scribe. A Writer rating, R.N.V.R. See preceding.

Roger or **roger.** Short for *Roger's blast*, a sudden gust of wind that takes a sailor unawares. Originally a Broadland term, it is used throughout East Anglia and among yachtsmen. *Roger* connotes fierceness or vigour—or both; it is a rural colloquialism for either a ram or a bull.

rogue sea. A wave that breaks unexpectedly inboard and damages the gear or boats on deck. Cf. :

rogue ship. A ship which is constantly causing trouble through engine defects, boiler troubles, etc. (Cf. CONDENSERITIS.) On the analogy of *rogue elephant*.

rogue's salute = ONE-GUN SALUTE.

rogue's yarn. The coloured threads in the heart of government rope. Devonport-made rope has a yellow thread; Chatham, red; and government-made, blue. Originally a colloquialism, the term has long been Standard English. The name arises from the fact that the thread was inserted in order to facilitate the detection of thieves. Cf. HEART YARN.

roke. A sea mist. An East Coast variant of *sea fret*, a Yorkshire coast term for the heat fog which hangs over the coast between Whitby and Flamborough Head in early summer. Dialectal rather than unconventional; *roke* probably derives from Dutch *rook*; cf. the mainly Scottish *reek*.

Roll on my bloody twelve! Often preceded by ' I heard the voice of Moses say '. A heartfelt cry of BLOODY-MINDEDness to which the matelot will give vent at least a dozen times a week. Active Service ratings usually engage for twelve years' service, and in spite of this expression, many TAKE ON to complete time for pension.

rolling-motion dicky. The first design of R.N.V.R. ' jean ' collar, which had three rows of wavy tape to distinguish the wearers from Active Service ratings, whose ' jeans ' had straight tapes. In the 1914–18 War the wavy ' jeans ' went out of fashion; all men dressed as seamen wore the same straight-tape collars and the Volunteer Reserve ratings wore the letters R.N.V.R. on their sleeves four inches from the cuff, as they do at the present time.

rompers. Ships that forge ahead of a convoy instead of keeping station as ordered. Cf. *stragglers*.

rooker. A fish similar to a skate. (East Anglian fishery term.)

rooster. A roster. (By mispronunciation: lower-deck.)

rooti (or **rooty** or **ruti**) **wallah.** A ship's baker in the Merchant Navy. From Hindustani *roti*, ' bread '; the term has been adopted from Army regulars.

rope-hookey hands. Hands that are curled by the constant handling of ropes. They are the distinguishing feature of an

OLD VET, but New Entries affect a deep-sea roll and curl their hands when on shore-leave in the hope that the local girls may admire their toughness. See SPIT BROWN.

rope-yarn Thursday. The original naval MAKE AND MEND day or half-holiday.

Ropner's Navy. Vessels of the Ropner Line.

rort. To shout in argument or act truculently when charged with indiscipline. (Lower-deck.) The adjective is *rorty*: unruly, drunken and obstreperous. Liberty men on pay night in a dockyard port are apt to be *rorty*. (The verb is a back-formation from the adjective. The adjective is of uncertain origin: Professor Ernest Weekley has suggested that it rhymes upon *naughty*; I, that it blends *roary* and *naughty*.—E.P.)

rosy, the. The Merchant Navy's GASH BUCKET. 'A rose by any other name . . .'

Rotten Row. A row of old ships awaiting the breakers in the knacker's yard.

round the bend. Mentally deranged; BATCHY. Cf. YARMOUTH.

round-house, the. The officer's lavatories in an H.M. Ship, situated in the stern of the ship. Cf. HEADS.

round-house ranger. A species of fish that swims round the stern of a ship at anchor. The allusion is to the preceding entry.

roundly! The naval order to do a job smartly and vigorously, e.g. hoisting a boat. Cf. HANDSOMELY.

round-the-world drink. A very potent drink popular with naval engineers: sherry, gin, whisky and brandy in one glass.

round turn, brought up with a = BROUGHT UP ALL STANDING.

rover. An inferior cod.

roving bridge. A bridge taking a towing path from one side of a canal to the other.

Royal. The vocative for a Royal Marine. (General Navy slang.) The plural is generic for the Corps of Royal Marines.

Royal Proclamation. A CHIT sent to all Naval Reservists on General Mobilization in a state of ' National Emergency '. It demands the presence of all officers and men at the place stated. See IMMEDIATE RESERVE. (Neither of these terms is slang, but they are included for their intrinsic interest.)

R.P.C. See N.C.D.

rub. A loan of any kind. ' May I have a rub of your mac tonight? '
' Can you let me have a rub of five bob till pay-day? ' (Probably
from a *rub* of a pal's cleaning-rag or boot polish.)

rubber. A loan of money, clothing, toilet gear, in fact of anything at all. See preceding.

rubber firm. A mess-deck money-lending concern. See preceding.
A *rubber* is a variant of *rub*.

rub-up. A refresher course in any subject. To *rub-up* a subject
is to ' swot ' at it.

rudery. Any marked attention from the enemy; an air raid or a
surface attack. (Wardroom.) A delightful meiosis, with a
reference to the civilian colloquialism, *rudery*, a rude remark,
' fast ' conversation, too-ardent behaviour.

rumble. To see through a ruse or a person's ' façade '. (Lower-
deck.) ' He tried to get it out of the ship but the Jaunty
rumbled him.' Adopted from civilian slang.

rumble-bumble. A shooting-up of enemy E-Boats or coastline
by motor torpedo (and gun) boats in the years 1940–45. Echoic.

rumbo. Short for *rummage* or contraband. Rope, paint, ironmongery stolen from a naval dockyard. From dialectal
rummage, litter, rubbish, a confused mass of things.

run. (1) A routine trip escorting merchant ships. *The Malta run*,
Atlantic run, etc. (Colloquial.) Cf. CLUB RUN. (2) To desert
the Navy or break out of ship for a period longer than twenty-
four hours. Cf. R, PAWN AN.

run ashore. Evening leave in a dockyard port or naval base, as
distinct from week-end or annual leave. Cf. DICKY RUN and
DICKY FLURRY. (Lower-deck colloquialism.)

run in. To put a man in the Commander's Report. ' If I have
any more lip from you I'll run you in to the Officer of the
Watch for insubordination.' From civilian *run in*, to arrest
(someone).

runners. Scratch crews provided by the dockyard to ' run ' a new
ship to her base. They are made up of dockyardees and
technicians, but the ship is commanded by the C.O. who will
commission her.

running. In submarines, exercising as opposed to active patrol duty.

running fix. Obtaining a ship's position on the chart by taking fixes at sea when running along the coastline. (Colloquial. See FIX, GET A.)

running Flotilla. A flotilla of torpedo boat destroyers attached to a fleet at sea. (Before and during 1914–18 War.) A colloquialism.

running rigging. All movable gear, halyards, boats, falls, etc., as opposed to standing rigging. (Technical.)

Ruskie or **Russki.** A Russian. The 1941 version of the 1919 *Bolshie*. By adoption of the Russian word (*Russki*).

Russian Finn. A superstitious or ' fey ' type.

ruti wallah. See ROOTI WALLAH.

S

S. The Captain S(ubmarines) in charge of a flotilla or parent ship. He is usually known by the short title: ' " S " took a poor view of the way the boat was handled, and Shorty got a whale of a blast.'

S.O.B.s. Silly old baskets: wardroom officers above the age of thirty. Cf. D.Y.F.S.

Saccony's. The firm of Saccony and Speed, wine merchants to the Royal Navy, which blessed them throughout the difficult war years 1939–45, supplies never failing to reach the fleets wherever they might be. (This firm published an excellent little book of wine wisdom and naval lore and legend entitled *Red Wine and Blue Water*; I understand, however, that it is not available at the moment [1949].)

sacks of coal. Heavy black clouds that foretell a storm.

saddle tanks. The external buoyancy tanks of a submarine.

safer. A load of fish. (East Anglian; recorded by Edward FitzGerald in his small glossary *Sea Words and Phrases*. I have, myself, heard the term used by old fishermen.) *Safely* landed.

sail close to the wind. Colloquially, to take risks by infringing rules and regulations of the Service. To skate on the thin ice of discretion.

sailor's best friend, the. A hammock, which, if lashed in the orthodox way with seven hitches, will keep him afloat for twenty-four hours.

sailor's pleasure. Grousing. Cf. DRIP.

sailorman. A barge or bargeman. The term *bargee* is taboo on the London River. (Colloquial, verging on technical.)

Sails. The sailmaker, a time-honoured nickname.

St George's banner. The White Ensign of the Royal Navy and the Royal Yacht Squadron. It has the cross of St George on a white field.

St Peter's fish. The haddock, because of the popularly supposed finger-print of St Peter on its sides. He caught a haddock to pay tribute.

Saliva, H.M.S. Liverpool Naval Headquarters in Liver Building. Cf. MATERNITY HOME.

salmon, catch a. To find a corpse in the Thames. (River police.) A euphemism.

salt eel. A rope's end, in so far as it is associated with corporal punishment. At one time an eel-skin was used as a lash.

Saltash catch or **Saltash luck.** ' A wet arse and no fish.' (A West Country term, used in the Royal and Merchant Navies and probably throughout the whole of the seafaring profession. It is believed to have derived from those luckless fishermen at Saltash near Plymouth, who sit on the bridge and catch nothing but the tide.) Cf. WET SHIRT.

saltbeef squires. Warrant Officers. (Old Navy term.)

salthorse. A non-specialist naval officer. ' I should specialize if I were you; there's a better chance of getting a brass hat that way than as a salthorse, especially these days.' (Wardroom.)

salt-water spoiler. A ship's cook. Cf. SLUSHY and GRUB SPOILER.

salvo. A ' broadside ' answer that clinches your argument and sinks your opponent. (Wardroom.)

Samson. A combined magnetic and acoustic mine. From its devastating strength.

Sand King. The bo'sun, the ' king ' of the SAND-SCRATCHERS.

sand strake, the. The garboard strake, which lies next to the keel. It rests upon the sand when the boat runs aground.

sandpaper the anchor. To do an unnecessary job. (General nautical slang.)

sand-scratcher. A seaman rating, one of whose jobs is the sanding of the deck.

sandy head. The pochard. (A wildfowlers' term.) The name is pronounced with the first element long and the *ch* hard, *po*-kard; hence the East Anglian slang name POKER.

Sardine. The nickname given to H.R.H. the Prince of Wales—the present Duke of Windsor—when he was a cadet at the Royal Naval College, Dartmouth.

sardine tin. A submarine. (Lower-deck.) Cf. TUBE.

Saturday Night sailor. A member of the Royal Naval Volunteer Reserve which, in peacetime, trains at week-ends. (A name given by the Royal Navy in the pre-1939 days.)

Saturday while. Leave from Saturday until (North-Country *while*) Monday, the short week-end leave given in naval barracks. See FRIDAY WHILE.

Saucy Arethusa, the. The cruiser *Arethusa*, Rear Admiral Tyrwhitt's flagship of the Harwich Force, 1914–18.

save-all. A metal trough under a scuttle (port-hole) to catch any water trickling through the rim when it is closed. (A colloquialism.)

saw-back. A species of *spiked* stickleback. It finds its way into shrimp nets.

sawbones. A nickname for a ship's doctor. (Lower-deck.) Cf. CHEMIST and QUACK.

Sawdust Club, the. A popular naval drinking-haunt in Plymouth. A converted chapel with a sawdust-strewn floor. (Wardroom.)

Scabby Liz. Scapa Flow, which, in the 1914–18 War, was a very grim place with little to offer in the way of entertainment. (Lower-deck.) Cf. SCAPATHY.

Scaldings! A warning cry from the duty cook that anyone getting in his way while he is carrying hot liquid food is liable to be scalded.

scales. Plain gold shoulder-straps worn by Sub-Lieutenants in full-dress uniform, less elaborate than the epaulettes worn by Lieutenants and above.

scaly back. A variant of SHELLBACK. A man who has been at sea many years and knows all the answers.

Scandinoogian. A Scandinavian seaman or ship. (Cf. SCOWEGIANS.) *Scandin*avian + Norwe*gian*.

scapathy. The state of mind induced by the dull monotony of days at anchor in Scapa Flow after the Battle of Jutland. This wind-swept anchorage was described as ' miles and miles of water surrounded by sweet Fanny Adams '. There was nothing to do ashore, for in the 1914–18 War there were few amenities; but in the 1939–45 War conditions at Lyness were much better. A telescoping of *Scapa* and *apathy*.

Scarborough warning. A blow and a word, in that order. A York-shire fisherman's term that dates from 1557, when Thomas Stafford captured Scarborough Castle and *afterwards* ordered the inhabitants to leave the town.

Scarborough whiting. Young haddocks when skinned and put up for sale in the fish shops. (Yorkshire coast.)

School of Wind, the. The Royal Naval School of Music at Scar-borough.

Schoolie. An Instructor Officer or *School*master. (Wardroom.) So too in the Army.

Scillonians. Scilly Isles fishing boats. Rather journalese than native.

scissor-grinder. An engineroom artificer. (Lower-deck.) Humor-ously pejorative.

scolter. A large porpoise peculiar to the North Sea. Etymology?

Scotch geese. Brent geese. (Fishermen's.)

Scotsman, the. A leather or zinc fender at the place on a ship's hull where duty boats come alongside. A protection for paintwork. (Reference to Scottish carefulness.)

Scotty. Captain Robert Scott, that gallant leader of a South Pole expedition who, in 1912, lost his life in a blizzard with four companions. The story of his poignant end can be read in *Scott's Last Expedition.*

Scouse. Short for *Lobscouse*, the nickname for all Liverpool-born men. From a local dish of that name.

Scowegians. Scandinavian ships or seamen. Cf. SCANDINOOGIAN.

scram bag. A bag already packed with essential things in case one has to *scram* or leave the ship hurriedly (i.e. take to the boats). (Not to be confused with SCRAN-BAG.)

scran. Food. (Lower-deck; originally tramps' underworld term.) ' Any gash scran loafing? ' Cf. MUNGY.

scran-bag. The receptacle in which are kept all articles of clothing, toilet, gear, etc., left on the mess-deck after it has been ' squared-off ' for ' rounds '. Petty Officers finding such gear place it in the scran-bag until it is redeemed by the loser at the cost of a bar of Navy soap. Nowadays the bag is a locker. (It was originally the receptacle for waste *food*. See preceding.)

scran oppos. Two men who cater for their messmates when the mess is run on the ' canteen ' as opposed to the ' general messing ' system. They choose the food and arrange the menus. Cf. SCRAN, OPPO, and COOKING OPPOS.

scraper. (1) A naval officer's cocked hat worn with full-dress uniform. Cf. FORE-AND-AFTER. (2) A steam trawler which ' scrapes ' the ocean's bed for fish.

Scratch. The Captain's Secretary. A wardroom vocative. From the scratching of his pen. Cf. SEC.

scratcher. A trawler that fishes off the east coast of Britain, as distinct from a LONG TRIPPER.

scratting. Scratching in the sands for coins, etc., after high tide. A beachcombing term used on the Yorkshire coast. Cf. FRETTING.

scribe. A Writer in the Royal Navy. Also used as vocative. A Writer is a clerk, and his duties vary. As a Captain's Writer he acts as typist and filer and generally performs the routine work of a civilian clerk. If he is a Ship's Office Writer he is responsible for keeping a section of the ship's ledger, which is a full-time job. In order that Writers may be thoroughly efficient in their rating they each do a period of Captain's and Ship's office duty. Often in ships where no Writer rating is carried a seaman will act as Captain's or Engineer's Writer and help to prepare the many returns that the Admiralty demands, and to make the amendments issued from time to time in King's Regulations and sundry Fleet Orders. This is regarded as a SOFT NUMBER by his messmates. See ROCKY SCRIBE and SPROG SCRIBE.

Scribe, a Chief. A Chief Petty Officer Writer.

scriggler. A small eel. It *scriggles* or wriggles about in the water.

scrimshaw. A naval collective term for toys, ship models, woolly ' mats ', etc., made on board by sailors during their watch below. From the Standard English sense; making designs with sea shells, bones, etc.

scrub. (1) To cancel an arrangement or order. (2) To reprimand (a subordinate). (3) (*Scrub round*) to fail to carry out (a job). In the ' reprimand ' nuance it is less used today than BOTTLE or BLAST; but, being traditional Navy, it is still used by conservative naval officers, who frown upon new Navy terms.

scud. To shake herrings out of the drift-net. From the Standard English sense, ' to cause to scud ' (to pass quickly).

scuffler. A small coasting vessel with low freeboard. She scuffles along.

scull. (Of a person) to wander aimlessly; (of a thing) to be left lying about. ' What are you doing sculling about here? Which watch are you in? ' ' Who's left all this gear sculling? Get it squared off before it goes in the scran-bag.' (General Navy.) Cf. LOAF. From an aimless sculling about in a rowing boat.

scuppered. (Of ships) sunk; (of men) killed or drowned. From opening the scuppers to let in the water—the easiest method of sinking a ship.

scurze. A naval nickname for bearded types. From whi*skers*.

scuttle. The Navy's name for a port-hole. (Technical.)

scuttle drill. A gunroom evolution carried out by junior midshipmen. In bad weather with a high sea running all scuttles are closed to prevent seas from invading the mess and in consequence the atmosphere becomes distinctly frowsty; the WARTS, as the junior MIDS are called, stand by the scuttles to open them ' between seas ' to let in pure air.

sea brief. A document that specifies the nature and destination of a ship's cargo.

Sea Cows = WOBBLY EIGHTS.

sea daddy. An elderly ' active service ' rating who takes a good-natured interest in one of the New Entries and helps him to avoid the many pitfalls in his first ship. Cf. SEA FATHER.

sea devil. (1) An angler fish. From its bad temper. (2) = FISHING FROG.

Sea Devil, the. Count von Luckner, commanding officer of a German raider which roamed the High Seas capturing or sinking ships. He was the soul of courtesy and always gave his victims time to take to the boats. The nickname was one of affection and is the title of a book on his adventures by Lowell Thomas. Count von Luckner survived the 1914–18 War and afterwards skippered a sailing ship.

sea eagle. The sting fish.

sea father. The second-termer at the Royal Naval College, Dartmouth, who looks after a first-termer (his *sea son*). Thus an eleventh-termer has a complete *sea-line* behind him: his *sea son*, his *sea son's sea son*, and so forth right down to a first-termer. (Cf. SEA DADDY.)

sea frog = FISHING FROG.

Sea Gallopers' Society. The Imperial Maritime League, which was inaugurated in 1901 in opposition to the Navy League.

sea lawyer. A nautical nuisance, one who is for ever standing up for his ' rights ' and is fond of quoting the regulations, etc. An unpopular messmate.

sea needle. The garfish, long and slender with a pointed head. Known as *guardfish* on the East Anglian coast.

sea owl. The lump fish. Somewhat like an owl in appearance.

sea parrot. The puffin. Cf. POPE, TOMMY NODDY and BOTTLENOSE.

sea pens. *Pennutulidae*, a feather-like sea coral found on the north-east coast of England.

sea pheasant. A bloater or kipper. Cf. SPITHEAD PHEASANT.

sea pie. An oyster catcher. (Marshmen's.) Cf. OLIVE.

sea pigeon. The black guillemot. (Manx term.) Cf. GREENLAND DOVE.

sea raker. The old type of beam trawler that used to work out of Great Yarmouth at the end of the last century; now almost, if not entirely, extinct.

sea rovers or **sea wanderers.** Herrings. Cf. ATLANTIC RANGERS and OCEAN RAMBLERS.

Sea Sammy. A shore crab. (Marshmen's.)

sea son. See SEA FATHER.

sea swallow. The tern. (Wildfowlers'.)

sea time. *Service* time spent at sea, as distinct from that spent in employment at a shore establishment. (Colloquial; almost technical.)

sea trumpet. A conch shell.

Seabees. Men of the Royal Engineers who worked with the Royal Navy in Combined Operations in the 1939–45 War.

sea-duty man. A helmsman or engine-telegraph man.

sea-going Wren. A C. W. CANDIDATE. A lower-deck sarcastic reference implying effeminacy.

sea-gull. Chicken served at the Royal Naval College, Dartmouth. From its (occasional) toughness; but partly also from a general tendency in regimented mankind to depreciate its food.

sea-legs. Ability to preserve equilibrium at sea. (A colloquialism verging on Standard English.)

sea-maw. A sea-gull. Cf. CHIEF STOKER and ANCIENT MARINER.

sealed pattern. The strictly orthodox specification, as laid down by the Admiralty. (Also known as *Admiralty pattern*.) It applies to clothing, food, even special rules of conduct.

Sec. An Admiral's or Captain's Secretary, a member of the Supply and Secretariat Branch with the rank of Lieutenant (s) or Lieutenant-Commander (s). Cf. SCRATCH and SECRET HARRY.

second class buff. A stoker second class.

Second Dicky. A Second Mate of the Merchant Navy.

seconds. Defective herrings, broken or otherwise unsuitable for the market. Second-rate. (Now a technicality.)

Secret Harry. The Secretary (Navy). (Wardroom.)

sedge marine. The sedge-warbler, a small marsh bird.

sedgy. The sedge-warbler. (Marshmen's.)

see off. To make short shrift of; to defeat in battle or sport; to reprimand a junior. ' The whaler's crew ought to see off the *Nonesuch* in the Regatta '; ' Jimmy saw me off for making a cock of that wire splice '. Probably from *see off the premises*.

Seehund. German two-man midget submarine. (German: literally, sea-hound.)

seek. To carry out an abortive search for herring. Steam drifters sometimes spend hours *seeking* and return to harbour without a catch. (Colloquial.) See CLEAN SHIP.

Selborne's Light Horse. Short-service men enlisted under the scheme instituted by Lord Selborne in 1907 to provide a Royal Fleet Reserve. Under this scheme men served five years at sea followed by seven ' on the reserve '. Cf. TICKLERS. Some of the *Light Horse* units recruited for the Boer War were somewhat lacking in discipline and generally behaved in a ' Harry Tate ' manner.

sell before the mast. To auction a dead messmate's effects on deck. An old naval custom. The amount raised is sent to his dependants.

Sell the pig and buy me out! A naval catch-phrase used by anyone who is feeling liverish and fed up with the Navy. See WHO'D SELL HIS FARM AND GO TO SEA?

Semaphore. A nickname for anyone who is addicted to gesture.

Senior. The Senior Engineer Lieutenant. (Wardroom vocative.) Cf. CHIEF.

Senior Watchkeeper. The senior Lieutenant in the WATCHKEEPERS' UNION.

serang. A Lascar bo'sun. (Not slang.) From the Persian *sarhang,* ' commander ' (literally ' chief power ').

serve out a drink. To give someone a BOTTLE. (Lower-deck euphemism.)

services. Lengths of spunyarn used for ' servicing ' rope to protect vulnerable parts from chafing. In the Royal Navy, cordage is wormed, parcelled and served; and the rule is: ' Worm and parcel with the lay; turn and serve the other way.'

set. (1) The moustache and beard demanded by King's Regulations when permission to ' grow ' has been given to an officer or rating. Cf. BUG WHISKERS and PLAYER'S PLEASE! (2) A long pole used for thrusting boats through the breakers. (An East Anglian colloquialism, especially among fishermen.)

seven imperial turns. The seven marline-hitches in a hammock lashing. (Lower-deck.)

seven-bell boat. A leave boat for officers at seven bells (3.30 p.m.).

seven-bell dinner. A special meal served to men at seven bells (11.30 a.m.) who are going on watch at mid-day. Cf.:

seven-bell tea. Wardroom tea at 3.30 p.m.

seven-beller. A slangy synonym of SEVEN-BELL DINNER.

seven bells out of (someone), knock. To give someone a thorough beating-up. (Lower-deck.) Cf. FILL IN.

seventh wave is the worst, the. A popular traditional belief, often disproved.

seven-whistle. A whimbrel, because of its seven-pipe cry.

sewn-up. Completely drunk and incapable: so dead drunk that he might as well be sewn-up in his hammock and dropped over the side. Cf. STITCHED.

sew-sew boy. A member of a lower-deck JEWING FIRM.

sex appeal Pete. A semi-armour-piercing shell. From the initials S.A.P. (Lower-deck.)

shaft. To propel a canal barge through a tunnel by means of a shaft. (Canalmen's colloquialism verging on technicality.)

Shagbat. A supermarine Walrus aircraft used by the Fleet Air Arm. Humorously depreciative.

shake book. The book kept by the Quartermaster of the Watch. It contains the names of ratings who are to be roused for duty during the night. ' Put me down for a shake at seven bells, Q.M.'

shake-down cruise. A cruise made by a newly-commissioned ship to help the ship's company to get used to her.

shake-up. Physical exercise in the gymnasium as punishment. At the Royal Naval College, Dartmouth, this is given to a class that has been particularly lethargic or inattentive.

shallow-waister. A flush-decked craft that is inclined to be ' wet ' in a seaway. (Colloquial.)

shambling. Ragging Authority at the Royal Naval College, Dartmouth.

shanghai'd, be. (In the Royal Navy) to be drafted to special service, e.g. Combined Operations or a shore assignment. ' Did you volunteer for Combined Ops? ' ' Not Pygmalion likely, mate, I was shanghai'd; I put in for general service in destroyers.' From *Shanghai*, where once it was common nautical practice to drug, or intoxicate, men and then ship them as crew.

shanks. Pink shrimps. The name is peculiar to the Fleetwood district.

sharks. Tinned sardines. (Lower-deck.)

Sharky. A sharp-featured messmate. (Lower-deck.)

sharp end, the. The landlubber's term for the bows of the ship, often used derisively by seamen. Cf. BLUNT END.

shebo. Soap. (Lower-deck.) With a pun on the beauteous Queen of *Sheba*?

sheep-tracking. A zig-zag method of searching for fish shoals.

Sheer Nasty. Sheerness in the Thames Estuary. (General Navy slang.)

Sheer Necessity. A variant of the preceding. The only thing that takes anyone to the place.

She's all legs and wings. Said of an over-sparred sailing ship.

She has lines like a butter-box. A disparaging phrase applied to an ugly ' utility ' ship. One with no grace of line or anything to commend her. Cf. HAYSTACK.

She sails like a witch. Said of a sailing boat that is so well rigged that she goes well to windward.

She smells the ground. Said of a ship that is nearing harbour.

She wouldn't have cracked an egg. A Midshipman's boast of the neat way he brought his picket boat alongside the ship or jetty. As delicately as Agag.

sheer. Clear. (East Anglian term.)

shellback. A veteran sailor who hangs round the sea-wall and recounts ANCIENT MARINER stories. Cf. SCALY BACK.

Shieldsman. A fisherman or fishing craft from North and South Shields.

shifting backstay. One who, not being brilliant, is moved from job to job in the hope that he may be found a niche where he can cause the least trouble. Backstays help the shrouds to support the mast in heavy weather.

shimmer. A catch of herring. From the glittering of fish as they are drawn through the water in the drift net. One of the most poetic of the nouns of assembly.

shiner. A black eye. (Lower-deck.) Adopted from civilian slang.

Shiney or **Shiny.** A variant of SHINER as nickname for men surnamed White or Wright. (Lower-deck.) From the idea inherent in '*shining white* in the moonlight'.

shingle-tramper. A coastguard. (Cf. GOBBY.) From their patrol.

ship. (1) To put an article in its right place. 'Ship warheads to torpedoes.' (2) To take on board. 'She ships a heavy sea in bad weather.' (3) To assume a rank or wear an expression, e.g. *to ship one's killick* on becoming a Leading Hand and therefore entitled to wear the anchor as badge of rank. 'He shipped a face like a scrubbed 'ammick when I told him that his leave was jammed.' (Lower-deck.) Incidentally, a Petty Officer daringly *shipped* a monocle and caused an Admiralty Fleet Order to be promulgated permitting lower-deck ratings to wear monocles if advised to do so by a naval eye surgeon.

shippie or **shippy.** A shipmate. (Fishermen's.)

Ship's Company. The full complement of officers and men. (Technical.)

ship's husband. A captain of a ship who is so proud of his command that he is for ever spending his salary on her, doubtless heedful of the advice of Ronald Hopwood in his sage poem, *The Laws of the Navy*:

> *Dost deem that thy vessel needs gilding,*
> *And the dockyard forbear to supply?*
> *Place thy hand in thy pocket and gild her,*
> *There be those who have risen thereby.*

ship's price. The charge for food and sweetmeats, cigarettes, etc., smuggled ashore and sold for double the cost. (Training-ships'.)

ship the swab. To wear epaulettes on the shoulders of one's full dress uniform. A Sub-Lieutenant does this when he is promoted to Lieutenant.

shittled. Tangled. Used of nets that have become so when drying in the wind. (Originally, euphemistic.)

211

shoe horn. An avocet. (Marshmen's.) (Also known in East Anglia as a *cobbler's awl*. Mentioned in the works of Sir Thomas Browne in the seventeenth century.)

shonkey or **shonky.** Any stingy person; one who hates paying for a round of drinks but is not averse from accepting treats from others. (Lower-deck.) From low civilian slang *Shonky*, a Jew.

shore billet. An appointment at the Admiralty or on the staff of any naval shore establishment. (Colloquial.)

shore saint and sea devil. One having the characteristics of a CARNEY.

shore-going. A naval adjective descriptive of anything connected with ' the Beach '. E.g. a shore-going parson, as distinct from a naval chaplain.

shore-loafer. A civilian. (Royal Navy.) Hence *shore-loafing*: ' In this sort of weather don't you envy your shore-loafing pals? '

shore-side. The BEACH. (Pidgin English: used by old ' China Birds '.) ' Coming shore-side after lunch? We might have a round of golf.'

shore wallah. A shore-based naval officer.

short-arm inspection. The periodical medical inspection in naval barracks to detect incipient venereal disease. Also known as *F.F.I.*, ' free from infection '.

Shorty. The traditional Navy nickname for any undersized man. Some synonyms are *sawn-off*, *stumpy* and *short-arse*. (Lower-deck.) Cf. LOFTY.

shottens. Spent or ' shotten ' herrings. (East Anglian drifter-men's.)

shovel-noser. One of the very early type of torpedo boats, which had shovel-nosed bows.

showing the flag. The paying of courtesy visits by H.M. Ships to foreign countries in peacetime.

shrieker. A black-tailed godwit; from its piercing cry. (Marshmen's.)

Sick Bay cocktail. Any dose of medicine. (Lower-deck.)

Sick Bay goose. A bed pan. From its ' neck ' and squat appearance. (Navy.)

Sick Bay lounger. A cadet who goes to the Sick Bay in order to miss Divisions or studies. (Royal Naval College, Dartmouth.)

Sick Bay moocher. The training ship *Conway's* version of the preceding.

Sick Bay tiffy. A sick berth attendant. He wears a uniform like a TIFFY. (Lower-deck.)

sickle bill. A curlew, whose beak is shaped like a sickle.

side party, the. Men engaged in painting the ship's side.

sig. (Short for) a signal rating.

signalitis. Disease from which a Flag Officer with a tendency to frequent signal-making is said to suffer. Cf. PROMOTIONITIS.

Signals. (1) Signal Officer. (Wardroom.) (2) The Signal Departments in Admiralty, each dealing with the signals of its own Division. 'I know nothing about this business, ring up Signals.' (Colloquial.)

silent hours. Those hours during the night when ships' bells are not sounded. (Colloquial.)

Silver Phantom, the. The cruiser *Aurora*, which was laid down at Portsmouth in 1935 and launched in 1936, the eighth *Aurora* in the Royal Navy. She did splendid work in the 1939–45 War and her nickname was given to her by the Italian Navy.

Silver Streak, the. The English Channel. (Verging on journalese.)

simple sailor. The self-depreciatory nickname of a naval officer. ' Look here, I'm a simple sailor; this stuff is too brainy for me. Try the P.M.O., he's a whale at crosswords.'

Sims' Circus. The first flotilla of American warships that sailed to their English base in 1917 when the United States entered the war. Admiral Sims was the Commander-in-Chief of the U.S. Navy.

sin bo'sun. The Chaplain. (Lower-deck.)

Sinbad. A Royal Naval Reserve officer. (Wardroom.) All R.N.R. officers are deep-sea sailors, the ' real ' sailors. Cf. ROCKY and CARGO BILL.

single-boating. Lone fishing—as opposed to FLEETING in the days of the smacks, which were still working at the beginning of the twentieth century.

sippers. A sip from the tot of a messmate's rum.

sitter. An enemy submarine on the surface, a ' sitting target '. Any enemy ship taken unawares. From the shooting of a sitting bird; cf. *sitter*, cricketing slang for a very easy catch.

sitting on a draft chit. Waiting to go ' on draft ', but unable to leave until one's relief arrives.

six on four. Six men living on the rations usually allowed to four.

sixpenny sick. A pleasure steamer; but since this term was coined the price of *mal de mer* has become somewhat higher.

sixteen bells. It is an Old Navy custom to have sixteen bells sounded by the youngest member of the ship's company at midnight on New Year's Eve. (Naval lore.)

skate. (1) A 1939–45 variant of BIRD. A leave-breaker, womanizer and general bad hat. (2) To leave the ' straight and narrow path of virtue '; to ' act RORTY ' and cheerfully face the Commander at Defaulters the next morning.

skating rink. Nickname for any bald-headed rating.

Skeggy hat. A cap of distinctive shape worn by trainee ratings at the Skegness shore establishment, H.M.S. *Royal Arthur*, in the 1939–45 War. *Skeggy* was the ratings' abbreviation of Skegness.

skettle. To change into full-fig dress uniform in pre-war days. The term may be a variant of *skiffle*, to hurry. Wright in his excellent *Provincial Dictionary* gives *sket*, an adverb meaning ' quickly; immediately '.

skimming dishes. Fast ' planing ' motor launches used as picket boats in the Fleet. They replaced the old steam pinnaces and are not, in the opinion of many naval men, nearly so picturesque, although they are very efficient. Usually shortened to *skimmers*.

skin. Cheek, ' nerve '. ' I don't know how Nobby Clark had the skin to ask the Bloke for week-end leave after the BOTTLE he had from him last Monday.'

skin out. To leave a ship with the intention of permanent desertion. Cf. RUN.

Skipper Woods. A haunt of cadets at the Royal Naval College, Dartmouth.

skipper's daughter. A crested wave, from the cock's comb suggestive of a ' hair-do '.

skipper's doggy. See DOGGY.

skips. An infrequently heard term for the Captain of a ship. Short for skipper. (Lower-deck.)

skulk. To dodge work; to be slack at whatever job is being done; generally, to behave in a lubberly and contemptible manner. (A special Service application of a Standard English word.)

skull. A narrow cod basket used in the cod-banging boats. From the shape.

sky pilot. An old nautical nickname for a Chaplain. Cf. SIN BOS'UN and HOLY JOE.

slack in stays. Slow in the uptake; dull-witted. A sailing vessel is so when she is slow in going about. See MISS STAYS.

slack party. Those punished for slackness at the Royal Naval College, Dartmouth. They are given special work to do.

Slackers. A Royal Canadian Navy term for Halifax, Nova Scotia. *Halifax—Halifacks—Slacks—Slackers*; the end of a tour of duty.

slacks, work the. To tow a lighter or barge against a tide. (Tug-men's term.) The tugs keep close to the edge of the river in ' slack ' water. When a tug is seen to be *working the slacks*, other vessels give her the right of way.

slap in. To make a request for leave. ' I'll slap in for FRIDAY WHILE this week '. (Lower-deck.)

slap-tailer. A vessel which has a low counter and is frequently slapped by a following sea. Also known as a *drabble-tailer*.

sleep. (Of a yacht) to have her sails filled but not flapping.

Sleeper's Hole. The Yacht Basin in Newhaven Harbour, Sussex.

slick. Spruce, TIDDLEY. (On the training ship *Conway*, through American influence.)

slide and glitter. Marmalade. (Lower-deck.)

Slim. An inevitable nickname for a fat man on the lower-deck.

sling. To sling a hammock. ' What's the name of the bloke who slings abaft the trunk? ' (Lower-deck.)

sling the donkey. To take dunnage on board by means of a donkey engine and tackle.

sling the hash. To pass the food. Cf. FAIR WIND. (Merchant Navy.)

Slinger. A naval nickname for men surnamed Wood. Also *Timber*. Cf. the Army's *Lackery*.

slingers. Ship's biscuits or bread soaked in cocoa. A snack eaten before slinging a hammock. Supper is very early in the Navy and *slingers* help to fortify the men until breakfast the next day. (Lower-deck.)

slip. (1) (Of an H.M. Ship) to leave her buoy and proceed to sea. ' Let me know when the *Nonesuch* has slipped, Number One.' (2) Colloquially, to lose one's mental hold of a situation; to seem obtuse.

slip one's cable. To die. (General nautical.)

slop chest. The ship's store, where *slops*—ready-made clothing, etc.—are sold. Cf.:

slop chit. A form supplied to a rating which enables him to buy ' slops ' from the ship's clothing store. Hence, colloquially, the amount of work one has to do: ' Let *him* do it, I have enough on my slop chit already.'

slops. Ready-made clothing obtained from the ship's SLOP CHEST.

slow-hauler. A slow-moving cargo ship in a convoy; a nine-knotter.

slow-match. Any red-nosed individual. Literally a slow-burning fuse for lighting an explosive charge.

sluggers. Sloe gin. (Wardroom.)

slush. Any ' sloppy ' food, e.g. soup or stew. (Lower-deck.) Hence:

slushy. A sea-faring cook. Cf. GRUB SPOILER and SALT-WATER SPOILER.

sluther. A large jelly-fish. (A trawlermen's term, which may be a dialect form of *slither*.)

Smack it about! 'Get a move on!'; PLAY LIVELY! A naval exhortation to the hands to 'put some beef' into the job. From the smacking about of paintbrushes by the SIDE PARTY painting the hull of the ship.

smart ticket. A certificate (officially known as a *Hurt Certificate*) awarded to any naval officer or rating who is injured in carrying out his duties on board ship if it is determined that such injury was not brought about by his own negligence.

smash-ankle. Deck hockey in the Royal Navy. Proleptic.

smashing. A 'surpassing' adjective used *ad nauseam* on the lower-deck. Adopted from civilian use. 'The Commander's a smashing bloke'; 'I met a smashing party last night.' It is closely rivalled by LUSH. Cf. modern civilian *devastating*.

Smell the spot. An invitation to a Midshipman to bend over to receive 'half a dozen of the best' for having committed some sin of omission or for transgressing a gunroom law.

smigget. A good-looking messmate. A Maltese word which I owe to Ldg. Stoker S. Hobson, R.N. (Lower-deck.)

Smokey Joe. (1) The officer in charge of smoke-screen operations. (2) A 'Fleet' Class coal-burning minesweeper.

Smudge. A variant of BIFF as nickname for Smith. Suggested by '*black*smith'.

smug boat. A Chinese *smug*gling junk.

Snake Pit, the. The Ladies' Lounge at the Union Club, Malta, the haunt of the FISHING FLEET.

Snakey. Any tall, thin rating. Cf. DRAINPIPE and TACKLINE. The vocative is *Snako*.

Snap! The classic signal made by the battleship *Queen Elizabeth* when she met her liner namesake in mid-ocean. (From the juvenile card-game.)

snatch. A tow. 'Give us a snatch, chum, we've got engine trouble.' Cf. PLUCK.

snobber. A member of a lower-deck SNOBBING FIRM; any cobbler.

snobbing firm. A lower-deck boot-repairing party. From the old civilian-slang *snob*, a boot-repairer.

217

snod. The end of a fishing-line to which the hook is attached. Probably a dialectal variant of *snood*.

snorter. One of the German submarines fitted with the *schnorkel* device, which enabled them to recharge batteries under the surface and to keep the seas for a considerable time. ' Schnorkels ' first appeared in late 1944.

snotty. A Midshipman, so called from the time when Their Lordships decided that three buttons should be worn on the sleeves of the Midshipmen's ' round jackets ' to prevent the sleeves being used as a substitute for handkerchiefs or ' snot rags '.

snotties' nurse. The Sub-Lieutenant in charge of the gunroom. See preceding.

Snowball or **Snowy.** Any fair-haired rating. (Lower-deck.) Cf. FROSTY.

snowball hitch. A ' knot ' that easily falls apart. Cf. GROCER'S HITCH.

snowbird. The ivory gull, an Arctic bird often seen in the Orkney and Shetland Isles.

snowflake. A night illuminant used by the Royal Navy to prevent surface attack on convoys in the Battle of the Atlantic (1939–45). It revealed the attacker to the gunners.

snub up. To bring a ship up to her buoy without jerking.

snurge = SKULK. From dialectal *snudge*, to lie quiet or snug.

soap and baccy paymaster. An Accountant officer in the Royal Navy. He carries out victualling as distinct from secretarial duties.

soap and flannel. Bread and cheese. (Lower-deck.) Physical resemblance.

social tits. Naval officers who are fond of attending dances and parties ashore. Cf. POODLE-FAKER.

Sot you, Jack, I'm inboard! A lower-deck catch-phrase meaning ' Pull the ladder up, I'm all right '. It doesn't matter about anyone else as long as the speaker is safe and sound. Cf. the Army's —— *you, Jack, I'm all right!* and the Air Force's —— *you, Jack, I'm fire-proof!*

sot's opera. An unofficial concert held in the canteen in a naval depot. Highly amusing but very, very low and also very libellous. Cf. FUNNY PARTY.

soddick. Soft tack; bread, cakes, etc. (Lower-deck.) Via the slovenly *soddack* from *soft tack*.

sodduk. The training ship *Conway's* version of the preceding term.

sodge. See SOJ.

sodger. A soldier, a term of abuse for a lubberly deck-hand. From the traditional naval seamen's attitude towards the Marines.

soft number. An easy job. (Lower-deck.) Cf. LOAFING NUMBER.

softers. Soft soap, soapy water used for SOOJYING the decks and cleaning generally. (Lower-deck.)

soj or **sodge.** A shortened form of SODGER; a corruption of *Soldier*, which is a wardroom form of address to a Royal Marine officer.

soldier's weather. Good sailing weather, when even a soldier could handle a boat without difficulty.

soldier's wind. A breeze such as one finds in SOLDIER'S WEATHER.

Solent seabirds. A class of sailing yacht peculiar to the Solent.

solid. 'Wooden', stupid=block-headed (person). (Lower-deck.)

Soo. *S*taff *O*fficer *O*perations. (Navy.)

soojy. To scrub or sand the deck. 'Who'd join the Navy? Nothing but soojy, soojy, soojy all the bloomin' day.' From *squeegee*. Hence, by rhyming reduplication:

soojy moojy. A mixture of soap, soda and sundry ingredients for scrubbing decks and washing paintwork.

sooner. A shirker. He would *sooner* (rather) do the job tomorrow —or never. Cf. MIKER.

sorrow on the sea, There's. A traditional warning to one who would 'sell his farm and go to sea'. Cf. WHO'D SELL HIS FARM AND GO TO SEA?

So'ton. Short for Southampton. (Local and general nautical usage.)

souse the gurnet = BLOW THE GRAMPUS.

southerly buster. A strong wind from the south.

spam medal. The 1939–45 Star, whose ribbon has the same colours as the N.A.A.F.I. girls' arm 'flash'. As spam was sold in the N.A.A.F.I. what more obvious term could suggest itself?

Spanish pennants = MALTESE LACE.

spark-box. The wireless cabin in a merchant ship.

sparker. A naval telegraphist. The vocative is *Sparko.*

Sparks. Nickname for the wireless operator in a merchant ship. Cf. SPARKER.

spasm. Synonymous with a FLAP or a PANIC, though *spasm* had the additional sense of *a false alarm.* (1914–18 War.)

spat. The ova of oysters.

special entries. The 'Public School Entry' Midshipmen who enter direct from schools and not through the Royal Naval College, Dartmouth. Cf. DARTS.

specialist. A naval officer versed in some such subject as gunnery, torpedoes, navigation, engineering. Cf. SALTHORSE.

speet. The spit or rod used for drying herrings. (East Anglian pronunciation of *spit.*)

spello. A *spell* of rest or 'stand easy'.

sperling. A sprat. (East Anglian: a dialectal form of *sparling*, a smelt.)

Spider. The inseparable nickname for Webb. From *spider('s) web.*

Spider's web, the. A patrol area of the Royal Naval Air Service in Felixstowe district. Seen on the operational chart, the patrol looked like a spider's web. (1914–18 War.)

spidereen. A non-existent vessel with nine decks and no bottom; a putting-off answer to those who ask what ship a man is ' on ' instead of (correctly) ' in '. Short for *spidereen frigate*, it is an old naval term that has survived the last century.

Spike. Nickname for men surnamed Sullivan or Hughes.

spike-boozle. To render ineffective, to sabotage, blow up or otherwise destroy (a ship or a plan). A merging of the senses of ' *spike* a gun ' and ' bam*boozle* '.

spin a cuffer (or **spin a bender** or **spin a twister**). To tell an improbable story, as in a seaman's pub. Cf. BENDER, CUFFER, TWISTER.

spit brown. To chew tobacco, which makes the spittle brown. ' A reg'ler Jack-me-'earty, ain't yer, spittin' brown and actin' rorty! ': the old Navy type of ' crusher's ' lecture to youthful law-breakers.

spitcher. To destroy or render useless. (From Maltese.) ' This gadget's spitchered, chuck it in the drink.' In 1914–18, especially to sink an enemy submarine.

Spithead nightingale. The bo'sun's pipe. The trilling of these pipes can be heard for miles when the Fleet is lying at Spithead.

Spithead pheasant. A bloater. (Naval lower-deck.) Compare ABERDEEN CUTLET and BOMBAY DUCK.

spit-kid. A United States landing craft. An American Navy term adopted by the lower-deck in 1943–44. Literally, a spittoon.

Spitter. A Spitfire aircraft. Also *Spitty*. (Lower-deck.)

splice the main-brace. To issue a double tot of rum on an occasion for celebration.

split chums. To quarrel. A term from the training ship *Conway*. Cf. PART BRASS RAGS.

split yarn. See EVERYTHING ON A SPLIT YARN.

spoonie (or **-y**). The spoonbill. (Marshmen's and wildfowlers'.)

sport ship. The supply and entertainment ship *Borodine*, a Grand Fleet tender at Scapa Flow in the 1914–18 War. Any ship with like functions.

spotty fishing. (In the herring fishery) unequal catches in one area, some drifters getting good hauls and others practically no fish. Good in *spots*.

spouter. (1) A whale. (2) A ship employed in the whaling industry. (3) A member of the crew of such a ship.

sprat loon. See RAIN GOOSE.

sprat mow. The common or herring gull. (An East Coast term.)

sprat weather. Dull wintry days on which good catches of sprats can be expected. (Fishermen's traditional term.)

sprat's eye. A silver threepenny piece.

spring-heeled jack. The early type of rocket-propelled torpedo.

springs. Spring tides. (Colloquial.)

spritty. A *sprit*sail barge. Cf. STUMPY.

sprog. A New Entry into the Navy. Originally applied to second-class stokers; probably is a corruption of *spr*ocket, a *c*og in the wheel. A sailor's first-born is usually referred to as a *sprog*. 'Jimmy Green's gone on compassionate leave, his missis has just had a sprog.' (Lower-deck.)

sprog scribe. A probationary Writer rating. See SCRIBE.

spud. (1) An obvious nickname for anyone surnamed Murphy. A *murphy* is a *spud* or potato: Murphy is a common Irish surname: potatoes form a staple Irish food. (2) A pierhead of a MULBERRY harbour.

spud barber. The galley hand who peels the potatoes. Also *spud skinner*.

spud net. (1) A string bag. Carried by husbands on shopping expeditions with their wives ashore. (Lower-deck.) (2) A scrambling net, as used in assault vessels for descending into the boats and for climbing back on board again. But for the *spud nets* many men in the 1939–45 War would have been unable to come aboard again and so save their lives.

spudoosh. A species of stew in which potatoes preponderate: *spud* + *oosh*. Cf. OOSH-ME-GOSH.

spunian. An occasional (fishermen's) pronunciation of *spunyarn*.

spunyarn major. A Lieutenant-Commander, a rank equivalent to that of Major in the Army.

spunyarn Sunday. A sabbath on which there are no Divisions and church is voluntary.

Squadron, the. The Headquarters of the Royal Yacht Squadron at Cowes, Isle of Wight. Cf. WHITE SQUADRON.

squall. Figuratively, a quarrel; a row, trouble with Authority. ' You'd better keep to windward of the Bloke; there's a squall brewing '. (Lower-deck.)

square number. An easy job in depot or shore base; what the lower-deck terms a LOAFING NUMBER or SOFT NUMBER. Cf. also SWING ROUND THE BUOY.

square off. To make things ship-shape and generally tidy. To straighten, as in the order ' Square off your caps '.

square one's yard-arm = CLEAR ONE'S YARD-ARM.

square rig. That worn by ' men dressed as seamen ', the bell-bottomed trousers, jumper, flannel and jean collar. See FREE AND BLOWING and cf. FORE-AND-AFT RIG.

square yards with. To settle accounts, get even, with someone. Also, to come to an agreement.

square-bashing. Squad drill in naval barracks or a gunnery school. Cf. GRAVEL-GRINDING.

square-face. Gin. From the square-faced bottles that contain it.

Squarehead. Any Dutch or German seaman. Cf. DUTCHY.

square-mainsail coat. A naval officer's frock coat donned on occasions of ceremony in peace-time.

square-rig ticket. A Master Mariner's certificate for sail only. Cf. STEAM TICKET.

square-rigger. A square-rigged sailing ship.

squashed flies. Garibaldi biscuits—very popular with cadets of the Royal Naval College, Dartmouth. From the currants therein; adopted from civilian slang.

squeaker. A very small and talkative cadet. He has a squeaky voice. (The training ship *Conway*.)

squeegee band. A ship's band of the FOO FOO or comb-and-paper variety. A band made up of whatever instruments are possessed by the ship's company. Rough-and-ready, like a *squeegee*, an implement used to dry the decks.

squeeze. A ship's steward's (Merchant Navy) term for a tip. Cf. the Cockney term, *dropsy*.

Squeeze him and he'll fill a bucket. Said of a particularly ' wet ' or useless rating. Cf. WET AS A SCRUBBER.

squeeze off a fish = SQUIRT A MOULDY.

squeeze-box. A concertina or a melodeon. (Lower-deck.)

Squibbley. Esquimault, Vancouver. The naval college and town.

squid-box. The housing of the *squid*, a triple-barrelled mortar for firing depth-charges. Placed on the sterns of modern destroyers (1948).

squillgee. Literally, a swab; hence a skulking, unpopular fellow who tries to PASS THE CAN whenever possible. Cognate with *squeegee*—and just as ' wet '.

squirt a mouldy. To fire a torpedo. Cf. MOULDY and FISH.

stabber. A marline-spike or pricker. (Lower-deck and Merchant Navy.)

stack. A ship's funnel.

Stack of Bricks, the. The Merchant Navy Memorial Hostel, London.

stacker, two- (three-, four-). A two- (three-, four-) funnelled ship.

Staffy. A staff officer. (Wardroom.)

stagger juice. Navy rum. (Lower-deck.) Cf. BUBBLY and WINE.

stagger off the wall. To put to sea. (Coastal Forces.)

staggers, get the. To be flustered or confused. Cf. DIZZY, GET (Royal Navy.)

staid hand. A long-service rating; a STRIPEY; a thoroughly reliable hand, who acts as SEA DADDY to New Entries.

Stamshaw nanny-goat. A quick-tempered messmate, apt to ' fly off the handle ' on the least provocation. The nanny-goats on Stamshaw Common, Portsmouth, were noted for their butting propensities. Cf. TORPOINT CHICKEN.

stand-easies. Articles of food left with the cook in the galley for baking in time for eating during *Stand Easy*. (R.N.)

standing watches. Watches kept at the same time each day—as in the Merchant Navy, where they do not have dog watches as in the Royal Navy. (Technical.)

standing water. Any tideless stretch of water. (Colloquial.)

stand-up prayers. A make-shift Divine Service, alfresco. (Royal Navy.)

star. To pass certain courses, e.g. the staff course, at the Royal Naval College, Greenwich, and so have an asterisk placed against one's name in the Navy List.

starboard light. The drink, *crème de menthe.* A ship's starboard light is green.

Stars and Bars, the. The United States Ensign.

Start, the. Start Point, Devon.

Starve 'em, Rob 'em and Cheat 'em. Strood, Rochester and Chatham, localities well-known to naval personnel. A good-natured libel, dating from the Eighteenth Century.

Stash it! The lower-deck form of the civilian's *Stop it!*; meaning, ' Be quiet! ' or bluntly, ' Shut your trap! '

steady. A regular girl-friend; a fiancée; a matelot's PIECEE ONE party. ' Was that Ginger's steady I saw him with last night? ' Adopted from civilian slang; *steady*-going. Girls likewise have *steadies*.

Steady Barker! A catchphrase from the Navy's radio revue *Merry-Go-Round* featuring Eric Barker. A popular show during the 1939–45 War.

steady double, the. The shambling movement adopted by ratings on their way to the defaulters' table. Ironic. Cf. DOUBLE SHUFFLE.

steam antics. Fleet exercises in peacetime. See P.Z.

steam bo'sun. A Warrant Engineer, R.N.

steam bus. A steam pinnace used as picket boat before the adoption of motor boats. Cf. STEAM PUNCHER.

steam chicken. A carrier-borne aircraft. Cf. PUSSER'S DUCK.

steam ditty-box. A steam pinnace. Ironic on DITTY BOX.

steam duster. A steam pinnace or cutter. (Lower-deck.) She often has a dusting in a seaway. Cf. STEAM PUNCHER.

steam jaunty. The Regulating Chief Stoker. See JAUNTY and CORDITE JAUNTY.

steam Navy, the. The Navy during the coal-burning era between the ' tar and spunyarn ' days and the modern oil-burning period.

steam puncher. The old-time steam pinnace, which was used as picket-boat. She punched her way through the short seas between the parent ship and the shore. Cf. STEAM BUS and STEAM DUSTER.

steam ticket or **steamer ticket.** A Master Mariner's certificate for steamships only.

steaming blind. Sailing in thick weather at night with visibility nil. (Colloquial.)

steeps. Shallow vats filled with water; in them, herring are drained. The spits are laid across the steeps and the fish suspended therefrom are thus immersed.

steerage, the. The gunroom, the home of the Midshipmen. (Old Navy.)

steerage hammock. A boiled steam-pudding done in a cloth that is lashed hammock-wise.

Steeroins! A cadet who calls ' Bags I steeroins! ' is given the privilege of coxing the boat. This is purely an ' off-service ' custom and applies to boats hired for pleasure, skiffs, pair-oars, etc. *Pairoins* means rowing a skiff double-banked, each man using a single scull. (Both terms are peculiar to the old *Britannia*, and I am not certain whether they have survived her passing; they are used in *One Hears a Drum*, by Allan Baddeley. The *oins* part is simply a perversion [i.e. deliberate]—or perhaps a corruption [i.e. a folk-growth]—of *ing*, the verbal-noun ending, with *s* added for luck.)

steer small. To use discretion, to ' watch one's step '. Literally, to steer within the nearest point of the compass course.

stem Jack. The small union flag worn in the bows of a battle-ship when she is at anchor and lowered when she is aweigh.

stemmed. Aground. (Canalmen's.) The *stem* of the boat is hard and fast in the mud.

stick. (1) A submarine's periscope. (2) A mast in a sailing craft.

sticks. A ship's drummer.

sticks and string. A naval reference to the days of sailing ships, the ' masts and yards' era.

stitched. Very drunk. A variant of SEWN-UP. (Lower-deck.)

Stitcher. An alternative nickname for SAILS, a ship's sailmaker.

stocker. Any small or unmarketable fish used as bait. (Fishermen's.) Short for *stock-bait*.

stodge. See ' BRITANNIA ' SLANG.

Stodger. (1) A 1914–18 War nickname for H.M.S. *Warspite*. Cf. OLD LADY OF THE NAVY. (2) The ' tuck-shop ' at the Royal Naval College, Dartmouth. Cf. *stodge*; see ' BRITANNIA ' SLANG.

stokehold bo'sun. The Warrant Engineer in a coal-burning vessel.

stoker. A cinder or smut in one's eye.

Stokes. A lower-deck form of address to a stoker.

stonachy. See STONNICKY.

Stone Frigate. One of the naval barracks or shore establishments which are named after the old-time frigates. For instance, H.M.S. *Pembroke*, the 22-gun frigate so named by Oliver Cromwell after his capture of Pembroke Castle, about 1648, has given its name to Chatham Barracks. *Victory*, the 100-gun ship launched in 1765, is the name for Portsmouth Barracks. *Vernon* was the torpedo school ship at Portsmouth, launched in 1858; the present-day establishment is still known as H.M.S. *Vernon*. *Excellent* (formerly *Hardy*, a coastal defence gunboat) became gunnery school tender, and when Whale Island became the Portsmouth Gunnery School it retained the name. *Ganges*, at one time a Boys' training ship at Falmouth, gave its name to the present establishment in Shotley Barracks. Other establishments are H.M.S. *St Vincent* (Gosport), *St George* (Isle of Man) and *Unicorn* (H.Q. of the East Scottish Division of the R.N.V.R. at Dundee); several bases established during the 1939–45 War were given ships' names.

stone ship. One of the concrete vessels built during the 1914–18 War. Not to be confused with a STONE FRIGATE.

stonnicky. A corruption of *stonachy*, a three-tailed ' cat ' used for mild ' chasing ' at naval colleges and in training ships, and forming also a prominent feature in the traditional naval game PRIEST OF THE PARISH. Perhaps akin to *stunner*.

stop one. To get killed or wounded; that is, stop a bullet or piece of shell. ' I'm afraid the Owner has stopped one, you'll have to take over, Number One.'

storm finch. The stormy petrel. A local variation. Cf. MOTHER CARY'S CHICKEN. (Fishermen's.)

storm-breeders. Heavy clouds. Cf. SACKS OF COAL.

stormy petrel. A nautical trouble-maker; a SEA LAWYER. As the stormy petrel portends bad weather, so does he portend trouble.

Stornowegian. A seaman hailing from Stornoway. A blend of *Storno*way and Nor*wegian*.

stort. Misused for the Standard English *scart*, a shag or cormorant. (Wildfowlers'.) Probably a confusion—an unconscious blend—of *scart* with *stork*.

straight bake = STRAIGHT RUSH.

Straight Navy, the. The Royal Navy, the wearers of straight braid as opposed to *the Wavy Navy*, the Royal Naval Volunteer Reserve, whose officers have curly stripes. In the 1939–45 War the Wavy Navy numerically exceeded the Straight Navy by seventy-five per cent.

straight rush. Meat and potatoes prepared for cooking which are rushed straight from the ship's butcher to the galley. Cf. MARCH PAST.

straight-laced. An R.N. officer, the wearer of straight stripes as opposed to the wavy-laced Reserve officer. (A wardroom pun.)

straight-stemmer. Any sailing craft with an up-and-down stem, e.g. a Thames bawley, a Colchester oyster smack, or old-type yacht: as distinct from a spoon-bowed yacht.

Straw House, the. A seamen's doss-house in Gravesend where out-of-work merchant seamen slept on straw and conditions were as bad as could be. It no longer exists.

Stream, the. (1) The Gulf Stream. (2) A roadstead off shore.

stretch = BIG-SHIP TIME. (Wardroom.) ' At the time I was doing a year's hard in the old *Nonesuch*, one of the worst stretches I've ever done. Give me destroyers every time.' Humorous on the underworld *stretch*, a period—especially, a year—in prison.

stretch off the land. A short sleep, a ' masts-and-yards ' term that has survived the last century. When a ship was sailing towards the shore nobody was allowed to sleep, but when she was making an off-shore tack or ' stretch off the land ', those so disposed could have a sleep. Cf. CAULK.

strike. A catch of herring. Also as verb: ' We struck them off the Lemon and we brought in a hundred cran.' Almost a technicality.

Stringbags. The Swordfish biplane of the Fleet Air Arm used during the 1939–45 War.

stripey. A three-badge Able Seaman. See BADGEMAN.

stroppy. From the solecistic *obstropulous* (obstreperous). (Lower-deck.) See JACK STROP.

stug. (Of a ship) to roll heavily when stranded. ' I don't like the way she's stugging; if we don't get her off next tide she'll break up.' Echoic.

stumpy. A Thames barge that carries no topsail. (Bargemen's.)

Sub. (1) A Sub-Lieutenant. (Wardroom.) Hence **Sub's Course.** The Sub-Lieutenant's Course at the Royal Naval College, Greenwich. (2) A submarine. Cf. SARDINE TIN and TUBE.

Subby. Sub-Lieutenant. (Lower-deck.)

submariners. The officers and ratings of the submarine service. Cf. WATERPROOF SAILORS.

suck the monkey = BLEED THE MONKEY. (The old type of rum casks were known as *monkeys*.)

sugar-loaf sea. A lumpy, confused sea with no wind to take the tops off the waves.

Suicide Club, the. Members of any particularly hazardous operational party, e.g. in the Dieppe Raid, the attack on St Nazaire, the battle of Walcheren—any ' party ' in which the odds are against survival.

sun fog. An early morning mist which hangs over marshlands in summer and is indicative of a hot sunny day. (Verging on Standard English.)

sun over the foreyard. The time for drinking in the wardroom, eight bells in the forenoon watch. ' Seeing as 'ow the sun's over the foreyard, what about a noggin? ' It is a traditional naval convention never to drink before the sun is over the foreyard.

sundog. A rainbow that has its curve broken by the sun; said to portend stormy weather. (Colloquial.)

supplementary officers. Reserve officers who are listed in the Navy List but do not serve unless called upon in a ' national emergency '. (Technical.)

Supply Chief. The Chief Supply Petty Officer in charge of the ship's stores.

Supreme Example of Allied Confusion. A sarcastic play on the initials S.E.A.C. (South-East Asia Command). The Navy got this from the Americans, who coined it.

Sure Shield of the Empire, the. The Royal Navy. A journalistic coinage that is also a truism.

swab. An epaulette worn by a Lieutenant in full dress uniform. Cf. SCALES. Hence *to ship a swab* (cf. SHIP), to be promoted to Lieutenant.

swaddy. A soldier. (Lower-deck.) Cf. GRABBIES and PONGO.

swain. Short for *coxswain*. (Lower-deck.)

swak. To censor naval mail. From the letters S.W.A.K. frequently on the back of envelopes and meaning *Sealed With a Kiss*.

swallow a sailor. To get drunk on rum. (A colloquialism amongst harbour and dockyard workers. Recorded by J. Redding Ware in his excellent *Passing English*, 1909.)

swallow the anchor. To leave the sea for all time; to retire on a pension.

swallow-tail. The points of a burgee.

sweat-rag. A piece of cotton waste used by an engineer to remove perspiration.

swede, crash down the. To place one's head on the pillow and sleep. Hence, *swede-bashing*, for sleeping. (Lower-deck.)

Swedish. More commonly, *jerks*. Swedish drill. (Lower-deck.)

sweeps. (1) Routine patrols by H.M. Ships and vessels in time of war. A colloquialism that became official. (2) Very long oars used for propelling becalmed fishing boats.

sweet william. Known to piscatology as the *mustelus vulgaris* or ' smooth hound '.

sweetheart. To ingratiate oneself with Authority or dockyard officials. ' I'll have to sweetheart the dockyard for some more paint.'

Sweethearts and wives! The Saturday night toast at sea in the wardroom—usually followed by the waggish, 'and may they never meet '. At one time there was a toast for every night in the week: ' Absent friends and those at sea ' (Sunday); ' Our Native Land ' (Monday); ' Our Mothers ' (Tuesday); ' Ourselves ' (Wednesday); ' The King ' (Thursday); ' Fox Hunting and Old Port ' (Friday). The Saturday night one is the only surviving toast. (Naval lore.)

Swift. The ironic nickname for anyone who is slow-moving or slow in the uptake. (Lower-deck.)

swim, the. The great movement of herring on the fishery grounds. (Fishermen's.)

swimmy. A swim-headed lighter. See preceding.

swims. (Short for swim-heads) the bow and stem of a lighter, which, unlike a stem-headed Thames or Medway barge, has a punt-shaped bow. As it is a double-ender, the plural is always used.

swindle sheet. A naval expense sheet completed by an officer who has been on detached duty or on such a journey as to cause him to incur unusual expenses. He claims these on the sheet.

swing. To postpone or cancel. The term is purely naval and akin to the Royal Air Force's *skip*. ' What shall we do about these letters, Chief? ' ' Swing 'em until next week, there's no panic! ' *Swing* is also used in the sense of ' forget ' as in : ' Thanks very much, it is decent of you to go to so much trouble.'—' Oh, swing it, anybody would have done the same.'

swing round the buoy. To hang on to a soft job in a shore establishment. Cf. BUOY, GO ROUND THE.

Swing that lamp, Jack! A phrase directed against a man who is boasting or telling a tall story. (Lower-deck.)

swing the lead. To malinger. (To swing the lead-line and call out fictitious depths instead of taking correct soundings. An old nautical term.)

231

Swinley's Circus. The officers and men of Coastal Forces, trained by Commander Swinley, R.N. (1939–45 War.)

swipes. The rinsings of a beer barrel. Inferior beer. (Lower-deck.) Adopted from civilian slang.

switchel. A brew of molasses, vinegar and water. An ' Old Salt's ' drink. (Adopted from U.S.A.)

T

T.124's. Men enlisted under the T.124 Scheme in the 1939–45 War. This was a contract under which merchant seamen or civilians could serve under the white ensign for a limited period at Merchant Navy rates of pay and in one ship. They wore naval uniform, were subject to the Naval Discipline Act, and could be discharged to shore if they proved unsatisfactory or inefficient. As the M.N. rates of pay were much higher than those of the Royal Navy there was some friction at first between the *T.124's* and naval ratings, but the scheme worked fairly well, especially in the larger ships and armed merchant cruisers. (Colloquial.)

tabby. A stewardess in a passenger liner.

Tabernacle Tim. Any narrow-minded, intolerant rating with a tendency to ' preach '. One who is for ever trying to convert his messmates. (Lower-deck.)

table money. An allowance for entertainment paid to senior Naval officers.

tab-nabs. Buns, pastry and confectionery which are reserved for the passengers in a liner and are not for the crew. (Merchant Navy stewards' term.)

tack, hard. Ship's biscuits. (General nautical.)

tack, soft. Bread. (General nautical.) Cf. SODDICK.

Tackline. Naval nickname for a tall, slim man, the regulation length of a tackline being six feet.

Taffy. A Welsh seaman; *Taffies*, Welshmen.

tail-arse Charlie. The junior boat in a flotilla of Motor Torpedo (or Gun) Boats. She is last in the line. (Coastal Forces, 1939–45 War.)

tailor. A term of abuse addressed to an unhandy seaman.

233

tailor-mades. Cigarettes made from Navy (TICKLER'S) tobacco and sold on board to men who prefer them to loose cigarette-tobacco.

take a swim. To be compelled to abandon ship and swim to the safety of a DOUGHNUT. Like *compulsory bathing*, this means that your ship has been mined or torpedoed and you have not been lucky enough to get on to a DOUGHNUT.

take bottom. (Of a submarine) to rest on the bed of the ocean and lie ' doggo '.

take felt. To be invalided or discharged from the Navy. Cf. BOWLER HAT, GET A.

take on. To elect to complete time for a pension—twenty-two years' service. ' Are you going to take on when you've done your twelve? '

take pension out of. A naval ' pensioner ' (a Royal Fleet Reserve man) often refers to the last ship in which he served as the one he *took his pension out of.* ' I took my pension out of the old *Nonesuch* in '25, and I came back for this lot in 1939.'

take your paravanes in. A request made to a messmate who thrusts his elbows into his neighbour at table. Paravanes are towed at right angles to the ship's side and are fitted with a serrated wire which cuts mine cables.

taking it green. Shipping heavy seas in bad weather, taking water and not spray on board. See GREEN 'UN.

takle. See TAYKLE.

Talbot Booth. Any of the many reference books on ships compiled by the indefatigable Commander Talbot Booth. ' I don't recognize this ship; look her up in Talbot Booth, will you? ' These reference books are illustrated with photographs or silhouettes from which it is easy to recognize a vessel and check a house flag. (Colloquial.)

talk last commission. To make frequent—and wistful—reference to one's last ship. There is no ship like one's last ship, though allusion to it may be somewhat irritating to one's messmates. ' He's always talking last commission, he makes me chokker.' (Lower-deck.)

talkee talkee. Any conference or mess meeting. (Pidgin English: China-side.)

talking. (Of a ship's anchor) dragging.

tally. A name. Hence, *cap tally*, a cap ribbon bearing the name of one's ship; PUSSER'S TALLY, a false name; DEATH TALLY, an identity disc. ' I know your face, Jack, but I can't remember your tally.'

Tanky. The Captain of the Hold, a leading seaman who looks after the ship's freshwater tanks. Until fairly recently the Navigating Officer's assistant carried out this duty and was known as ' Tanky '; he was usually a Sub-Lieutenant or Midshipman.

tap, do a. To DRIP, constantly complain or grumble. Cf. DRIP PAN. From the *tap-tap* of water dripping into a metal vessel.

tarpaulin muster. A whip-round amongst the crew, either for drinks or to relieve a shipmate in financial straits. The term has been used as the title of a book of short stories by John Masefield.

tarpot. An old name for a Jack Tar or, as he is known today, MATELOT.

taste the timber. To test the quality of the wood by chopping and knifing it. An owner wishing to sell an old boat will invite a surveyor to *taste her timber*.

tattics. This is the traditional naval pronunciation of *tactics* and is used by officers and men. Cf. TAYKLE.

taut hand. A very strict disciplinarian. From *taut*, tight. Hence the adjective *taut-handed*.

taut ship. One run by a taut-handed captain. Very PUSSER indeed. (Navy.)

taykle. Tackle; always so pronounced in the Navy; *luff-taykle*, etc. Cf. TATTICS.

T.B.D.s. Destroyers. (Term used in 1914–18 War when these vessels were known as *T*orpedo *B*oat *D*estroyers. An official abbreviation rather than an unconventionality.)

tea boat. A tea-making firm on the lower-deck. Anyone who decides to brew a pot of tea is said to *run a tea boat*.

tea trolley. The shell-hoist from the magazine to the gun in an H.M. Ship.

tea wagon. An East Indiaman, a tea-carrying vessel.

Tea-kettle Hole. A favourite fishing ground E. half N. from Great Yarmouth.

Teacher Cap. A submarine captain acting as instructor at the Periscope Course for submarine commanders. One who knows the answers. See PERISHER.

tear off a strip. To dress down a junior. ' The Commander tore him off a strip for not calling away the duty boat.' From the ' raspberry '-like sound of tearing cloth.

teased out. Worn out, tired. Like a ' fagged-out ' or *teased out* length of cordage.

teaser. A small rope with a ' hangman's knot ', used for chastising *Conway* cadets. Cf. Dartmouth's TOGIE and H.M.S. *Worcester's* BIMSTER.

Teddy. Nickname of EVANS OF THE BROKE.

Tel. Short for telegraphist. Hence, *P.O. Tel.* and *Leading Tel.*

temperance men. Those who do not *draw*. They receive three-pence a day in lieu of the rum issue.

ten-A matches. Non-safety matches. The only matches allowed in H.M. Ships were safety ones, and anybody in possession of wax vestas or ordinary non-safety matches was awarded *number ten-A punishment*.

Thames-tonnage length. From the forepart of the stem to the afterpart of the stern-post at the level of the deck. (Technical.)

Theatre Ship, the. Any converted merchantman which functions as a theatre. A notable example was the old *Gourka*, the Fleet Theatre Ship at Scapa Flow in the 1914–18 War. These ships are fitted like any theatre ashore and can seat quite large audiences.

They don't pipe dinner outside. A naval warning to those who would desert, or leave the Navy on completion of their twelve years' service. Neither, incidentally, are duty-free tobacco and tots of rum available. Nor is gin threepence a tot, as many an N.O. has sorrowfully realized when going on the BEACH.

thick knees. A stone curlew. (Marshmen's and wildfowlers'.)

236

thick 'uns. Sandwiches made of thick bread and fried fish. (Fishermen's.)

thickers. (1) Strong mess-deck tea noted for its ' bite '. Cf. obsolescent Cockney *thick*, cocoa. (2) Thick soapy water for scrubbing decks.

thirty-knotters. A class of destroyers built in 1900 and used in the 1914–18 War.

three naval turns, the. *Turn in*, *turn out*, and *turn to*. (Lower-deck.)

Three O. A *Third O*fficer in the Women's Royal Naval Service.

three-sixty-five. Eggs and bacon. From the commercial travellers' term—they used to eat them on 365 days in the year and would order them thus: ' Call me at seven-thirty—365 ' (i.e. eggs and bacon for breakfast).

thunder-box. The HEADS in a submarine. The term arose in India, where it denoted a commode.

ticket. A Pilot's certificate. A legacy of the Royal Naval Air Service. Hence, any nautical certificate of proficiency.

ticket, branded. A naval Service Certificate with a CLIPPED CORNER. Cf. BLANKER.

ticket, get one's. To obtain one's discharge from the Service.

tickler, roll a. To make a cigarette from TICKLER'S tobacco.

tickler machine. A cigarette-rolling machine. (Lower-deck.) See TICKLER'S.

Tickler's. Tinned tobacco—pipe or cigarette—issued to officers and men of the Royal Navy at duty-free prices and so called because it was tinned by the firm of Tickler who also supplied the Navy with jam.

Ticklers. Men who joined the Navy under the short-service scheme in 1903. They joined for a term of five years' active service and seven on the reserve. As their entry into the Navy coincided with the improved messing and other refinements they were dubbed *Ticklers* after the firm that provided the marmalade. Cf. preceding and SELBORNE'S LIGHT HORSE.

tickler school. A party of seamen engaged in *rolling Tickler's*: see TICKLER'S and TICKLER, ROLL A.

Tickytackytoo. The title of a low ballad known throughout the Navy. Another like it is ' Ringarangaroo '; the words vary with each Port Division.

tiddler. A one-man submarine. Humorous, from *tiddler*, the nursery colloquialism for a stickleback.

tiddley. An adjective connoting the very acme of naval smartness and efficiency. Hence, *tiddley ship*, one in which ' spit and polish ' is very much in evidence; *tiddley suit*, a sailor's best shore-going uniform with gold badges and usually made by a shore-going tailor; *tiddley turn-out*, a very smart church parade. (Cf. GYVO.) From *tidy*, influenced by *titivate*.

Tiddley Chats. The Chatham Depot, H.M.S. *Pembroke*. TIDDLEY in the best naval sense.

tiddley bull. Excessive spit and polish; great ceremony. (Lower-deck.)

tiddley quid. The nickname of H.M.S. *Royal Sovereign*. By a pun on TIDDLEY and *quid*, ' a sovereign (coin) '.

tiddleys = NUMBER ONES.

tiddly. A spelling variant of TIDDLEY.

tiddy-oggy. A variant of *taty-oggy*, a Cornish pasty made of meat and *potatoes* and very popular in Devonport Barracks.

tidgen. Night work; a term used by tugmen and lightermen of the London River. Origin obscure; perhaps from *tiring*, exhausting.

tie-up. (An unseamanlike term for) to *make fast*; to warp to a jetty. Hence, colloquially, to get married, to tie the ' Gordian knot '.

tiffics. Bits and pieces of ironmongery. A baffling term to define. Perhaps from dialect-slang, *tiffany*, a sieve: with it, one can shake out screws, bolts, etc., that a TIFFY has no further use for. The transition from ' a flour sieve made of *tiffany* ' to ' any sieve ' is a natural one.

tiffy. Short for Engineroom Arti*fic*er. (Lower-deck.)

tiffy bloke. A variant of the above. See HIP HIP HURRAHS.

tiffy school. The School for Engineroom Artificer apprentices.

tiger piss. A brand of beer sold at a foreign port. From the tiger depicted on the bottle label. (Lower-deck.) Cf. PANTHER PISS.

tiller-soup. Much the same recipe as BELAYING-PIN SOUP. (Merchant Navy.)

Tilly. A U*tili*con car used by the Royal Navy. (Wren Transport Drivers'.)

Timber Town, H.M.S. The name given to the prisoner-of-war camp at Groningen in Holland where most of the men of the Royal Naval Division were sent when captured on the Belgian coast in the 1914–18 War.

time-expired. (Of men) having completed time for pension and awaiting discharge.

tin-clads. The first battleships of the ' sail-to-steam ' transition. Also known as *ironclads*.

Tin Duck. The veteran battleship *Iron Duke* which was Admiral Sir John Jellicoe's flagship in the Battle of Jutland in 1916.

tin hat. (1) A steel helmet. (2) A variant of BRASS HAT.

Tin Lizzie. H.M.S. *Queen Elizabeth*.

tin titfer. A steel helmet or TIN HAT. Cockney rhyming slang: *tit-for-tat* = hat. (Lower-deck.) Cf. BATTLE BOWLER.

Tin Training Squadron. The first training squadron in the Royal Navy to dispense with sails—a squadron of TIN-CLADS.

tinfish. A torpedo. Hence, *be tinfished*, to be torpedoed. See FISH.

tinfishmen. Torpedo operators in H.M. Ships. From preceding.

tin-opening ticket. Said to be possessed by an incompetent cook, who can cope only with canned food. These men being supplied by the Board of Trade, the term is a play on the B.O.T. Master's *ticket*. (Merchant Navy.)

tip the grampus. A variant of BLOW THE GRAMPUS.

tipple bows. Lines used in fishing for dabs or codling. (Fishermen's.)

Tirps. Admiral von Tirpitz, Commander-in-Chief of the Imperial German Navy in the 1914–18 War.

tit, press the. See PRESS THE TIT.

titterel. A whimbrel. (Essex fishermen's term, adopted from dialect.)

tizzy snatchers. Naval Paymasters. TIZZY, adopted from civilian slang, is Lowerdeckese for sixpence.

tobacco charts. Unreliable charts; those stained by tobacco juice.

tobacco juice. A jelly-like marine growth that clogs a herring net. (Driftermen's.) This organism is known to science as *Phaeocystis.* In smell and colour it resembles tobacco juice.

Tod. Inevitably all men named Sloan are so nicknamed, after the once famous jockey Tod Sloan; so too all named Hunter, from the surname *Todhunter.*

toddy blossoms. A variant of GROG BLOSSOMS. From imbibing rum toddy.

toe-pitch. The muster at the defaulters' table. The defaulters come up to *pitch* by *toeing* the line.

togie or **togey.** A rope's end used at the Royal Naval College, Dartmouth, for ' chasing' slack cadets. (Cf. *Worcester's* BIMSTER and *Conway's* TEASER.) It is wielded (mildly) by senior cadets. Probably from civilian slang *toco* or *toko* (chastisement), especially in the phrase *give* (someone) *toco,* to thrash.

Tom. Any good-natured rating who is willing to do another man's share of the work as well as his own. ' Let Tom do it, he won't mind.' Used sarcastically by heads of departments when their underlings seem anxious to knock off work. ' All right, push off, " Tom " will square off for you; trust the old pack mule.' The Navy's equivalent of the R.A.F.'s *Joe Soap.* Probably suggested by the obsolescent *tomfool* (= *Tom fool*), a half-wit or a blockhead.

Tom Collins. A character in naval history who seems to have acted permanently as CAPTAIN OF THE HEADS. Anyone carrying out an unpopular duty is said to be *doing a job for Tom Collins.* (Lower-deck.)

Tom Cox's traverse. Up one hatchway and down another. In everybody's mess and nobody's watch. The art of work-dodging. The term is well over a hundred years old; Richard Henry Dance heard it used in 1835. Presumably from the name of some notorious naval, or at least nautical, shirker.

240

Tom Pepper. That magnificent liar of legend who was expelled from hell for his mendacity.

Tom pudding. A compartment boat worked ' in trains ' on the Aire and Calder Navigation Canal.

Tom Tug. A Thames waterman, one who tugs his ferry-boat with oars.

tombola. What ashore and in the other Services is known as ' House ' and ' Housey-housey '. The only gambling game allowed in the Royal Navy.

tombstone. The lower-deck mess menu. (Cf. BEEF CHIT.) The grave of many hopes.

Tommy. All naval men surnamed *Thomas* are so called.

Tommy Noddy. A puffin. Cf. POPE and BOTTLENOSE. (Wild-fowlers'.) A more familiar form of *tomnoddy*.

tommy shop, the. A Royal Naval Victualling Yard. *Tommy*, originally slang, has acquired Standard English status and is defined as food, soft bread. At Bedford and elsewhere, loaves of bread have, for centuries, been distributed by charity on St *Thomas*'s Day (December 21) and are known as *tommy*.

tonsil varnish. Lower-deck tea, very sweet and full of tannin.

Toosie. St Osyth near Brightlingsea on the Colne, Essex. A resort of yachtsmen. The nickname is taken from the local dialect pronunciation, *Toosith*.

toot. (1) To drink in an impressive way. *Exercise Toot* describes a mild session but *Operation Toot* is a spectacular ' binge '. Cf. HONK. (Royal Navy.) Echoic of the noise that normally results. (2) (v.) To grouse or complain, (n.) a complaint. ' He's always doing a toot.' (Lower-deck.) (3) Money. (Lower-deck.) An obscure term, it perhaps is rhyming slang for the New Zealand and Australian synonym, *hoot* (from Maori *utu*).

tooter. A seasoned drinker. One who can see the rest of the party ' under the table '. See TOOT (1).

Toothie. The Dental Surgeon. A wardroom nickname and vocative. See TOOTHWRIGHT and FANG-FARRIER.

toothpick. A sword. (Wardroom.) Borrowed from the Army, which, about 1913, abandoned the term in this sense and endowed it with the more up-to-date meaning, *bayonet*. A pleasing instance of meiosis.

toothwright. The Dental Surgeon. (Wardroom.) Cf. TOOTHIE.

top. The unit into which the watch is divided in H.M. Ships. The *tops* are maintop, foretop, fo'c'sle and quarter-deck. The men's ' parts of ship '.

top gear. Clothing above the waist. When a man undergoes a medical examination of a ' routine ' kind, he is ordered by the Sick Berth Attendant, ' Take your top gear off '. (Lower-deck.)

top-hat party. (1) In the 1914–18 War, the City men who enlisted in the R.N. wearing their ' City ' clothes and silk hats. (2) In 1939–45, a flotilla of landing craft commanded by Lieutenant R. O. S. (Ross) Salmon who, whenever he led them into action, wore a top hat made of brass that was always beautifully burnished.

Top, please! A request on the training ship *Conway* to pass through a mess to which one does not belong. In the course of a cadet's duties he may have to pass through a mess to reach his own *top* or part of ship.

topsail-yard voice. A voice that is loud and capable of being heard at considerable distance. Technically known as *power of command*.

topsides. Aloft, on deck as distinct from 'tween decks. Hence used in colloquial reference to senior officers. ' I don't know how those topsides are going to view the matter.' (Wardroom.) Cf. UP TOP.

Topsy. All naval men surnamed Turner are so nicknamed. Perhaps influenced by (*turn*) *topsy-turvy*.

tore-out. Any converted lifeboat or similar craft. The thwarts, etc., are torn out and the hull re-designed. (Yachtsmen's.)

Torpedo Jack. The Torpedo Lieutenant. Cf. TORPS.

Torpoint chicken. A quick-tempered messmate. An aggressive type. Cf. STAMSHAW NANNY-GOAT. *Torpoint* is a suburb of Plymouth.

Torps. Wardroom vocative for the *Torp*edo Officer.

242

Torture Chamber, the. The Board of Trade examination room. (Merchant Navy.)

tot. The official issue of Navy rum. All men listed as GROG receive this before dinner each day. (Colloquial, but knocking at the door of Standard English. From the primary sense of *anything small*; apparently of Scandinavian origin.)

tot, bottle the. See BOTTLE THE TOT.

tot, deep sea. A short measure tot—caused, presumably, by the roll of the ship.

tot, shaky. Same as preceding. Spilt by the shaky hand of the server.

Tott's. Totterdell's Hotel in Portsmouth, a rallying-point of naval officers.

touch and go. (Of a vessel) to touch the bottom but be able to steam across without actually stopping. She touches and goes on.

tower. A fish-curing house in Great Yarmouth, Lowestoft, and other herring ports. (From the shape.)

towing. (Of a ship) having her trawl down and fishing. When she has the trawl inboard she is *steaming*. (Trawlermen's.)

towny. A man who hails from one's home town: ' He's a towny of mine.' (Lower-deck.) Cf. the colloquial French *pays*, a man from one's own part of a *pays* or country.

toy box. A ship's engine-room, full of *toys* for the engineers to play with.

Trade. Trade Division, Admiralty, which deals with all matters concerning merchant shipping in wartime: convoys, casualties, statistics, etc. Staffed by naval officers and civil servants, this division works a 24-hour day.

Trade, the. The submarine service, a colloquial term seldom used by submariners themselves. Many people believe it to have been coined by Kipling in his *Sea Warfare*, 1916. Perhaps from the fact that submarines sank enemy *trading* vessels; more probably from the service being a highly specialized one—' *the* trade '.

Trades, the. Trade Winds. A colloquialism that has become Standard English.

Traffy, the. H.M.S. *Trafalgar*. (Lower-deck.)

trailing the coat. Uneventful patrols by H.M. Ships in time of war. The Grand Fleet did this, *ad nauseam*, after the Battle of Jutland in 1916—after which, apart from an odd brush with enemy patrol vessels, nothing spectacular happened until the surrender of the German High Seas Fleet in 1919.

train smash. Fried tomatoes. (Lower-deck.)

tramlines, the. Convoy routes or swept channels in wartime. Familiar routes.

trap ships. British Q-SHIPS used in the 1914–18 War to *trap* U-boats.

Trawler Section. A section of the Royal Naval Reserve in the 1914–18 War, confined principally to those trawlermen and driftermen who manned the converted fishing vessels—vessels whose sea-behaviour they were better able to endure than were the ' hostilities only ' ratings recruited from shore. In the 1939–45 War the minesweeping trawlermen were enlisted under the new title, the Royal Naval Patrol Service. Included were armed yachts and every kind of small vessel that could be usefully employed in the war effort at sea.

treacle factory. Any R.N. Boys' training ship. Plenty of treacle pudding is available.

trek boat. One that is towed along a canal or river. A translation of the Dutch *trekschuit*, a covered boat used on the Dutch canals: from *trekker*, to draw or tow + *schuit*, a boat. (Technical.)

Tribals. A class of destroyers named after famous tribes, *Cossack*, *Zulu*, etc.

trick. A spell on watch or any turn of duty;   a trick at the wheel '. (Colloquial.)

trim tram. A Yarmouth herring lugger. Humorous—from dialectal *trimtram*, a trifling thing or a piece of nonsense.

trimmed down. Drunk. (Submariner's colloquialism.) When a submarine is *trimmed down*, her tanks are full of water.

tripe hound. An aircraft used by the Royal Naval Air Service in 1914–18, the Sopwith *trip*lane, which was a ' *bitch* ' to handle.

trooped. A variant of LINED-UP. Haled before the Commander as a defaulter.

Troops, the. Generic term for the lower-deck. (Wardroom.) Adopted from the Army's use of the term for ' the rank and file; the men in general '.

trot. A line of vessels moored to buoys or alongside a jetty. Cf. CAB RANK.

trot boat. A duty boat that plies between the ship and the shore with liberty men, stores, etc. Always *on the trot*—always on the go.

trot boat queen. A Wren member of a trot boat's crew.

trot fob. The moving away of submarines in the TROT alongside their parent ship, to make way for a ' boat ' (i.e. a submarine) to draw alongside her, for ammunitioning or victualling, etc.

trot lines. Worm-baited lines for catching whelks. See:

trotting. Fishing for whelks with a *trot line*—a baited, hookless line. The fish cling so tightly to the bait that it is easy to pull them out of the water.

trouble-box. A mine fuse-box. (Slang of Bomb Disposal parties 1939–45.) Difficult to handle with safety.

trout line, the. A stationary line of ships acting as screen on the flank of the Eastern Invasion Force off the Normandy beaches in 1944. Its chief function was to prevent enemy surface craft from attacking the ships of the ' build-up ' force taking men and materials. The *trout line* was made up of support landing craft such as the river gunboat *Locust*, L.C.F.s (Landing Craft Flak), and M.L.s (Motor Launches). Officially this Force was known as ' Support Squadron, Eastern Flank '. Excellent and gallant work was done by the *trout line*, which met many examples of German ' frightfulness ', such as the ' circling torpedo ' and the explosive motor boat; in fact, the Support Squadron had as ' sticky ' a time as any section of the Invasion Force.

trow. A type of barge peculiar to the river Severn. Also a boat used on the Tyne for salmon fishing.

truck. The top of a ship's mast. Cf. PRIVATE TRUCK.

true water. The exact depth of the water at any given spot. (Virtually a technicality; included only because of its instructional interest.)

trunnions. Hair worn over the ears and protruding from a sailor's cap. From the technical Gunnery sense, the projections on each side of a gun.

trymoon. A Chinese river craft.

tub. (1) A ship of any kind. A term of affection or disparagement, according to a man's feelings. ' She's not a bad old tub, it's the blankety blanks wot's in 'er '; ' I'm chokker with this old tub and the sooner I get a draft chit the better '. (Lower-deck.) (2) To puzzle or bewilder. (Lower-deck.) Perhaps from the idea of *cold tub = cold douche*, literal and figurative. Cf.:

tubber. A difficult question in an examination. From preceding.

tube. A submarine. (Submariners'.) Suggested by *torpedo tube*, the tube through which a torpedo is fired.

tuck. That part of a ship immediately under the stern or counter.

tuck net. A small net used for taking fish from a larger one.

tuck strands. To curry favour; usually as verbal noun, *tucking strands*, ingratiating oneself with the authorities. From the technical sense of *tuck*, to tuck a strand between or under other strands, so that all the strands will fit snugly.

Tudgy yarn. Spunyarn. (Dartmouth College.) From the name of a seamanship instructor.

Tug. The naval nickname for anyone surnamed Wilson. According to naval tradition after one Admiral Wilson, *Tug* being a corruption of his first nickname *Chug*. But in fact Admiral Sir A. K. Wilson was nicknamed *Tug* because already all naval (and military) Wilsons were nicknamed thus. Probably *Tug* comes either from the Winchester College *tug*, an adjective meaning ' ordinary '—thus *Tug* Wilson would, at Winchester, have been plain, ordinary Wilson as opposed to a hyphenated Wilson, e.g. Sturt-Wilson—or from the Winchester noun *tug*, a Colleger, *Tug* Wilson being, at Winchester, Colleger Wilson.

tumble. A very rough passage at sea; in the Portland Race, for instance. (Cf. JOBBLE; LOP; and POPPLE.) Proleptic.

tunnel throat. A sore throat which assailed men who slept in the *tunnels* at the Royal Naval Barracks, Chatham, during the 1939–45 War. These *tunnels* were air-raid shelters built in the chalk down, or ' The Lines ' as they are known locally, and they could accommodate the whole of the Barracks personnel. They were built at the instance of Admiral Lord Mountevans (' Evans of the *Broke* ').

tunnyman. A vessel engaged in the tunny fishery. On the analogy of *East Indiaman.*

turkeys. The Royal Marines, because of their red tunics and ruddy complexions.

turn. (Short for *turn of duty*) a period on watch. (Term peculiar to lightships.) Cf. TRICK.

turn it up at that. ' Call it a day '; stop working; etc. Often shortened to *turn it up,* as in: ' Turn it up, can't you? You're always dripping about something or other.' (Lower-deck.) (Derived from the turning-up of a rope when belaying.)

turn over. When a naval officer goes off watch at the end of his TRICK he *turns over* to his relief; that is, puts him *au fait* with whatever of importance has happened during the watch and the course, speed, revolutions, etc., of the ship. Likewise when an officer leaves a ship to take up a fresh appointment he *turns over* the salient features of his job, including the snags, to the officer who relieves him. (Colloquial.)

turn-over bridge = ROVING BRIDGE.

turret rat. A turret-sweeper in a tramp steamer.

'tween decks. Inside the ship, below upper-deck level. (Colloquial.)

twenty-four hours to sling one's hammock. A full day is allowed a man to settle down in a new ship. ' You are the new bloke, are you? All right, you can sling your hammock today, but report to me in the morning.' (Colloquial.)

twice laid. (1) Cordage laid up from the sound strands of old rope. (2) Hence, any warmed-up or re-cooked meal.

twister = BENDER. (Lower-deck.)

two blocks, be. To have reached the limit of one's endurance. To be fed up and CHOKKER. When two blocks of a purchase are drawn together, they are said to be *chock-a-block* and cannot move any farther. ' I'm chokker with this ruddy hooker!' ' So am I, chum, absolutely two blocks.' (Lower-deck.)

247

two ends and the bight of a fool. A complete idiot. (Lower-deck.) Based upon the technical sense; two ends and the bight of a length of cordage.

Two O. A Second Officer, W.R.N.S.

two-and-a-half-striper. A Lieutenant Commander, a rank which came into being in the year 1914. He wears a thin stripe (half stripe) between two thick ones on his sleeve. A Lieutenant, R.N., automatically becomes a Lieutenant Commander after eight years' service; formerly he was known as an *Eight Year Lieutenant*. In time of war Reserve officers can qualify for the half stripe after three years' service as Lieutenant if they have been recommended.

two-eyed steak. A kipper. (Lower-deck.) Cf. ABERDEEN CUTLET.

two- (three-, four-) funnel bastard. The sailor's term of abuse for his ship. ' Roll, you two-funnel bastard, roll! ' There is a lower-deck couplet, current in the 1939–45 War, that runs:

> *Send out the Rodney, the Nelson and Hood,*
> *This two-funnel bastard is no bloody good.*

two (three, four) piecee all same. ' Same again, please ', when ordering a round of drinks. (Wardroom.) (China-side. Pidgin English is very common in naval officers' conversation.)

two- (three-, four-) sticker. A sailing ship with two, three or four masts.

two-striper (wardroom); **two-ringer** (lower-deck). A Lieutenant of the Royal Navy or of the Reserves.

two-water rum. Grog, two parts water to one rum.

Tyne handicap, the. The race for home by merchant ships in a north-bound convoy when restrictions were relaxed and ships might proceed independently. Most of the ships in these convoys were colliers with the Tyne as their destination. (1939–45 War.) (Recorded by John Batten in *Dirty Little Collier*, 1947.)

tystie. An Orcadian name for the black guillemot, probably echoic of its cry. Cf. SEA PIGEON.

U

U.A. A naval Boy or Ordinary Seaman who is too young (*under age*) to draw his tot of rum. In the Ledger, men are classed as *G.* (grog), *T.* (temperance) and *U.A.* (under age). Cf. GROG and TEMPERANCE.

U-boat. Any round-shouldered rating. A 1914–18 War adjective derived from the rounded conning tower of a German submarine. (German *Unterseeboot*, literally ' under-sea boat ', abbreviated by the Germans themselves as *U-boot*.)

U-jeep. A two-man submarine. (1939–45.)

uckers. A popular naval game, known as *ludo* ashore. The board, marked out on the deck, can be anything from four to fourteen feet, with dice of proportionate size which are shaken out of a bucket. (An arbitrary formation.)

ullage. Literally, the useless dregs at the bottom of a rum cask; hence a useless rating.

Ultima Thule. For the Royal Navy this is Shetland, the most northerly land known to the Romans, who regarded it as the ' world's limit '.

unbutton. To decode (a signal). (R.N.)

under control. See EVERYTHING UNDER CONTROL.

under full sail. Well on the way to being drunk. Pleasantly *on*. I.e., sailing along on a buoyant sea.

under the truck or **climbing the rigging.** Angry, ' het up '. (Naval lower-deck.) Cf. DIZZY, GET.

underground fruit. Potatoes, carrots, radishes or any vegetables that grow in the earth. (Lower-deck.)

unemployed time. Time to a maximum of six months on full pay. Naval officers without appointments in peacetime receive this. (Technical.)

unhead. To remove the top lid of a barrel and prepare it for packing by rinsing it with water and brine. (Herring-fishery term.) A colloquialism verging upon technicality.

unhook. To purloin or ' borrow ' without permission. ' Who's unhooked my oilskin? ' (Lower-deck.)

Union Jack, the. Civilian for the Union *Flag*. The *jack* is a small union flag worn in the bows of an H.M. Ship at anchor. See STEM JACK.

up along. See DOWN ALONG.

up and down. When the anchor chain is UP AND DOWN the anchor is about to break out. (Colloquial.)

up and down the mast. *The wind's all up and down the mast today*, there is not enough wind to fill the sails.

up and downer. A fierce lower-deck argument.

Up Spirits. The daily pipe which sends the duty ratings to draw the exact amount of rum for the issue at mid-day.

up the line. On leave. ' Are you going up the line this week-end? ' (Lower-deck.) I.e. up the railway line leading from the port to home. Cf. ON DAGS, GENS.

up the Noo. On leave in Edinburgh. (Lower-deck.)

up the pole. Annoyed or DIZZY. ' What's he up the pole about? ' (General nautical.)

up the River. Serving in river (FLATIRON) gunboats on the Yangtse Kiang, a very popular appointment with junior officers.

up the Smoke. On leave in London. (Lower-deck.)

up the Straits. On the Mediterranean Station. I.e., through the Straits of Gibraltar.

up top = TOPSIDES.

up-killick. To weigh anchor; hence, colloquially, to depart (usually hurriedly): ' I up-killicked and skinned out of the place as fast as I could.' (General naval slang.)

upper, the. Short for the upper-deck. (Lower-deck.)

Upper Yardmen. Active Service (i.e. permanent) ratings in the Royal Navy who are candidates for commissioned rank. They are trained in H.M.S. *Hawke*, a shore establishment near

Beaulieu in Hampshire. In Nelson's day *upper yardmen* were the seamen who could be relied upon to do the most difficult work aloft; the pick of the lower-deck. *Upper yardmen* must not be confused with C.W. CANDIDATES.

upsets. Newly packed herring-barrels that are placed on their sides.

uranium. See OUNCE OF URANIUM.

Uriahites. The Third Battle Squadron in the 1914–18 War. Perhaps because *David* (Admiral Sir David Beatty) led them to battle.

urn, carry the. A variant of CARRY THE CAN. (Lower-deck.)

us. One's ship. ' The C.-in-C. will be boarding us tomorrow'; ' She passed us at the rate of knots.'

usher. A naval Schoolmaster or Instructor. Cf. SCHOOLIE.

V

V. and A., the. The Royal Yacht *Victoria and Albert.*

Vs and Ws, the. A class of destroyers whose names begin with V or W; *Vesper, Vixen, Woolston, Wolsey, Winchester,* etc. Built shortly after 1918, they did magnificent service throughout the 1939–45 War.

V-class battleships. The two armed merchant cruisers *Voltaire* and *Vandyke,* sunk in the early part of the 1939–45 War. (This nickname is recorded by Lieutenant David James, M.B.E., D.S.C., R.N.V.R., in his fascinating book *A Prisoner's Progress,* 1947.)

V.C.s, the. A class of steam trawlers named after the naval V.C.s of the 1914–18 War, Commander Holbrook, Commander Nasmyth, Commander Horton, and others.

V.I.P. A *V*ery *I*mportant *P*erson—e.g. a cabinet minister— ferried in H.M. Ships in wartime.

van John. A wardroom shape of the game *vingt-et-un,* very popular in the Navy.

'Vast heaving! 'Who do you think you're kidding?' 'Stop hauling my leg.'

Vectis Two. The Globe Hotel at Cowes, Isle of Wight. In the 1939–45 War the naval base at Cowes was given the name H.M.S. *Vectis.* Its headquarters was adjacent to the Globe Hotel whose saloon bar became extremely popular with the officers; in fact, so often were they to be found therein that the Globe was christened *Vectis II.* When the base expanded, the Globe, to the sorrow of all, was requisitioned as part of the naval barracks. But the *Vectis II* will be remembered with affection by all who visited her in the days of her unofficial ' commission '.

Vernon. H.M.S. *Vernon,* the Navy's torpedo school at Portsmouth.

Vernon's Private Navy. A flotilla of minesweeping drifters— *Silver Dawn, Fidget, Jacketa, Lord Cavan,* and *Fisher Boy.* These craft dealt with every type of mine and did excellent work at the Dunkirk evacuation and when the Allied forces returned to the Continent in 1944. H.M.S. *Vernon,* a shore establishment at Portsmouth, is the Mine and Torpedo School.

vicarage, the. The Chaplain's cabin in an H.M. Ship.

Victoria, the. The Royal Victoria Yacht Club, Ryde, Isle of Wight.

victualled up. Having a good time ashore with friends; ' doing very nicely ' with one's girl friend. ' Nobby's nicely victualled up there, lucky dog.' (Lower-deck.)

villa. A seamen's mess. Ironic. Also known as *the drum,* THE COTTAGE and *Donelly's Hotel.*

Vinolia. See PUSSER'S VINOLIA.

violets. Onions. Ironic on the smell. (Lower-deck.)

Virgin, the. The Petty Officer's mess. (Broadcast by the B.B.C. from the weather-ship, *Weather Observer,* the former Flower Class corvette *Marguerite,* on February 20, 1948.) The term may derive from *the virginity curtain,* a screen over the lower gangway preventing ratings from gazing at the women visitors using the upper one. The name symbolizes privacy, the Petty Officers' mess being a screened portion of the general mess-deck.

Vittles. An old name for a Victualling Paymaster in the Royal Navy.

voyage, the. The autumn voyage of the Scottish herring drifters to Great Yarmouth and Lowestoft for the great herring season.

W

W.C.s. See C.W. CANDIDATES.

W.M.P. ' With much pleasure .' See N.C.D.

wad. A Commissioned or Warrant Gunner, R.N. (A term now obsolete, but current at the beginning of the century.) From the *wads* used as stoppers in cannon.

wagon. Short for BATTLE-WAGON.

Wailing Winnie. The preliminary sound made by the ship's broadcasting system. It precedes the ' Do you hear there! ' that prepares the men for an important announcement. Cf. MOANING MINNIE.

walk the chalk. To walk along a chalked line to prove sobriety.

Walker's knot = MATTY WALKER.

wallop. Beer. (Lower-deck.) Adopted from civilian slang. It used to ' pack a punch '.

war babies, the. The cadets who went straight to H.M. Ships from the Royal Naval College, Dartmouth, when it closed down in 1914. Many lost their lives in the first year of the war.

War Reg. The War Registry in the Admiralty where signals, etc., are sorted for the various departments.

wardroom, the. Collective noun for the officers of the Royal Navy: ' The wardroom takes a dim view of the matter.' Cf. TROOPS. The wardroom is the officers' mess. It was once known as the *wardrobe* and was a repository for the prizes captured in battle as, at that time, there was no separate officers' mess, officers feeding in their own cabins (which were built round the wardrobe). The officers used to foregather in the space for conversation, etc. It was not until about 1750 that the *wardrobe* space became the officers' mess and named the *wardroom*. Cf. QUARTERDECK.

wardroom joint as mess-deck stew. Officers' conversation heard aft and retailed, usually inaccurately, on the mess-deck.

warm the bell. See BELL, WARM THE.

warn for draft. To post a man's name on the list of names of men nearing the top of the foreign draft ROOSTER. This *warning for draft* allows men to break the news to their families; and, if they feel that they are being unfairly drafted, they can request to see the Drafting Commander. Only in the case of extreme urgency can a draft be cancelled. (Technical.)

warning. A note from the authorities to the parents of a cadet who is not making satisfactory progress. It intimates that if he does not improve he will have to be removed. (Royal Naval College, Dartmouth.)

warp. Four herrings. An East Anglian fishery term, which John Nall, in the valuable appendix—' Dialect of the East Coast ' —to his *Great Yarmouth and Lowestoft*, derives from the Anglo-Saxon *weorpan*, to throw or throw out. The fishermen usually take two herrings in each hand and throw them into a *swill* (local name for basket) when counting. A swill holds approximately five hundred herrings.

Warrant Officer's champagne. A drink of Navy rum and ginger beer mixed.

wart. A naval Cadet or junior Midshipman, the ' lowest form of naval life '; an unseemly excrescence. Cf. WONK, DOGSBODY and SNOTTY.

wash out. To cancel. The term dates from the time when slates were used to take down messages, a cancelled signal being washed out. The term has become popular in civilian life.

wash-deck. Mediocre. A *wash-deck musician* is a bad performer on his instrument. Hence:

wash-deck bo'sun. A non-specialist Warrant Officer.

washes clean and dries dirty, he. A classic excuse for a slovenly rating who disgraced his Division on an important occasion by appearing unshaven and unwashed: now a part of naval folk-lore.

washers. Steam trawlers. They are frequently washed by heavy seas.

waste-paper basket. The cage-like mast of an American warship in the 1914–18 War.

watch and watch. Keeping alternate watches, four hours on and four hours off. (Colloquial.)

watch ashore. The watch on leave.

watch below. A general nautical colloquialism for time off duty. ' Blue Watch is watch below tonight; how about a run ashore? ' (Lower-deck.)

watch below, called to the. Killed in action or dying from natural causes.

watch coat. Short for *watch-keeping coat*, a long overcoat worn by naval ratings on sentry duty or on watch at sea.

Watch my smoke! A sailor's catch-phrase when he is in a hurry. From the smoke made by a ship that is going full speed ahead.

watch on watch or (R.N.) **watch on, stop on.** An eight-hour instead of a four-hour watch.

Watcher. (1) The Fishery Protection Cruiser, which keeps a look-out for poachers within the three-mile limit. (2) Mr Chad who appeared on the hoardings in 1945–6 with his long nose peering over a wall and the legend *Wot no beer!* and *Wot no*—anything of which there was a shortage. (Royal Navy.) Such Chad-signs as *Wot no leave!*, *Wot no Tickler's!* were chalked on black fences in the vicinity of naval depots.

watching buoy. One that is properly afloat and *watching* the approaching shipping. Sometimes buoys become water-logged and have to be ' bled ' and re-floated.

Watchkeepers' Union, the. Those officers who perform the duties of Officer-of-the-Watch in H.M. Ships.

Water Carnival. The weekly cleaning-up of a ship which takes place on Saturday morning for Captain's inspection and Sunday Divisions. There is an orgy of hosing, sand-scratching, brass-polishing, etc.

water crow. A cormorant. (Fishermen's.)

water haul. A fishermen's term for an empty net. It contains only water.

Water Rats, the. The Thames River Police, dreaded by those engaged in illicit activities on the London River.

water smoke. A sea mist. (Old term used by East Anglian fishermen.)

water stoup. The common winkle.

water Wren. A Wren member of a boat's crew; a Wren coxswain, ' bow and stern sheet woman ' or stoker.

waterborne. Description of the troops of the INLAND NAVY. (After *airborne.*)

water-bruiser. (1) A blunt-nosed vessel. (2) A harbour ferryman.

Wateries, the. A Naval Exhibition that used to be held in South Kensington at the beginning of the twentieth century.

waterproof sailors. The submarine service.

Waves. Members of the United States service equivalent to the Wrens: *W*omen's *A*uxiliary *V*olunteer *E*xpeditionary *S*ervice.

Wavies. R.N.V.R. personnel. (R.N. term.)

Wavy Bill. A pre-war nickname for an R.N.V.R. officer doing his period of training in an H.M. Ship. The implication being that he was not sure of his sea legs. See ROCKY.

Wavy Navy, the. The Royal Naval Volunteer Reserve. Cf. ROLLING-MOTION DICKY.

wavy ringer. An officer in the Royal Naval Volunteer Reserve.

Way Hi. The treaty port of China, Wei-Hai-Wei. (Wardroom China-side.)

we; our. The use of the first person plural is traditional among Petty Officer instructors: e.g. ' Some of us don't know our left feet from our right, do we? '; ' How long 'ave we bin in the Navy? Three weeks and we don't know a reef knot from a granny.'

We don't get much money, but we do see life! A naval catch-phrase of 1914–18, meaning much the same as the 1939–45 NEVER A DULL MOMENT! Usually uttered in the middle of an air raid or any form of PANIC or excitement. (Wardroom.)

We want make-and-mends, not recommends. A lower-deck catch-phrase. Cf. MAKE AND MEND and RED RECOMMEND.

weasel. An explosive motor boat used by the Germans as a counter weapon during the invasion period in 1944. It was ingeniously contrived to explode on impact with a ship, the ' bumper ' in the bows acting as a detonator of the explosive charge set in the nose. These boats were very speedy and driven by twin engines.

weasel duck. The smew, a diving bird whose head somewhat resembles that of a weasel. (East Anglian term.)

weather line. When two lines of battleships are running on parallel courses the line nearest the wind is known as the *weather line*, the other being the *lee line*. A survival of the sailing days.

weather-ship. A sea-going meteorological vessel carrying scientists who study and report upon weather conditions in special areas. (Colloquial.)

weaver. A fish of about the same size as whiting which has sharp, poisonous spikes in place of fins. Anyone stung by it suffers intense pain until sundown.

web-foot. Any Devonport rating. See DUFFOES and WESTOES.

webs. A sailor's feet. A sailor takes to the sea as a duck to water.

weed, bitter. See BITTER WEED.

weed on, have a. To have a grievance, to be annoyed with life. Cf. COB ON, HAVE A.

Week, the. Cowes Regatta Week, a very important social event.

week's Navy. Seven tots of rum bottled by the drawer in order to barter for a special favour. ' I'll give you a week's Navy if you'll swap week-end leave with me.' (Lower-deck.)

week-end sex wagon. A gaudy cabin-cruiser or motor yacht. See WHORE'S PARLOUR.

weekly boats. Coasters which take a week over their trips down the English coast, e.g. colliers plying between Newcastle and the London River. (Colloquial.)

weevil bo'sun. A Victualling Warrant Officer; he issues *weevilly* biscuits. Cf. JAM BOS'UN.

weigh off. To serve (punishment or sarcasm). ' Jimmy weighed him off three days' Number Eleven.' (Lower-deck.)

weigh, the. The purport of anything. ' Have you got the weight? ' is Navalese for ' Do you understand this? ' or ' Have you got my drift? ' A variant of the instructor's ' All right? '

Welsh Navy, the. The Blue Funnel Line owned by Alfred Holt, Ltd. The crews were at one time predominantly Welsh.

West Country parson. The hake, from the black mark on its back and its being found in the West Country. Cf. ISLE OF WIGHT PARSON.

Western Ocean, the. The blue-water sailor's name for the Atlantic.

Westminster Palace of Varieties, the. A long-standing nickname for the Admiralty, also known as the MAD HOUSE.

Westoes. Devonport ratings. *West* Countrymen.

wet. Stupid, half-witted. (Lower-deck.) ' Did you ever see anyone so blinkin' wet? ' ' Jimmy gets some wet ideas at times! '

wet a stripe. To drink to anyone's promotion. (Wardroom.)

wet as a scrubber. The description of any exceptionally inane rating.

wet as a shag. Very wet indeed. The shag is a diving bird. See SALTASH CATCH, and cf. WET AS A SCRUBBER for a different sense.

wet ship. (In the naval sense) a ship whose wardroom has a heavy drinking reputation. Literally, a ship that takes a lot of sea on board. ' I don't like the look of her, Jack, she'll be a wet ship in a seaway.'

wet shirt. A thorough soaking. See SALTASH CATCH or SALTASH LUCK. (Wardroom.)

Wet Triangle, the. An area of submarine patrol in the Kattegat during the 1939–45 War. The seas there are short and ' lumpy ' and a submarine on the surface is apt to have a wet passage.

wetto. A stupid, inefficient person to whom the adjective ' wet ' is applied with full justice. (Wardroom.)

Whacker. The traditional lower-deck nickname for Payne or Paine.

whack-up. To increase speed. ' Whack her up, Snotty, I have a train to catch.'

Whale Island show. An attack upon an enemy ship by gunfire as opposed to torpedoes. See WHALEY.

whales. Tinned sardines. (Lower-deck.)

Whaley. Whale Island (H.M.S. *Excellent*), the Naval Gunnery School at Portsmouth.

wharf rat. A dockyard pilferer who prowls round wharves breaking into deserted ships or warehouses.

what Cromwell had on his nose. A wart, hence a Midshipman.

What's the form? A phrase borrowed by the Royal Navy from the Army and the Royal Air Force during Combined Operations; it means, 'How does one go about the job?'; 'What's the place like and the inhabitants?' or simply, 'How's things?'

whatter and whyer. A naval officer who is always asking *what* is the reason for this and *why* one has done that. One who expects 'reasons in writing'.

wheelbarrow religion. Going to church when 'pushed'. (Lower-deck.) Cf. FANCY RELIGIONS and NON-CAN-GO-ISTS.

wheel-box. The wheelhouse in a steam trawler or drifter. It is square and box-like.

whiskers. The detonator in the nose of the warhead of a torpedo.

whistler. A widgeon, from its long whistle. (Marshmen's and wildfowlers'.) Adopted from dialect.

white as a hound's tooth. The colour of his decks expected by a fastidious captain.

white ensign ship. Any commissioned ship of the Royal Navy or Auxiliary Fleet; also a yacht whose owner is a member of the Royal Yacht Squadron, the only club in the British Isles to have the privilege of wearing the white ensign.

white feather, the. A plume of steam from a ship's safety valve.

white-line day. That on which a ship's company musters by *Open List*, and according to the Ship's Ledger. Each man, as he steps up to the line, gives an account of himself to the Captain: 'Able Seaman Jones, number so-and-so, three good conduct badges, first class for leave,' etc., what he says tallying with his description in the Ledger.

White Man's Grave, the. The port of Freetown, Sierra Leone. Because of its very unhealthy climate. A derisive adoption from journalese.

white nun. A seamew. (Wildfowlers'.)

White Paper candidate. A candidate for a temporary commission in the Royal Naval Volunteer Reserve. A White Paper was passed in Parliament for a scheme of promotion for those suitable ratings who had spent three months at sea in time of war. Cf. C.W. CANDIDATE.

white rat. A mess-deck sycophant, a ' crawler ' who is always trying to curry favour with officers. (Lower-deck.)

white rope. Untarred cordage. (Colloquial.)

White Squadron, the. The Royal Yacht Squadron, Cowes, the senior yacht club of Great Britain, so named because its members are privileged to wear the white ensign in their craft, provided these are over thirty tons; the burgee is white, with the St George's cross superimposed by a gold crown. Founded in 1815, it was first known as *the Yacht Club*, but in 1833 King William IV desired that it should in future be known by its present title. Cf. BLUE and RED SQUADRONS.

white squall. A white mist accompanied by a high wind and confused seas, highly dangerous to ships caught unawares. These squalls appear without warning on clear calm days and pass as suddenly. ' Said by naval officers to be outside of their experience, and probably a popular myth' (*Webster's New International Dictionary*).

white wings. Sailing vessels seen at a distance.

whites. Tropical clothing. (Colloquial.)

whizzer. A ship's screw or propeller. Also known as FAN.

Who called the cook a bastard? Who called the bastard a cook? Complementary, but scarcely complimentary, rhetorical remarks passed in disparagement of the cook's efforts.

who'd sell his farm and go to sea? An old naval expression varied occasionally by SELL THE PIG AND BUY ME OUT! (Wardroom.)

whore's parlour = WEEK-END SEX WAGON.

wifflo gadget. Like the FOO FOO VALVE and DOO HICKY this is a name for any mechanical device of whose name you are ignorant. (Naval officers'.) *Wifflo* is an arbitrary formation.

Wiggy. The traditional naval nickname for Bennet(t).

Wight, the. The Isle of Wight.

willock. A razorbill. Echoic from its cry. (Wildfowlers'.)

willock eaters. ' An old nickname for Eastbourne fishing boats, suggesting that their men ate the willock or guillemot. ' (Frank C. Bowen, *Sea Slang*, 1929.)

will-o'-the-wisps. Lights seen on the shore at night. At one time crown and anchor—a game forbidden on the lower-deck —was very popular in the Navy, and men used to go ashore for evening leave and walk into the country where, in the light of candles or torches, they played in the lee of the hedges or on the beach.

wind. To go about on to the opposite tack. (Bargemen's.) (Technical.)

wind rose = FLOWER OF THE WINDS.

wind-bag. A sailing ship of any kind. A variant of WINDJAMMER.

wind-banks. Banks of cloud which portend a gale.

wind-hammer. A pneumatic riveter used in dockyards.

winding hole. A ' bulge ' in a canal provided as a turning place for boats. They WIND round.

windjammer. A sailing ship, full rig, barque, brigantine, schooner, or any ship that depends on the wind. Most of the real old *windjammers* are extinct or moored up West Country rivers as show-pieces.

windward of, get to. To have the advantage of anyone. Also to get on the right side of Authority, especially dockyard officials, from whom one obtains paint or materials for smartening a ship. Cf. SWEETHEART.

windy. ' Long-winded '; prosy, etc., e.g. *a windy bore*. (Submariners'.) Also a general slang term for nervous, having ' the wind up '. (The lower-deck has a more expressive but unprintable version.)

Windy Corner. (1) Any particularly dangerous part of a coastline which is exposed to enemy gunfire or aerial bombardment; the Straits of Dover, for instance. (2) Wicers Corner in Fareham Creek, Portsmouth, exposed to south-easterly ' blows ' from Portsmouth.

wine = BUBBLY: dark Navy rum.

winger. An assistant or pal. Someone taken under another's wing. The term has lately largely displaced RAGGIE as a name for a friend.

winger, do a. To ' pull a fast one ' over someone. To take an unfair advantage of a messmate. (Lower-deck and obsolescent.) Cf. the Air Force's *flanker*.

wings. Short for WINGER.

winkers. Anti-gas respirators.

winkle barge. A Landing Craft (Flak). (Combined Operations slang.)

winkling. Bayonet exercises or fighting. One extracts winkles from their shells with pins. (Lower-deck.)

Winnie and Pooh. The two coastal guns in the Dover Command (1939–45). The former was named after the Rt. Hon. Winston Churchill, and Pooh was no doubt inspired by A. A. Milne's *Winnie the Pooh*.

Winston. The Rt. Hon. Winston Churchill, First Lord of the Admiralty in the 1914–18 War and Prime Minister, 1940–45.

wipe up. To shoot one's nets across those of a neighbouring vessel. (Fishermen's.)

Wir. The short title of *W*eekly *I*ntelligence *R*eports, issued by the Admiralty to ships and shore establishments. All the important items of war news are set out rather more fully than would be allowed in a civilian newspaper.

with-but-afters, the. Officers of the Naval Reserves. They rank *with, but after* officers of the Royal Navy.

wizard. A ' surpassing ' adjective borrowed from the Fleet Air Arm, who took it from the Royal Air Force. Much used by Wrens employed on R.N. Air Stations.

Wobbly Eights, the. The King Edward VII Class of cruisers—the Third Battle Cruiser Squadron in the 1914–18 War. They were also known as the BEHEMOTHS.

wolf packs. German submarines that operated in ' nests ' against the Allied convoys in the 1939–45 War.

wonk. A junior Midshipman or Cadet.

wood-and-iron men. Carpenters and shipwrights serving their apprenticeship in an H.M. Dockyard.

Woodcock Pilot. The golden crested wren, which usually appears in this country two days before the woodcock. Cf. HERRING SPINK.

wooden men and iron ships. The Old Navy's taunt at the New Navy. Cf.:

wooden ships and iron men. The motto of the minesweepers working in converted herring drifters which have wooden hulls. These men are as hard as iron.

wooden topsails. Oars that one uses in the dinghy when towing a becalmed yacht.

Wooden Walls, the. The old frigates or RATERS.

woods. Slats of greased wood used in launching small boats.

wood-spoilers. Ship's carpenters. (Lower-deck.)

Woolworth Carriers. Aircraft carriers converted from merchant ships and used for the protection of convoys in the 1939–45 War.

work double tides. To perform extra duty. (An old Coastguard Service term.) Cf. the naval WATCH ON WATCH.

working fly. Travelling through a canal by horse-drawn barge, using relays of horses. A craft working thus is known on the canals as a *fly-boat*.

worm. To remove the ' beard ' from an oyster or mussel. (Fishermen's and East London.) From the beard's resemblance to a small worm.

Worms. (1) Nickname for a gardener in naval barracks. (2) Macaroni. (Lower-deck.)

wreck heap. An old unreliable engine.

Wrecker's Retreat. The Royal Naval School of Navigation, which was destroyed by enemy action during the ' blitz ' on Portsmouth in 1941. Cf. NAV HOUSE.

Wren. A rating member of the Women's Royal Naval Service; originally slang, but long (pre-1939) official. *W.R.N.* with an *e* interpolated for the sake of euphony. Cf. JENNY WREN, HANNAH, and WREN O.

Wren O. A Wren officer; a female N.O.

Wren, Water. See WATER WREN.

Wrenlin. A Wren gremlin, a Fleet Air Arm term deriving from the R.A.F. sprite who is associated with trouble and mishaps. From Standard English folk-mythology.

Wrennery. The Wrens' quarters in a naval establishment. Cf. NESTING BOX.

Wrenpecked. (Self-explanatory.)

wrist-watch sailors. The Old Navy's term for the New Navy. A pre-1914 term when wrist-watches became popular with ratings entered under the short-service scheme.

wusser. A canal boat. A bargeman's term of obscure etymology: possibly dialect though Wright does not record it; but probably from *wusser and wusser*, worse and worse.

X

X-boat. A British midget submarine.

x-catcher or **x-chaser.** A mathematically minded officer; a DAGGER type. (Wardroom.) One who chases—and sometimes catches—the elusive x of mathematics.

X-ship. A type of shallow-draught vessel, with twin engines burning shale oil, having a speed of about six knots. The *X-ships* were built at the instance of Admiral ' Jack ' Fisher during the 1914–18 War for landing troops on enemy territory. They were the precursors of the L.C.I.s (see LICE) of the 1939–45 War. *X*, because they were ' hush-hush '.

Y

Yacht, the. The Royal Yacht, *Victoria and Albert*. It is interesting to note that the crew of the Yacht wear silver badges on their uniforms instead of the gold ones worn by general-service ratings.

yachting. Absent without leave. (Old Navy.)

Yachtsman's Bible. *The Riddle of the Sands*, by the late Erskine Childers; perhaps the best-written spy story in the language and still as popular as when it was published in 1903. A lovable and companionable book, esteemed by all who love the sea and ' messing about in boats '.

yachtsman's gale. A strong breeze that a professional sailor would regard with indifference.

Yachtsman's Navy. The name given to the Royal Naval Motor Boat Reserve (later to become the R.N.V.R.), which was largely recruited from amateur yachtsmen. A 1914–18 coinage revived in 1939–45.

yachtsman's ticket. A Yachtmaster's Certificate of competence in navigation, seamanship, etc.

yak. Dirt or refuse of any kind. (The training ship *Conway*.) Origin obscure.

yak tub. The training ship *Conway's* GASH bucket. See GASH and YAK.

Yankee. One of the American destroyers taken over by the Royal Navy in the early days of the 1939–45 War. Cf. FOUR-STACKERS.

Yankee dish-up. Throwing a dirty plate out of the scuttle instead of washing it up. Cf. DISH UP.

rdee. Short for *dockyardee*. See DOCKYARD MATEY.

267

Yarmouth. Mentally deranged; ROUND THE BEND. The naval hospital for mental cases is at Great Yarmouth, Norfolk. ' The man's completely Yarmouth.' (Wardroom.)

Yarmouth capon. A herring. The town is famous for its herrings. Cf. ABERDEEN CUTLET and SPITHEAD PHEASANT.

Yarmouth mittens. Bruised hands of the herring fishermen.

yarning a hammock. A trick played on New Entries. The foot of the hammock is unhooked and tied on with a piece of thin yarn which, strong enough to support the unoccupied hammock, gives way when the owner gets in and he falls on the deck.

yawlers. Half-grown herrings. (Fishermen's.)

Yellow Admiral. Such a Captain promoted to Rear Admiral on retirement as has never flown his flag as a Rear Admiral. From the yellow form that he received from the Admiralty.

yellowing. The making of YELLOW ADMIRALS.

yellow flag, the. The quarantine flag flown by a ship that has a case of infectious illness on board. (Colloquial.) Cf.:

yellow Jack. Yellow fever. A dangerous tropical disease that causes the skin to become yellow as in jaundice.

yellow peril. (1) Canteen cake, which is yellow and eaten at one's peril. (2) The Visual Signalling Instruction Book, which is bound in yellow cloth.

Yellow-Bellies. Chinese.

Y-mewdon. The fishermen's attempt to pronounce *Ymuiden*, the Dutch port.

Yorky. A Yorkshireman; a Yorkshire-born seaman in the Royal Navy; any Hull trawler or drifter.

You shouldn't have joined! A phrase of scant sympathy addressed to a mess-mate who is always grousing about his lot. (Lower-deck.)

Young Doc, the. The Junior Medical Officer in an H.M. Ship. A term that has displaced the Old Navy's *Pills*.

young flood. The beginning of a fresh tide. (Colloquial.) Rudyard Kipling uses the term in these lines from *Fringes of the Fleet*, 1916:

> *Dawn off the Foreland—the young flood making*
> *Jumbled and short and steep.*

Young Gentlemen, the. The Midshipmen of the Royal Navy.
Cf. SNOTTY.

young strops. Undisciplined New Entries in the Royal Navy.
They are apt to be STROPPY.

yow yow. A sampan, a Chinese river craft. (China-side.)

yum-yum. Love letters. (Lower-deck.) Echoic of osculation.
' Hi, Postie, any yum-yum this morning? '

Z

zeppelins in a fog. Sausages and mashed potatoes. A 1914–18 War lower-deck term.

zeps. Short for Zeppelins, dirigible airships invented by Count Zeppelin and used for reconnaissance by the German Navy in 1914–16 and for carrying out air raids on London and the Eastern Counties of England. Their ' scare value ' was small and, extremely vulnerable, these airships suffered crippling losses, the first two victims falling to the Royal Naval Air Service over the North Sea, the ' killers ' being Flight Sub-Lieutenants Warnford and Cadbury, based, I believe, on Great Yarmouth. The R.N.A.S. also raided the Zeppelin sheds at Düsseldorf, destroying a number of airships. After the Battle of Jutland in 1916 Zeppelins were little used.

zigging. The Navy's term for *zig*-zagging, a course adopted in convoy when enemy submarines are reported.

Zion's Hill. The old fo'c'sle head in the training ship *Conway*.

zizz. Sleep. ' If you want the Officer-of-the-Day, he's probably zizzing in the wardroom.' (Cf. CAULK.) Echoic. See *Forces' Slang*.

zizz pudding. A suet pudding. It induces sleep.

zob for drinks, to. A wardroom method of deciding who is to pay for drinks. The contestants face one another, repeat the word ' Zob! ' three times, then simultaneously make the sign of a closed fist, an open palm, or two fingers. The fist represents a stone, the palm a sheet of paper, and the fingers a pair of scissors: scissors can cut paper, stone can blunt scissors, paper can wrap up stone. The loser pays for the round of drinks.

Zone, the. The promotion zone for naval officers. Promotion is automatic up to the rank of Lieutenant Commander; above this it depends on selection. Those chosen for this further promotion are said to be *in the Zone*. Since the Navy has room only for a limited number of Commanders, many excellent officers must necessarily be passed over and forcibly retired. See PASSED-OVERS and PROMOTIONITIS.